THE DISCOVERY OF THE
TITANIC

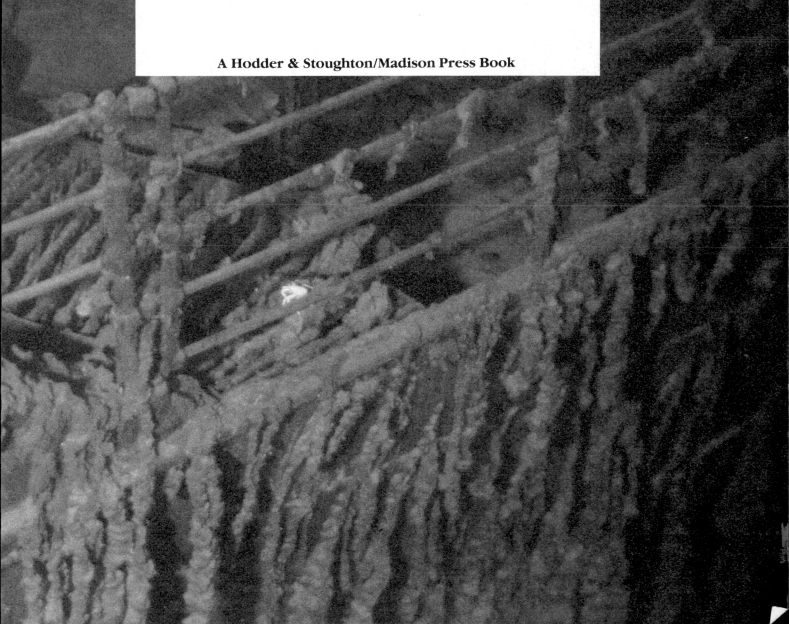

THE DISCOVERY OF THE
TITANIC

by Dr. Robert D. Ballard

with Rick Archbold

Introduction by Walter Lord

*Illustrations of the Titanic
by Ken Marschall*

A Hodder & Stoughton/Madison Press Book

First published in Great Britain 1987 by Hodder and Stoughton Ltd,
47 Bedford Square, London WC1B 3DP
First paperback edition published in Great Britain 1989

British Library Cataloguing in Publication Data

Ballard, Robert
   The discovery of the Titanic: exploring
   the greatest of all lost ships.
   1. Titanic, *Ship*   2. Underwater
   archaeology – North Atlantic ocean
   I. Title
   910′.091631   VK1255.T6

ISBN 0-340-50520-6

*(Title page) The curved forward bow
railing on the* Titanic *wreck.*

(Opposite) One of the Titanic*'s ghostly
portholes.*

**Produced by
Madison Press Books
40 Madison Avenue
Toronto, Ontario
Canada M5R 2S1**

Printed in Italy

Contents

*Poised in the stocks at the Harland &
Wolff shipyards, the* Titanic *is made
ready for launching.*

Introduction

by Walter Lord

WHAT IS THE MYSTIQUE OF THE *TITANIC?* Is it the sheer immensity of the disaster – the largest ship in the world, proclaimed unsinkable, going down on her maiden voyage with appalling loss of life? Is it the element of Greek tragedy that runs through the story – if only she had heeded the warnings; if only there had been enough lifeboats; if only...if only. Is it the built-in sermon, the irresistible reminder that "pride goeth before a fall"? Or is it because she so eloquently symbolizes the end of the Edwardian era, a final nostalgic glimpse of a whole way of life?

Certainly all these elements are present, but somehow they are not enough. Recently, I received word that *A Night to Remember*, a small book I wrote about the *Titanic* more than 30 years ago, is about to have a Bulgarian edition. Surely there can't be that many Bulgars interested in the end of the Edwardian era.

No, the appeal must be more universal, and the thought occurs that the *Titanic* is the perfect example of something we can all relate to: the progression of almost any tragedy in our lives from initial disbelief to growing uneasiness to final, total awareness. We are all familiar with this sequence, and we watch it unfold again and again on the *Titanic* – always in slow motion.

There is the initial refusal to believe that anything serious is wrong – card games continuing in the smoking room; playful soccer matches on deck with chunks of ice broken off from the berg. Then the gradual dawning that there is real danger – the growing tilt of the deck, the rockets going off. And finally, the realization that the end is at hand, with no apparent escape. Entranced, we watch how various people react: the Strauses embracing, the band playing, the engineers keeping the lights going. We wonder what *we* would do.

Whatever the explanation, the fascination continues; hence the universal excitement when word came in 1985 that an expedition led by Dr. Robert D. Ballard of the Woods Hole Oceanographic Institution and Jean-Louis Michel of IFREMER had located the wreck. At first I thought that the discovery might spoil some of the allure. Part of the spell seemed to depend on the great ship, still hauntingly beautiful in her final moments, disappearing beneath the sea forever. But it soon became clear that the discovery actually added to the mystique. The magnificent photographs of the ghost-like bow had a haunting quality all their own. Later, the close-up pictures taken in the 1986 expedition each suggested a fresh vignette: an empty davit, an opened porthole, the crow's nest. And what little girl owned the doll's head that shows up so clearly in one of the shots taken near the stern?

Now these classic photographs have been gathered together in a volume of their own. Looking at them and reading the story of the expeditions, we can understand why Bob Ballard himself finally fell victim to the *Titanic*'s mystique. Initially the search was, for him, basically a professional challenge – a sort of diver's Mount Everest – but by the time he came up from his final dive, he felt differently:

> A melancholy feeling of emptiness came over me. How could I be experiencing this sense of loss, I wondered? After all the *Titanic* was, in the final analysis, only a big wreck in deep water. Our mission had been a technological success. I should be feeling jubilation. Instead, I felt like a high-school senior saying good-bye to his steady girlfriend before heading off to college. I wanted to look to the future, but I couldn't help looking back.

One feels the same way on turning the last page of this magnificent book. The mystique of the *Titanic* lives on.

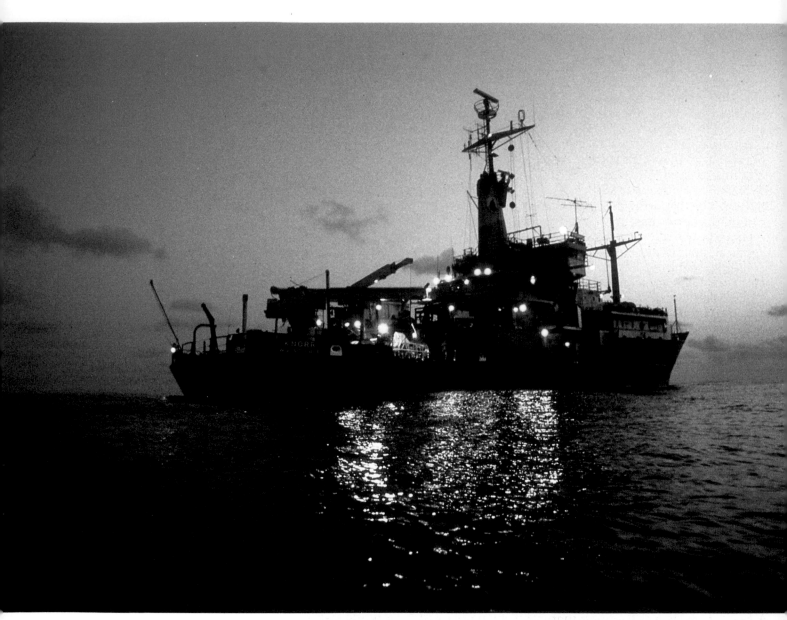

The research vessel Knorr *at night.*

CHAPTER 1

Search For A Legend

THE RESEARCH VESSEL *KNORR* HEAVED AND PLUNGED WITH THE OCEAN swell as I leaned out over the bow railing, squinting into the blackness. I was bone tired – a combination of fatigue and the beginnings of despair. This was the fifth week of our search for the *Titanic*; only five more days to go, and still nothing. All we had seen so far was an endless seascape of ocean above and a barren muddy bottom passing below. Did I expect to see the ghost of the *Titanic* coming at me through the dark? I thought of the *Titanic*'s lookout Fred Fleet, nearing the end of his watch on a clear but moonless night. Suddenly he sees something dead ahead and coming fast. There is barely time to react ....

By August 31, 1985, time had almost run out and still there was no sign of the Titanic.

Like that fateful April night 73 years ago, the August air was chilly – summer is fleeting in the North Atlantic – and the rail cold and wet to the touch. Through the cold steel I could feel the vibrations of the *Knorr*'s powerful engines as they drove the ship painstakingly forward at a speed of 1.5 knots.

Not for the first time, I reflected on the enormity of our mission: to locate a wreck two and a half miles down in the middle of nowhere. It was far worse than looking for a needle in a haystack, and yet I'd often boasted that finding the *Titanic* would be easy – with the right equipment and manpower. On this expedition we had both. What had gone wrong?

Both my French co-leader Jean-Louis Michel and I had prepared carefully for our expedition to find the legendary wreck of the R.M.S. *Titanic*, sunk in 1912 with great loss of life. We had followed our plan faithfully. But now time was running out. Had we somehow missed the ship? Or were we looking in the wrong place? Would we return with empty hands, like the three expeditions that had come and gone before us? I knew I would take such failure hard. I don't like losing under any circumstances. Besides, I'd sacrificed an awful lot in the struggle to fulfill this personal dream that went back 12 years.

I walked aft, alone with these thoughts, to *Knorr*'s deserted fantail. A few feet away was the long inanimate shape of ANGUS, its white paint glowing faintly in the deck lights. Not very lively company, but we planned to use this sled-like assemblage of steel tubing and underwater still cameras to take beautiful pictures of the wreck – if we found it. Beyond ANGUS I could just barely make out the even more ghostly silhouette of *Knorr*'s crane, used for launching and recovering ANGUS and its sibling *Argo* – a sled that took moving television pictures as it was pulled a few feet above the bottom of the ocean floor. In my current state of mind the crane resembled an arm bent at the elbow and ready to land a punch.

At this moment *Argo* was out of sight, trailing just above the sea floor at the end of a slender cable. With its high-tech video eyes, *Argo* was continuing our around-the-clock search for the *Titanic*. Meanwhile, I waited, ruefully reflecting on the vast gap between the glamorous stereotype of the underwater adventurer and the mind-numbing reality of our endless, often boring, search.

Only a few yards forward, a squat rectangle loomed in the darkness. This was the control van, the nerve center of our mission. All I had to do was walk over, open the door, and I'd enter a world of light, warmth, and companionship. Soft music would be playing on the tape deck and the day's shipboard gossip would be in the process of dissection. Since I wasn't there, there'd also probably be the inevitable griping. Morale was at its lowest ebb and some members of the team had even begun to question our search strategy....

What was it about the *Titanic* anyway? Why did she still exert such a powerful spell over so many? I'd certainly caught the bug, and I was supposed to be a hard-headed scientist using the sunken ship as an excuse to test some fancy new equipment. But long ago the *Titanic* had ceased to be just another shipwreck.

In the popular imagination the events of the night of April 14, 1912, have distilled themselves into a powerful morality play about overweening pride leading inevitably to a tragic fall. A great passenger ship, the largest and most luxurious yet built, sets out on her maiden voyage. She is widely believed to be "unsinkable" – although her builders and owners never make such a claim – and there are not enough lifeboats. Aboard are gathered a glittering array of the wealthy set of England and America, the celebrities of an age that worshipped old money and blue blood. In command is a veteran captain whose lack of self-doubt epitomizes his rich passengers' confidence in the world they control. Despite a number of warnings of ice ahead, he does not slow down and takes only the minimum precautions. He has made this passage countless times before and, besides, there is often ice in April.

The ship hits an iceberg at full speed, a glancing blow but a fatal one, and begins to sink. The passengers are at first simply curious, turning the event into a diversion from shipboard routine. But as the ship begins to show a pronounced tilt at the bow and a slight but definite list to starboard they begin, reluctantly, to enter the lifeboats, many of which leave not even half full. Less than three hours later, the great ship has vanished beneath the freezing water of the North Atlantic. Of the more than 2,200 on board, only 705 are saved. Somehow the world will never again seem quite so certain and controllable.

The disaster caused a sensation at the time. But people living then were too close to the event to realize that it would come to symbolize the end of one era and the beginning of another. They could only gasp in horror at the immensity of the tragedy – the number of lives lost, the size of the vessel, and the reputations that sank with it. In time the sinking of the *Titanic* would come to represent the point in our century when people lost their innocence and their sense of certainty. In those late-Edwardian days, before the carnage of the First World War, people still knew what they believed in. As Walter Lord eloquently put it in his recent book, *The Night Lives On*, "In 1912 people had confidence. Now nobody is sure of anything, and the more uncertain we become, the more we long for a happier era when we felt we knew the answers. The *Titanic* symbolizes that era, or more poignantly, the end of it. The

R.M.S. Titanic *on her maiden voyage.*

worse things get today, the more we think of her, and all that went down with her.''

All that went down with her .... As I stood there on the *Knorr's* stern, somewhere not far from where the real *Titanic* sank, not the one of legend and half-truth, I pondered the enduring fascination of this ship. I wondered what we would find in the blackness and crushing pressure below. What condition would the wreck be in if we located it? What changes would the deep sea have wrought over the years? Had the *Titanic* sunk in one piece like many other wrecks? It seemed probable. Was she lying intact on the bottom after falling two and a half miles, having been subjected to incredible underwater pressures, and hitting the bottom at considerable speed? There was every reason to expect that she was. Would the Grand Banks Earthquake of 1929 have unleashed an avalanche that left her buried beneath tons of mud, never to be found? I fervently hoped not.

I'd dreamed of sending my soon-to-be-completed seeing-eye robot vehicle down the *Titanic's* Grand Staircase. What would be left of this once-magnificent structure? Would the 1912 Renault car still be sitting in the hold, waiting to take a spin along Fifth Avenue, or would its tires have been eaten away by underwater organisms, and the gleaming metal of its body corroded into unrecognizable junk? Would the wood paneling in the first-class lounge still show its careful craftsmanship? And a darker thought: would there be human remains?

These questions would all be academic, though, if we didn't find the ship. I shivered and started toward my cabin. Five more days and then we'd be heading home – either as heroes or losers. Maybe the *Titanic* really was a cursed ship and our expedition, despite its high-tech excellence, would be only the latest to fall victim to her spell.

So much had been invested in this effort: so many years, so much money, so much labor. If we failed, no doubt many of my scientific colleagues would mutter about grandstanding and straying away from the proper precincts of science. And I would have to put a brave face on things, reminding the press that the official purpose of the trip was to test our new deep-sea visual imaging technology. The *Titanic* was merely incidental. The tests had gone well.

But I would be bluffing. As I walked through the darkened lab, past the constantly jabbering sonar printout, by the deserted galley, and up the stairs toward my cabin, I knew that sleep wouldn't come easily. Too many questions were waiting to be answered.

This fanciful view of the sunken Titanic *was featured in a French magazine shortly after the disaster.*

CHAPTER 2
What Happened That Night

I N THE WIRELESS ROOM ABOARD THE ROYAL MAIL SHIP *TITANIC* – ON THE fifth day of her maiden transatlantic voyage – Jack Phillips was busy dealing with the day's radio traffic, most of it private messages to and from the passengers on board. In 1912, wireless was a relative novelty – many ships still traveled without it – and Phillips, and his junior Harold Bride, as employees of the British Marconi Company, were not part of the established shipboard chain of command, and followed no routine procedure in the delivery of messages to the bridge.

At 9 a.m. that Sunday morning, April 14, the wireless room received a message from the Cunard liner *Caronia* reporting "bergs, growlers, and field ice at 42°N, from 49° to 51°W." This was not the first ice warning the ship had picked up during the trip and it would not be the last. When he had a moment Bride took the message to the bridge where it was probably received by Fourth Officer Joseph G. Boxhall. In all likelihood Boxhall noted the position on the ship's chart.

The officers on the bridge paid little attention to this information. Ice was not unknown in this part of the Atlantic during April crossings, and they were confident they would have no trouble spotting an iceberg in time. Indeed, the sea was calm, the weather cool and sunny and, besides, what danger could a few bits of ice pose to their magnificent new ship?

Elsewhere on board passengers went about the leisurely pursuits of a typical transatlantic passage – reading, writing letters, strolling along the promenade decks, chatting with old friends or new acquaintances, or reclining with a cup of broth and a biscuit in a sunny deck chair. Since it was Sunday, divine services were held. The first-class service, at 10:30 a.m. in the first-class dining saloon, was presided over by the redoutable Captain Edward J. Smith. At the age of 62, Smith was to retire after taking the *Titanic* on her maiden voyage – a fitting end to a sterling career with the White Star Line. To this assemblage of the rich and titled, the dignified and self-confident Smith must have seemed the perfect pastor.

The first-class passengers on board the *Titanic* represented the cream of Anglo-American society of the day. The wealthiest among them was indubitably 47-year-old Colonel John Jacob Astor, great-grandson of the wealthy fur trader, who had extended the family's wealth through real estate acquisitions – especially hotels. Astor had recently been the center of scandal when he was divorced by his wife and had then married an 18-year-old girl from New York. He and his now-pregnant bride Madeleine were returning from a long winter trip in Egypt and Europe where they'd been hiding out of the range of reporters.

Playboy scion of the American mining and smelting family, Benjamin Guggenheim was also on board. So were Isidor Straus and his wife

(Above) Captain Edward J. Smith, pictured here on the Titanic's *nearly identical sister ship,* Olympic.

(Opposite) The Titanic *dressed with flags at the White Star Dock in Southampton on Good Friday, April 5, 1912, five days before her maiden voyage.*

Ida. He was the owner of Macy's, the world's largest department store. The list of the very wealthy was rounded out by the presence of George Widener of Philadelphia along with his wife and 27-year-old son Harry. The Widener family had made their huge fortune building streetcars.

Besides these super-rich, there were many other merely wealthy people on the *Titanic*'s maiden voyage: for instance, Mr. Arthur Ryerson, steel magnate; John B. Thayer, second vice-president of the Pennsylvania Railroad; Charles M. Hays, president of the Canadian Grand Trunk Railroad; and Harry Molson of the Montreal banking and brewing dynasty. Among the representatives of the British upper classes were Sir Cosmo and Lady Duff Gordon; he was a British peer and she was a successful dress designer with stores in Paris and New York.

In addition to the very wealthy, the ship was well stocked with prominent personages. Among these were Major Archibald Butt, President Taft's military aide and a close friend of Theodore Roosevelt, returning to Washington after a leave of absence, and William T. Stead, renowned British spiritualist, editor, and political reformer who was traveling to New York to attend a peace rally.

The roll call of the rich and famous might have been even more impressive had some prominent people not canceled their tickets. Financier J.P. Morgan, whose shipping trust owned the *Titanic*, was too ill to take the trip. Alfred W. Vanderbilt and his wife decided at the last moment not to sail, but were too late to retrieve their luggage or their personal servant; both went down with the ship. And Lord Pirrie, chairman of Harland & Wolff shipbuilders in Belfast, who had built the *Titanic*, canceled because of poor health. In his place sailed Thomas Andrews, the company's managing director.

(Top) John Jacob Astor and his wife Madeleine. *(Above)* Isidor Straus.

While the wealthy brought retinues of maids and manservants and mountains of luggage, most members of the crew earned such tiny salaries that it would have taken years to save the money for a single deluxe first-class ticket. In fact, the *Titanic* was a kind of floating layer cake, composed of a cross-section of the society of the day. The bottom layer was made up of the most lowly manual laborers toiling away in the heat and grime of the boiler rooms and engine rooms located just above the keel. The next layer consisted of steerage or third-class passengers – a polyglot mixture hoping to make a fresh start in the New World. After that came the middle classes – teachers, merchants, professionals of moderate means – in second class. Then finally, the icing on the cake: the rich and the titled.

The ship that carried these passengers was absolutely the last word in floating luxury – with its opulent public rooms and splendid private staterooms. The finest quarters were the two first-class suites on B Deck, a full 50 feet in length, which included private promenade decks with half-timbered walls echoing the Elizabethan period. First-class cabins were decorated in various periods and styles from Louis Quinze to Queen Anne. Many of the public rooms were paneled in wood. There were elevators (for both first and second class); a gymnasium (with the latest in exercise equipment); a Turkish bath and a swimming pool; an à la carte restaurant (as well as the usual dining-rooms); the Café Parisien, a replica of a sidewalk café where the younger set gathered; and the most lavish Grand Staircase afloat. It added up to quite a conspicuous display.

Even the third-class compartments were impressive by the standards of the day, and the ship itself, as her name boastfully indicated, was

(Above) Lord Pirrie of Harland & Wolff and J. Bruce Ismay, Chairman of the White Star Line, inspecting the Titanic *before her launching on May 31, 1911.*

(Left) The Titanic *off the Isle of Wight on April 10, 1912, photographed by Frank Beken of Cowes.*

(Above) This rare picture shows a group of first-class passengers posing for a photograph on the Boat Deck of the Titanic at Queenstown. From left, they are: Stanley J. May; his sister, Mrs. Lily Odell; his brother, Richard May; and nephew, Jack Dudley Odell. Shortly thereafter, this group disembarked on the tender and went on a motor tour of Ireland. Before doing so, Jack Odell's aunt, Kate Odell, took several unique photographs of the Titanic.

(Above) Second-class passengers strolling on the starboard Boat Deck while the Titanic is anchored off Queenstown.

(Left) As the Titanic prepared to weigh anchor, Kate Odell snapped this picture from the tender Ireland of the liner's starboard side looking aft.

(Opposite, center, left) Furnished in Old Dutch decor, special stateroom B-59 was among the most luxurious on board.

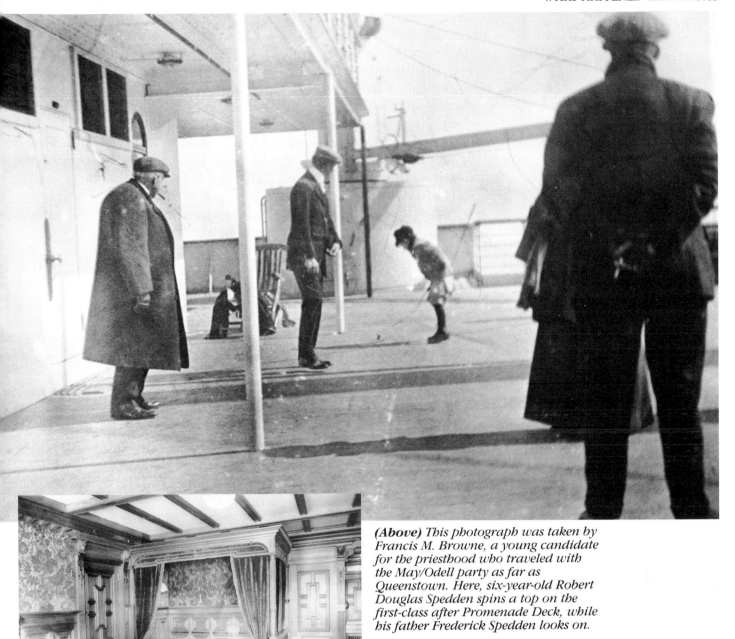

(Above) This photograph was taken by Francis M. Browne, a young candidate for the priesthood who traveled with the May/Odell party as far as Queenstown. Here, six-year-old Robert Douglas Spedden spins a top on the first-class after Promenade Deck, while his father Frederick Spedden looks on.

(Below) The Verandah Café and Palm Court on A Deck.

(Right) This advertisement claims that by offering Vinolia soap to its first-class passengers, the Titanic offers "a higher standard of toilet luxury and comfort at sea."

indeed the biggest afloat. She displaced 52,310 long tons, was 882 feet, 9 inches long overall, 94 feet wide at her widest point (the hull itself reached a maximum breadth of 92.5 feet), and 175 feet tall from the keel to the top of her four funnels. Put another way, she was the equivalent of an 11-stories-high building and a sixth of a mile long. It was no wonder that the more than 1300 passengers on board felt there was nothing that would threaten their safety.

At 11:40 a.m., the wireless room received a message from the Dutch liner *Noordam*, reporting "much ice" in about the same position as the *Caronia* earlier that morning. There is no evidence this message ever reached the bridge.

Around 1:30 p.m., Captain Smith was on his way to lunch when he ran into J. Bruce Ismay, president of the White Star Line, on the Promenade Deck. They stopped for a minute to chat about the performance of the new ship on her maiden voyage. Between noon Saturday and noon Sunday, the *Titanic* had made 546 miles – her best day so far. The next day, they were planning to bring her up to full speed for a short test to see what she was capable of, perhaps as much as 23 knots. The ship was performing well and to make matters even better, the fire that had been smoldering in the forward coal bunker of boiler room No. 5 had finally been put out the previous day. Perhaps they also commented on the weather, which remained unusually calm. Before Smith and Ismay parted, the Captain handed him a wireless message recently received from the steamer *Baltic*: "Greek steamer *Athinai* reports passing icebergs and large quantities of field ice today in latitude 41°51'N, longitude 49°52'W . . . Wish you and *Titanic* all success." That put the ice field about 250 miles ahead of the *Titanic*. Ismay casually put it in his pocket. Later that afternoon Ismay would wave the message at two prominent passengers, Mrs. Arthur Ryerson and Mrs.

(Above) J. Bruce Ismay.

(Below) A figure believed to be Captain Smith, walking aft on the Promenade Deck.

John B. Thayer. It was as if Ismay were reinforcing just how great and powerful the ship was. Despite the ice warnings already received, Captain Smith and Bruce Ismay, the two most important men on the ship, remained unconcerned. Yet another ice warning, this one intercepted from the liner *Amerika*, was received at 1:45 p.m. but was not sent to the bridge.

The daylight hours passed uneventfully. There were no rigid routines, no organized recreational activities. Even though it was Sunday, some passengers played cards in the first-class smoking room. As the day unfolded, the sound of a bugle announced lunch, then dinner. In the late afternoon, the temperature had begun dropping rapidly. On instructions from Captain Smith, the ship altered course slightly to the south, perhaps to avoid the ice ahead. Darkness approached.

Around 7:30 p.m. in the à la carte restaurant, Mr. and Mrs. George D. Widener were hosting a dinner party in honor of Captain Smith. The guest list included a select group of the more prominent Americans on board – most representing the high society of Philadelphia. As well as the Wideners' son Harry, there were Mr. and Mrs. John B. Thayer, wealthy Philadelphians Mr. and Mrs. William Carter, who were bringing over a 25-horsepower Renault car (for which they would later claim damages of $5,000); and finally, Major Butt.

While the captain sat at dinner, Junior Marconi Operator Harold Bride delivered yet another ice warning to the bridge. It was from the steamer *Californian*, well ahead of the *Titanic*, and on a course slightly to the north. The *Californian*'s master, Captain Stanley Lord, reported passing three large icebergs three miles to the south. This message was never given to Captain Smith.

Around 9 p.m., Captain Smith excused himself from dinner and went to the bridge where Second Officer Charles Herbert Lightoller was on duty – the 6-to-10 p.m. watch. He and Lightoller discussed the changing weather conditions – it was possible the drop in temperature indicated they were entering a region of ice and both were aware that some ice was ahead. They were also both aware that bergs could be very difficult to see on a clear, calm, moonless night with no wind or swell to cause surf. Lightoller informed Smith that with the temperature continuing to drop he'd ordered the crew to see to the fresh water supply which was in danger of freezing. Somewhat earlier, First Officer William Murdoch had ordered the forward forecastle hatch closed so that the glow from inside wouldn't interfere with the lookouts in the crow's nest above it. At 9:20, Captain Smith retired for the night, leaving Lightoller with these words: "If it becomes at all doubtful let me know at once. I shall be just inside." Ten minutes later, Lightoller had Sixth Officer Moody tell the lookouts in the crow's nest to "keep a sharp lookout for ice, particularly small ice and growlers." It was customary, at that time, for ships to travel at full speed until a berg was actually sighted, so it probably never entered Smith's mind to reduce speed on such a clear night. The sea was so calm, in fact, and reflected the starlight in such a way, that the horizon itself was difficult to discern. One sailor, a veteran of 26 years at sea, later said he had never seen the ocean so flat.

At this point, apart from the slight alteration of course to the south, the closing of the forecastle hatch, and the warning to the crow's nest, the officers of the *Titanic* had taken no precautionary measures to deal

(Top) This photograph shows what a shipboard wireless room of the period would have looked like.

(Above) An ice warning from the German steamer Amerika that the Titanic received and dutifully relayed onward.

with the hazards ahead. It was common practice to rely on lookouts and they seemed confident in their ship's ability to avoid a collision. Because of the lack of coordination between the bridge and the wireless room and the absence of any standard procedure for dealing with ice warnings, they seem to have been under the impression that the main body of ice lay to the north of their path. In the words of Walter Lord, "The result was a complacency, an almost arrogant casualness, that permeated the bridge."

Two more ice messages were received by the *Titanic* that night. None of the surviving officers remembered either of them making it to the bridge. The first one, which arrived in the wireless room at 9:40 p.m., might well have galvanized Lightoller into some sort of action. "From *Mesaba* to *Titanic*. In latitude 42°N to 41°25', longitude 49°W to longitude 50° saw large icebergs, also field ice, weather good, clear." This ice was quite clearly directly ahead of *Titanic*'s present course.

In the Marconi room, Harold Bride had now retired for a much needed nap – between the two operators they kept the wireless operating 24 hours a day – and Jack Phillips was busy trying to wade through the commercial traffic. The nearest North American shore station at Cape Race on the southeastern tip of Newfoundland had come in range and messages that had piled up all day could now be sent. In fact, Phillips was now so busy that he brushed off the final ice warning altogether. It was the *Californian* again, still ahead but now stopped in field ice on a course a mere 19 miles north of the *Titanic*'s line of travel. Her position was now so close to theirs that the message literally blasted in his ears. Irritated by the interruption, he cut off the sender with the words: "Shut up, shut up. I am busy. I am working Cape Race."

Altogether, the day's seven ice warnings indicated a huge field of ice some 78 miles long directly ahead of the *Titanic*.

In the crow's nest, lookouts Fred Fleet and Reginald Lee had passed an uneventful watch. It was now 11:40 p.m. In another 20 minutes they would be relieved and would head below, perhaps for a hot drink, before hopping into warm bunks. The sea was still flat calm, but the air was now bitterly cold. A few minutes earlier, they'd noted what looked like a slight haze extending a couple of miles to either side and dead ahead. But they were without binoculars, which had been misplaced before the ship left Southampton.

Suddenly, Fleet caught sight of something directly in the *Titanic*'s path. In a few seconds it grew larger. Automatically he rang the warning bell three times to alert the bridge, then picked up the phone.

Sixth Officer James Moody, the junior officer on watch under First Officer Murdoch, who had relieved Lightoller at 10 p.m., picked up the receiver and calmly asked, "What did you see?"

"Iceberg right ahead," replied Fleet.

The *Titanic*'s officers were experienced seamen. When Moody relayed the news, Murdoch reacted immediately. He moved quickly over to the telegraph and ordered the engines stopped, then reversed, at the same time telling Quartermaster Robert Hitchens to turn the wheel "hard-a-starboard," which would have the effect of turning the ship to port. Murdoch then pulled the lever to close the doors to the watertight compartments in the bottom of the ship. Hitchens spun the wheel as far as it would go. At the last moment the ship veered slightly to port.

It was too late. A head-on collision had been averted but the ship

(Above) *The crow's nest with the warning bell that was rung by lookout Frederick Fleet to alert the bridge to the iceberg.*

(Right) *Frederick Fleet, photographed after the disaster.*

rushed forward, hitting the iceberg a glancing blow along its starboard bow. At the bridge level it seemed as if the ship might have escaped unscathed. Several tons of ice fell into the forward Well Deck as it passed, but the ship only shuddered slightly and glided on. A few minutes later, she came to a stop.

Most passengers aboard the *Titanic* were unaware the ship had hit anything, let alone been fatally wounded. Because the air was so biting, most were inside and some had already turned in for the night. The Wideners' dinner party was finally winding down. The ladies had already retired to their cabins and the men had gathered for an after-dinner cigar in the first-class smoking room on A Deck, where a few other small groups were enjoying a nightcap before calling it a day. They heard a faint grinding jar. A couple of people jumped to their feet and ran out on the deck in time to see the iceberg vanishing astern. They were soon joined by others, curious to know what had happened. When they heard it was just an iceberg, they drifted back to their games, their drinks, or headed to their cabins to bed. When other passengers heard about all the ice in the forward Well Deck, they light-heartedly made plans for snowballing matches the following morning.

Lawrence Beesley, a young science teacher, was reading in his second-class cabin when ''there came what seemed to me nothing more than the extra heave of the engines and more than usually obvious dancing motion of the mattress on which I sat. Nothing more than that – no sound of a crash or of anything else: no sense of shock, no jar that felt like one heavy body meeting another.'' Divining nothing out of the ordinary in this, Beesley returned to his reading. His first intimation that something was wrong was when, a few moments later, the engines stopped dead.

Second Officer Lightoller was just drifting off to sleep when he felt ''a sudden vibrating jar run through the ship. Up to this moment she had been steaming with such a pronounced lack of vibration that this sudden break in the steady running was all the more noticeable. Not that it was by any means a violent concussion, but just a distinct and unpleasant break in the monotony of her motion.''

A number of other passengers and crew felt the gentle jar as the iceberg brushed by and described it in various ways: like rolling over ''a thousand marbles''; ''as though somebody had drawn a giant finger along the side of the ship''; ''a disquieting ripping sound like a piece of cloth being torn.''

Down at the very bottom of the ship, the collision was perceived very differently. Second Engineer J.H. Hesketh was in the forwardmost boiler room (No. 6) when the ''STOP'' sign lit up on the boiler-room indicator. Barely had he given the order to ''shut all dampers,'' thereby shutting off the flow of air to the fires, when there was a noise like ''a big gun going off'' – someone else compared it to ''the roar of thunder.'' Hesketh and leading stoker Frederick Barrett were immediately hit by a jet of icy water. The combination of noise and the shock of cold water was enough to send them both running aft through the short tunnel to boiler room No. 5 just before the watertight door glided shut. The remaining men in No. 6 raked out the fires before clambering up the ladders to the relative safety of E Deck.

Twenty minutes after the collision, Captain Edward J. Smith knew the worst. He and Thomas Andrews, chief among the ship's designers,

DIAGRAM II.—Scraping Past the Berg.

This drawing from The Illustrated London News *shows the iceberg towering over the Boat Deck as it scrapes past the* Titanic. *Most witnesses reported that the berg was actually no higher than the Boat Deck.*

had just completed a rapid tour belowdecks to assess the damage. The mail room was filling with water and sacks of mail were floating about. The forepeak tank was breached as were the three forward holds and boiler room No. 6.

The *Titanic's* hull was divided by 15 transverse watertight bulkheads into 16 "watertight" compartments. She was designed to float with any two of these compartments breached. In addition, she would survive if all of the first four were flooded – but not the first five. The critical compartment was boiler room No. 6. With these first five compartments breached, water would eventually fill them and overflow into the compartments aft, one by one. And the *Titanic* would inevitably sink. Andrews estimated the ship would be gone in an hour – an hour and a half at the most.

Captain Smith had no time to ponder the mistakes that had led to this disaster. Being a man of action, his thoughts turned to the orderly evacuation of his ship and the business of keeping her afloat as long as possible. This was his first real crisis in a long and remarkably uneventful career. Undoubtedly, he wrestled with the reality that the ship had lifeboats for barely half the estimated 2,200 on board. Incredibly, the *Titanic* actually carried *more* lifeboats than British Board of Trade regulations of the day required. Given her tonnage, she need only have had lifeboat space for 962. The actual lifeboat capacity was 1,178. Captain Smith knew that more than 1,000 people – assuming every lifeboat went away full – would be left on the ship. He would have to proceed carefully to delay the inevitable panic. Later, as he stood on the bridge, he would have time to contemplate what had gone wrong as he prepared to go down with his ship.

At 12:05 a.m., the squash court, 32 feet above the keel, was awash. Smith ordered Chief Officer Henry Wilde to uncover the lifeboats. Fourth Officer Boxhall was sent to wake up Second Officer Lightoller, Third Officer Herbert Pitman and Fifth Officer Lowe. Then the captain walked aft along the port side of the Boat Deck to the wireless room – a distance of about 20 yards – to personally give instructions to Phillips and Bride to send out the standard CQD distress call. Later that night, Bride decided to try out the new distress signal, SOS, which was just coming into use. And the *Titanic* sent out one of the first SOSes from a ship in distress. Her position, as worked out by Boxhall, was 41°46′N, 50°14′W.

Not far away, about 12:15 a.m., aboard the Leyland Liner *Californian*, Wireless Operator Cyril Evans had retired for the night shortly after getting that soon-to-be-famous brush-off from Jack Phillips aboard the *Titanic* and only minutes before the first distress call was

(Above) A double cylinder door to one of the Titanic's "watertight" compartments. These doors could be closed immediately by a switch on the bridge.

(Below) A drawing that shows how the Titanic *was divided by 15 transverse bulkheads into 16 compartments that were said to be watertight because the bulkheads extended well above the water line.*

sent. Third Officer Charles Groves had just finished his watch and had stopped by the wireless room. He liked playing around with the set – maybe he could raise the ship whose lights he could see coming up from the southeast. To him she appeared to be a passenger liner about ten miles away. But with Evans gone he couldn't get the receiver to work. After fiddling with the dials, he headed for his cabin several minutes before the *Titanic* was sending out her first distress call.

On the bridge of the *Titanic* a little after midnight, Fourth Officer Boxhall observed the lights of a steamer seemingly about five miles distant and pointed it out to Captain Smith, who gave him permission to send up distress signals. Boxhall then instructed Quartermaster George Rowe to begin firing white rockets, which he proceeded to do at about five-minute intervals. The first rocket went up at about 12:45. In the wireless room, Bride and Phillips feverishly continued to send out their distress signal. Although numerous ships heard and responded to their calls, the closest vessel they had been able to reach was the Cunarder *Carpathia* under the command of Arthur Rostron about 58 miles southeast of the *Titanic*'s position. Captain Rostron was incredulous at the news, but nonetheless turned his ship full steam toward the *Titanic* and raced to the rescue.

At approximately the same time, Second Officer Stone, alone on duty on the *Californian*'s bridge, observed a white rocket bursting above the strange ship to the south. Attempts to contact it by Morse lamp had been futile and no one wanted to wake up Evans, who as the only wireless operator on board worked an all-day shift from 7:00 a.m. to 11:00 p.m. The first rocket was followed at several-minute intervals by more white rockets – five in all. Stone called Captain Stanley Lord on the speaking tube. The captain had gone to lie down in the chart room but had asked to be informed if the strange ship came any closer. Lord

(Top) A distress message sent out by wireless operators, Jack Phillips (left) and Harold Bride (right).

(Below) The first rockets being fired.

BRAVE AS THE "BIRKENHEAD" BAND: THE "TITANIC'S" MUSICIAN HEROES.

(Above) Bandleader Wallace Hartley (center) and his musicians played lively ragtime tunes while the boats were being lowered. None of them survived.

(Above) "Molly" Brown is seen here with Captain Rostron of the rescue ship Carpathia *at a ceremony honoring his heroism.*

asked if the rockets were private signals and, when Stone replied that he didn't know, instructed him to attempt once again to raise the stranger by Morse lamp.

Stone was again unsuccessful. He and Apprentice Gibson, who had joined him on the bridge, now watched as three more rockets were fired, the last of these at 1:40 a.m. Around 2 a.m., the anonymous ship appeared to be sailing away to the southwest. Stone sent Gibson below to wake up the captain and bring him up to date. Lord again asked what color the rockets were and told his officer to continue signaling with the Morse lamp. Sometime between 2:00 and 2:20, the mysterious ship disappeared completely.

On board the *Titanic*, almost an hour after the collision, the seriousness of the situation had still not sunk in for the majority of passengers. By 12:30, Captain Smith had instructed his officers to start loading the lifeboats – women and children first. Most of first class was now on the Boat Deck wearing life belts as the stewards had instructed them, but despite what Beesley described as the thunderous "roar and hiss of escaping steam from the boilers," and even though the ship was slightly down at the bow and was beginning to show a discernible list to starboard, many people remained reluctant to exchange the seeming safety of the ship for the apparent risk of the tiny lifeboats. The ship's band added to a kind of party atmosphere from their position just inside the Boat Deck entrance to the Grand Staircase (they'd started playing in the first-class lounge) where they continued to play a medley of lively tunes.

Both First Officer Murdoch, in charge of the starboard side, and Second Officer Lightoller, looking after the port side, were having trouble persuading people to enter the boats. No later than 12:45, and quite probably earlier, the first boat was lowered – starboard boat No. 7. Although it had a capacity of 65 people, it left with only 28 aboard, among them artist's model Dorothy Gibson and several men from first class.

Below, in the steerage decks of the ship, there was considerably more confusion and alarm. Most third-class passengers had so far failed to get abovedecks; others had reached the Poop Deck – third-class space – or were milling about the forward Well Deck. Most of those who made it onto the Boat Deck had done so either by circumventing the barriers between third and first class – or breaking them down. The White Star Line would later deny that any favoritism had been shown to first-class passengers, but the naked statistics told a different story.

By 12:55 a.m. – with the ship distinctly down at the bow – the first port-side boat was sent on its way – No. 6. Denver socialite Margaret "Molly" Brown, who had been walking away from the Boat Deck, was picked up and dropped unceremoniously into the less than half-full boat as it was lowered with only 28 people aboard. When Lightoller realized that there was only one crewman – Quartermaster Hitchens – in the boat, he let Arthur Peuchen, a middle-aged manufacturing chemist and skilled yachtsman from Toronto, slide down the fall to join him. Back on the starboard side, boat No. 5 was lowered with 41 people aboard, then No. 3, with only 32, 11 of them members of the ship's crew. By 1:10, the second port-side boat, No. 8, carrying only 39 people, was finally lowered away. Since there weren't enough crewmen, the Countess of Rothes boldly took the tiller.

Of all the boats launched that night the most controversial was undoubtedly starboard boat No. 1. Although it had a capacity of 40, it left the ship with only 12 aboard, including Sir Cosmo and Lady Duff Gordon, their private secretary Miss L.M. Francatelli, and two American men. The remaining seven were members of the crew. Later, this boat – and many of the others that were less than full – would fail to return to pick up people dying in the water.

The band played on as the bow sunk further. With the firing of the distress rockets, the milling passengers began to realize that the *Titanic* was in genuine trouble. On the Boat Deck, there were numerous touching scenes as husband bid farewell to wife and children, then helped them into a waiting boat. Many women were reluctant to leave their husbands and some refused. The best-known story that has survived is that of Mrs. Ida Straus, wife of the owner of Macy's department store. At one point she almost got into boat No. 8. Then she changed her mind and said to her husband, "We have been living together for many years. Where you go, I go." Calmly, the two of them sat down in a couple of deck chairs and watched and waited.

As the slant in the deck grew steeper and more alarming, the boats began to go away more fully loaded – but seldom full. A number of male passengers behaved as if nothing at all was amiss. Archibald Gracie observed a scene in the first-class smoking room on A Deck. "There all alone by themselves, seated around a table, were four men, three of whom were personally well known to me, Major Butt, Clarence Moore and Frank Millet. All four seemed perfectly oblivious of what was taking place on the decks outside." Then there was Ben Guggenheim who, having realized the ship was sinking, went below to his cabin and exchanged his life belt and warm sweater for evening clothes. When he reappeared on deck, he declared that if he was going to perish he wanted to die like a gentleman.

Below in the engine room, Chief Engineer William Bell and a few crewmen kept the steam up in boiler rooms No. 2 and No. 3 so that the lights on the ship would remain lit and, more important, so there would be power to keep the pumps going. Anyone who wandered into

(Above) This 1912 drawing, showing the lifeboats being lowered, exaggerates the distance from the Boat Deck to the water. In reality, the distance was a still considerable 60 feet.

(Left) The first-class smoking room where Major Archibald Butt *(above)*, and three other men sat seemingly unconcerned as the ship sank.

(Left) Millionaire Benjamin Guggenheim changed into evening clothes, stating that he wished to die like a gentleman.

the deserted first-class dining saloon would have seen the lights still burning brightly.

By 1:30 a.m., the bow was well down and the list had shifted heavily to port. People found it hard to keep their balance, and signs of panic began to appear. As port-side boat 14 was lowered, a group of passengers rushed to the rails and threatened to jump in. The boat was already loaded with 40 people. Inside the boat, Fifth Officer Harold Lowe fired two shots to warn the crowd on deck away and the boat reached the water safely.

In the Marconi room, the wireless operators were still at their posts – but the tenor of their distress calls was becoming increasingly desperate. At 1:25 a.m.: "We are putting the women off in the boats." At 1:35 a.m.: "Engine room getting flooded." At 1:45 a.m.: "Engine room full up to boilers," meaning several of the boiler rooms had flooded.

By 1:40, most of the forward boats had gotten away and collapsible (canvas lifeboat) C had been fitted onto the davits for starboard boat No. 1. This part of the deck was now fairly deserted as the majority of passengers had moved toward the stern area, which was already beginning to lift out of the water. Chief Officer Wilde's call for women and children got no further response and he ordered the well-filled boat lowered away. As it left the deck, William E. Carter and Bruce Ismay, the latter having assisted in the loading of passengers since the first lifeboat was uncovered, stepped into the boat. Ismay would later be pilloried for this perceived act of cowardice.

Over on the port side, things had proceeded more slowly with the forward boats under Lightoller's charge. He had followed his orders to the letter and been much more strict than First Officer Murdoch about not letting men into the partly full boats. He made no exception for Colonel John Jacob Astor. At 1:55, Astor assisted his young wife into boat No. 4 and then requested permission to join her. Lightoller replied, "No sir. No men are allowed in these boats until the women are loaded first." Astor asked what boat number it was – Lightoller thought he

(Above) Second Officer Lightoller, who supervised the lowering of the port-side lifeboats, was the most senior officer to survive the disaster.

(Below) By 1:40 a.m., all the port-side boats were away, the forecastle was underwater, and collapsible D was being readied for lowering.

planned to lodge a complaint – then watched as the boat dropped away only two-thirds full. Astor went off to await his end like a gentleman. His body was later recovered, identified by the letters "J.J.A." on the back of his collar. Other prominent passengers in No. 4 included Mrs. Arthur Ryerson, Mrs. George Widener, and Mrs. John B. Thayer. The Thayers' son Jack had been separated from his parents for some time. He would jump for it at the last moment.

By 2:05 a.m., the forward Well Deck was deeply awash, the sea only ten feet below A Deck and, except for collapsibles A and B, only one boat was left – collapsible D fitted on the davits of port boat No. 2. More than 1500 people remained on the sinking ship and Second Officer Lightoller was taking no chances. He ordered his crew to lock arms and form a ring around the boat, allowing only women and children to come through. Collapsible D (capacity 47) left the ship with 44 people. Now Lightoller and several other crewmen climbed onto the roof of the officers' quarters to attempt to free collapsible B, but they had little success as the ship's tilt grew steeper. Meanwhile, Murdoch and Moody were faring somewhat better on the starboard side with collapsible A, which they managed to get down from the roof and attach to the davits where lifeboat No. 1 and then collapsible C had been launched. But before they could load it, it was washed off the deck and floated free.

As Walter Lord described the scene in *A Night to Remember*, "With the boats all gone, a curious calm came over the *Titanic*. The excitement and confusion were over and the hundreds left behind stood quietly on the upper decks. They seemed to cluster inboard, trying to keep as far away from the rail as possible." Captain Smith, who seems to have been a curiously passive figure throughout the final hours of his ship, made his way to the wireless room and told the operators they had done their duty. "Now it's every man for himself." Quietly, he walked around giving various crew members the same message. Then he headed back toward the bridge.

There were conflicting eyewitness reports about Smith's final words and final actions. But given his character and pride, it seems likely that he went down with his vessel stoically.

Probably the last glimpse anyone had of the *Titanic*'s designer, Thomas Andrews, was of him standing alone in the first-class smoking room, staring into space. (Although one witness recalled later seeing Andrews on deck, helping with the boat loading.)

Archibald Gracie was one of the unlucky ones left on the ship once all the boats were gone. "It was about this time, fifteen minutes after the launching of the last lifeboat on the port side, that I heard a noise that spread consternation among us all. This was no less than the water striking the bridge and gurgling up the hatchway forward." Gracie and his old friend J. Clinch Smith considered heading in the direction of the bridge to try to help those attempting to free collapsible A, but thought better of it and headed for the stern. "We had taken but a few steps in the direction indicated when there arose before us from the decks below, a mass of humanity several lines deep, covering the Boat Deck, facing us, and completely blocking our passage toward the stern." These were steerage passengers who had been languishing belowdecks. As the water surged over the bridge, Gracie managed to climb up on the starboard roof of the officers' quarters where a wave washed over him. "Before I could get to my feet I was in a whirlpool of water, swirling

(Above) The Poop Deck at the Titanic's stern where remaining passengers clustered after the lifeboats had gone.

(Above) Thomas Andrews, the Titanic's builder. *(Below)* Colonel Archibald Gracie.

round and round, as I still tried to cling to the railing as the ship plunged to the depths below. Down, down I went: it seemed a great distance.'' He swam underwater away from the ship, surfaced, and safely reached collapsible B, which had floated free upside down as the ship sank.

Moments before Gracie was engulfed, young Jack Thayer stood at the ship's rail until the water was only a few feet below and then jumped. He was sucked down in the icy water as he swam for his life – in a direction he hoped was away from the ship. When he finally surfaced, gasping for air and numbed by the water, the ship was perhaps 40 feet away and there was no sign of his friend Milton Long, who'd jumped seconds before. Thayer never saw him again. The ship's lights, which had burned almost to the end, had blinked once and gone out (according to Beesley). Now Thayer watched in fascination – almost oblivious to the killing cold – as the practically unsinkable ship went into its final death throes. It was now 2:18 a.m.

''The ship seemed to be surrounded with a glare, and stood out of the night as though she were on fire.... The water was over the base of the first funnel. The mass of people on board were surging back, always back toward the floating stern. The rumble and roar continued, with even louder distinct wrenchings and tearings of boilers and engines from their beds. Suddenly the whole superstructure of the ship appeared to split, well forward to midship, and bow or buckle upwards.

(Below) At 2:05 a.m., the stern begins to lift clear of the water and passengers move farther and farther aft. All boats are now gone and more than 1500 people remain on board.

The second funnel, large enough for two automobiles to pass through abreast, seemed to be lifted off, emitting a cloud of sparks. It looked as if it would fall on top of me. It missed me by only twenty or thirty feet. The suction of it drew me down and down struggling and swimming, practically spent.''

When Thayer surfaced he found that, miraculously, he'd come up against the overturned collapsible lifeboat B. Several men were already clinging to the upturned bottom of the boat. They helped Jack up to safety. He had a ringside view of the last moments of the *Titanic* as she disappeared beneath the still waters.

''Her deck was turned slightly toward us. We could see groups of the almost fifteen hundred people aboard, clinging in clusters or bunches, like swarming bees; only to fall in masses, pairs or singly, as the great part of the ship, two hundred and fifty feet of it, rose into the sky, till it reached a sixty-five or seventy degree angle. Here it seemed to pause, and just hung, for what felt like minutes. Gradually she turned her deck away from us, as though to hide from our sight the awful spectacle.''

During these final moments, the overturned collapsible was being sucked toward the ship and the men on her were desperately trying to row her away. ''I looked upwards – we were right under the three enormous propellers. For an instant, I thought they were sure to come right down on top of us. Then, with the deadened noise of the bursting of her last few gallant bulkheads, she slid quietly away from us into the sea.''

That was the end of the greatest ship the world had yet seen. Scattered over the sea were the lifeboats, many of them partially filled. Almost immediately, the silent night was punctuated with the calls of floating survivors, growing in number and anguish until in Thayer's words they became ''a long continuous wailing chant.'' Long before dawn the wailing had stopped.

The people who shivered in the drifting lifeboats, waiting for dawn, waiting for rescue, were the last people to see the R.M.S. *Titanic* for more than 73 years.

(Below, left) The heavily filled collapsible D was the last boat to be launched from the *Titanic*.

(Below) Boat No. 14, towing collapsible D, approaches the *Carpathia*.

An aerial view of Woods Hole, Massachusetts showing the Institution docks and the original administration building. In port are research vessels including the Atlantis II *(left) and the* Knorr *(center).*

CHAPTER 3

The Quest Begins

W HEN I FIRST BEGAN TO THINK ABOUT GOING AFTER THE *TITANIC*, IT was really only as a means to an end. I felt the magic of the lost ship would help attract funding that would enable me to make a major step forward in underwater research technology. But reaching the legendary wreck soon became an obsession. Over a period of more than ten years, I would try without success to mount an expedition to find and film this most famous of all shipwrecks. At one point I came incredibly close, only to be cheated of my chance by a horrible technical disaster beyond my control. Then, just when I'd pretty much given up hope and resigned myself to the fact that someone else was going to fulfill my dream, Lady Luck winked in my direction.

I've often been asked when the desire to find and film the *Titanic* first entered my mind. The precise answer to that is difficult to give. Certainly I'd known about the ship for many years before it ever occurred to me to go looking for her. You can't live your whole life as closely entwined with the sea as I have and not know the outline of her tragic story. As much as anything, however, it was the scientific challenge of actually visiting and filming the *Titanic* that first captivated me. And yet the *Titanic* also appealed to a romantic part of my personality – the underwater adventurer, the submarine cowboy. My childhood idols were imaginary explorers at the technological frontiers of science – people like Jules Verne's Captain Nemo and his *Nautilus*.

As long as I can remember I've been enthralled by the sea. But I've always been more interested in what goes on underneath the waves than on the surface. To me the surface of the ocean is beautiful but ultimately boring. As a boy walking along a California beach, I always found things the ocean washed up on the shore more interesting than the crashing surf. I was fascinated by the marine life you could discover in tidal pools. As a teenager, I became a scuba diver rather than a surfer and began to discover the world just beneath the surface. As an adult scientist, I began to go deeper still. But I wasn't particularly interested in shipwrecks. Up to the time the *Titanic* entered my head, the only wreck I'd had anything to do with was a sailboat I had helped a friend salvage and raise.

Still, I had no doubt that finding the *Titanic* would be a pioneering feat; and that visiting her and filming her at such a great depth would extend the known limits of undersea exploration. But I was not yet under her spell. She was simply a big wreck, down deep, out of reach of the technology then available when I moved from California to The Woods Hole Oceanographic Institution in Woods Hole, Massachusetts, in 1967 as a young scientist and ensign in the U.S. Navy.

Shortly after my arrival, I joined the legendary Boston Sea Rovers, one of the oldest diving clubs in the world, whose history goes back to the days before Jacques Cousteau invented the aqualung. The people I met at the club meetings talked about wrecks all the time and they began to infect me with their enthusiasm for exploring these archeological treasures of the deep. The Sea Rovers' members represented an incredible spectrum of humanity, where lawyers and surgeons mixed with stevedores and gas jockeys, all of them united in their love of the sea and the thrill of exploring it. In the late sixties, the club was still in its heyday and its annual get-togethers attracted many of the biggest names in the underwater world, people who walked in the same rarified circles as Jacques Cousteau. One of these was Jacques Picard, son of Auguste, the Swiss balloonist who really invented deep diving. Jacques had continued his father's work in the U.S. and French bathyscaphes *Trieste* and *Archimède*. Another was Captain George Bond, the Navy physician whose research into the physiological effects of scuba diving had led to the development of the Navy diving tables, now used by every diver. Bond had pioneered "saturation" diving, the technique that allows human beings to work below depths of 100 feet for hours or even days, but to go through the process of "decompression" only once. These gatherings were also attended by some of the finest underwater photographers and filmmakers in the business, people like Stan Waterman and Peter Gimbel, who filmed *Blue Water, White Death*.

A Boston Sea Rovers meeting in the early 1970s. Left to right: myself, Len Pinaud, and Stan Waterman.

I was young and completely in awe of these heroes of the underwater world, impressed not only with their professional achievements but with their skill as popularizers. Their adventures beneath the sea were breathtaking and so was their ability to communicate their exploits to the public. Stan and the others would sometimes speak about the *Titanic*, dreaming out loud of what it would be like to dive down and swim along her stately decks – and soon I had caught the bug.

But in my early days at Woods Hole I was hardly in a position to realize such a dream. I was young and I didn't yet have my Ph.D. – let alone tenure. My scientific reputation was barely in the making. Woods Hole, however, was a good place to be to make it.

The Woods Hole Oceanographic Institution was then and remains one of the two most important American institutions in the field. Our main rival was and is the Scripps Institute of Oceanography in La Jolla, California (close to home and where I'd always assumed I'd end up). Another important competitor is the Lamont-Doherty Geological Observatory in New York. During the sixties, Woods Hole geophysicists had helped gather important information about the ocean floor and the movement of the earth's crust. The Institution had grown with the boom in oceanography that happened when the space program was in its heyday, a time when there was talk of "wet NASA" concepts for the conquest of the oceans. In those days, oceanographers as well as astronauts appeared on the cover of *Time* magazine.

But to visitors, Woods Hole then as now must have seemed an unlikely place for such intensive scientific activity. The town itself remains by all appearances a sleepy New England village with a winter population of barely more than a thousand people, perched on a splendid natural harbor at the southwesternmost point of Cape Cod. In the distance you can see the waters of Nantucket Sound and the island of Martha's Vineyard and in the summer the tourists outnumber the locals as cars line up for the ferry boats.

The Woods Hole Oceanographic Institution (WHOI), referred to as

"Whooey" by local residents, was started back in 1930 by a few ocean-ographers who wanted a quiet place to work in the summer. It is dispersed over many acres throughout the town and on a nearby estate. For the most part, its buildings blend into the surrounding architecture, half-hidden by the foliage of century-old trees. On the surface, there's little about the Institution to dispel the town's image of a rural back-water, but since its founding the Institution has grown into a very sophisticated place.

It's a unique American phenomenon – a blend of cloistered academe and competitive free enterprise. Every tenured Woods Hole scientist is, in a sense, an independent entrepreneur operating under the Woods Hole banner. Woods Hole gives them the credibility of a respected name in ocean science. But they must go out and raise the money to pay their own salaries and the salaries of those who work for them. The scientists with vision and ambition eventually gather around them a scientific "company" that can be either a large and complex organiza-tion or a small and relatively simple one.

With Woods Hole scientist Dr. Wilfred B. Bryan aboard Alvin's original mother ship Lulu *in 1974 during the Project Famous expedition.*

Woods Hole is organized along the lines of a federal system with a weak and loosely defined central government existing primarily to serve a group of strong individual "states" – often in fierce competition with each other – and each ruled by its chief scientist. The management of the Institution – the central government – takes its cut of each state's annual income, but otherwise leaves them pretty much alone – unless it thinks they are doing something to hurt the image of the Institution or making promises they can't keep.

The first time I remember seriously thinking about going after the *Titanic* was in 1973. By then I had left the Navy and, as a junior scientist at Woods Hole, I was a brash 31-year-old member of the Alvin Group. *Alvin* is a small three-man submarine named after one of its early advocates – Al Vine – and the Alvin Group was then moving into the forefront of underwater research technology. Built in 1964, the sub had been developed as a tool in underwater scientific exploration. Its range was limited however by its HY-100 steel hull, permitting it to dive only to about 6,000 feet, far less than the average depth of the deep ocean (about 12,000 feet or two and a half miles).

In those days, oceanography was rapidly moving from a rather primi-tive science to a high-tech high-profile grouping of disciplines. In the forefront of the research that was developing the revolutionary theory of plate tectonics were the geophysicists with their fancy sonar equipment and deep-drilling ships. (Plate tectonics explains the phenomenon of continental drift – the fact that the earth's crust is divided into moving plates that carry the continents about with them.) These geophysicists were radically changing the way we viewed our living planet. They had already mapped the broad contours of the Mid-Ocean Ridge and vast areas of the ocean floor.

But I was a geologist, not a geophysicist. I have always had a strong bias toward the visual – toward observation and direct experience – and so had naturally gravitated to geology, which is an observational science: marine geologists are visual, hands-on oceanographers. The geophysi-cists, by contrast, are abstract scientists who love equations and abstruse theories, but in general don't like to get their hands dirty. One of their favorite tools is sonar; they prefer to bounce sound waves off the ocean's bottom rather than go down and look at it firsthand. There has long been competition between these two schools of earth science, even on land or in outer space.

In the early 1970s, the underwater geologists like myself – those who believed in direct observation – were somewhat in eclipse. We were pretty much stuck in the shallow waters of the continental shelves while the geophysicists pondered global questions. *Alvin*, with its limited depth capability, was out of the action. It couldn't dive to the deep parts of the ocean where the tectonic plates were actually drifting apart. In fact, the geophysicists sneered at us geologists who depended on a submarine and on our eyes, dismissing *Alvin* as an expensive toy. It was too difficult to see underwater, they said. Sonar was the better way.

But in 1973, *Alvin*'s steel hull was replaced with one made of a titanium alloy. *Alvin*'s new hull would double the sub's maximum depth to 13,000 feet, sufficient to dive to the crest of the Mid-Atlantic Ridge – and, incidentally, just enough to reach the ocean floor in the region where the *Titanic* had sunk. Finally, the geologists in the Alvin Group could compete with the geophysicists.

With the changes to *Alvin*, it would become the only modern submersible capable of reaching the *Titanic*. The only other manned submersibles that could go that deep were the bathyscaphes *Archimède* and *Trieste II*, but by comparison with *Alvin* these were primitive machines, big, unreliable, difficult to maintain and awkward to maneuver. Essentially they were underwater elevators. By contrast, *Alvin* was a tiny submarine with all the flexibility that that implies.

The *Alvin* conversion program was called Project Titanus. Titanium, Titanus, *Titanic*: perhaps I was struck then by the closeness of those three words. Perhaps the talk of the *Titanic* I'd heard over the years –

The Manned Submersible *Alvin*

The *Alvin* as it appeared in 1974.

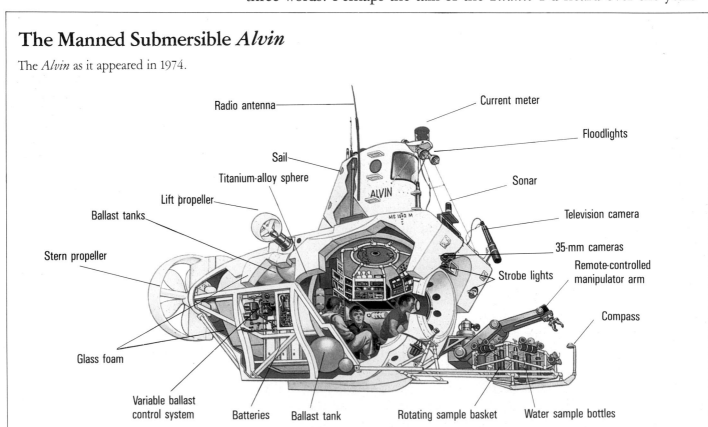

Radio antenna — Current meter — Floodlights — Sail — Sonar — Titanium-alloy sphere — Lift propeller — Television camera — Ballast tanks — 35-mm cameras — Stern propeller — Remote-controlled manipulator arm — Strobe lights — Compass — Glass foam — Variable ballast control system — Batteries — Ballast tank — Rotating sample basket — Water sample bottles especially from the redoutable Sea Rovers – had been working away in my unconscious. Whatever the reason, the *Titanic* now began to dominate my thinking. It became routine for me to imagine myself directing *Alvin* to a soft landing on the *Titanic*'s bow or exploring the famous gash made by the iceberg.

As part of the Alvin Group, I could combine primary research with my appetite for technological challenge and adventure. Diving to great depths in a tiny sub and seeing the features of the ocean floor with my own eyes seemed the only way to practice oceanography.

But at the same time, I began to dream of ways to improve our ability to see so far below the surface. It was exciting to dive two miles to the ocean floor like an underwater astronaut, but I knew there had to be a better way. I was already convinced that the best way to do this was with deep-towed vehicles mounted with special cameras and lights, eventually to be supplemented by remotely controlled robots. Among other things, such a system would save the enormous amount of time spent getting to and from the ocean floor in manned submersibles. But I also knew it would be hard to sell my dream directly, with the geophysicists still holding sway. So in 1973, the *Titanic* appealed to me not just as an adventure but as a means to fund the development of much better and revolutionary deep-sea visual-imaging technology. For the first seven years of my quest, from 1973-1980, this was in essence the approach I took. I thought that the prospect of searching for and finding this legendary ship might attract the money needed to develop the very means required to find and film her. And, as promoters like Jack Grimm would later prove, such money could be found.

But having the idea and getting the money are two quite different things. And I would see all of my *Titanic* proposals turned down over the next few years.

(Above) Alvin *comes home to the huge catamaran,* Lulu, *its floating garage. The pilot is standing in the sub's turret or "sail" and driving it toward a submerged cradle between* Lulu's *twin hulls. Once in place, divers attach lines and the sub is lifted onto a platform so technicians can prepare it for the next dive.* Lulu *holds sleeping and working spaces for the* Alvin *team and support crews.*

(Left) Just before the pilot floods Alvin's *air tanks for descent, a diver gives the sub a final check.*

During the years I was trying to raise money for a *Titanic* expedition, I was busy continuing the basic work in marine geology that earned me a Ph.D. in 1974, thereafter keeping me on Woods Hole's tenure track. In 1973 and 1974, I was part of Project Famous, the joint French and American expedition sent out to explore the Mid-Atlantic Ridge. This ridge is a mammoth mountain range running down the middle of the Atlantic Ocean and part of an even larger undersea range called the Mid-Ocean Ridge, which extends for 40,000 miles around the world. In 1973, the first year of Project Famous, I dove with French scientists in the French bathyscaphe *Archimède*. In 1974, *Alvin*, with its new titanium hull, joined *Archimède* and the French submersible *Cyana* as we continued our investigations. In the ensuing years, I made descents of 20,000 feet in the Cayman Trough, studied underwater oases of life in the Galápagos Rift – including giant tube worms and clams – a submarine ecosystem based on chemical rather than solar energy, and discovered on the East Pacific Rise the amazing "black smokers," hydrothermal vents that belch mineral-rich fluids hot enough to melt lead.

The second year of Project Famous, 1974, was also a test voyage for ANGUS (Acoustically Navigated Geological Underwater Survey), a by-product of the acoustical tracking system developed for *Alvin*. This tracking system, which would be critical in our search for the *Titanic*, allowed those in the sub and those on the surface to know exactly where *Alvin* was. Once we had the tracking system, it meant that any object equipped with a small sonar interrogation beacon could be precisely tracked underwater. So the Famous group developed ANGUS as an additional underwater tool. But initially we didn't use it in coordinated fashion with *Alvin*. That would come later.

The name is pretty impressive, but ANGUS was a homely fellow. In fact, its nickname soon became, "the dope on a rope." In 1974, it consisted of a heavy-duty steel sled mounted with black-and-white cameras, which was towed on the end of a long trawl wire over the area we wanted to explore, its down-looking cameras snapping away. The result was thousands of photographs adding up to a mosaic of the ocean floor – a visual survey.

ANGUS was fine up to a point. But before you could see what ANGUS had seen you had to wait until the sled was back on deck, and the film removed and developed. For instance, it wouldn't be very efficient for actually finding the *Titanic*. By the time the film was processed the wreck could be far behind the search vessel and would have to be found again. Even as early as 1974, I knew that another generation of deep-towed vehicles needed to be developed – one that would give us real-time visual presence on the ocean floor – something I came to call "telepresence." I didn't then have a name for the piece of hardware I would develop – but when it finally was built, it would be known as *Argo*.

In 1976, during our expedition to the Cayman Trough, ANGUS began to play a vital role in our discoveries. It became an indispensable exploration tool, identifying dive sites for our sub. Pretty soon the Alvin Group wouldn't go to sea without ANGUS. It was the beginning of the ascendance of the unmanned submersible in underwater exploration.

At the same time as I was exploring the potential of ANGUS for underwater mapping, I was working on more sophisticated techniques for taking pictures underwater. My collaborators in this effort were the

(Top) On board Lulu, *I examine the largest tube worm we brought to the surface – its body filling more than half of a 2.5 meter tube.*

(Above) Giant tube worms from the underwater oases we discovered in 1977 near hydrothermal vents along the Galápagos Rift, west of Ecuador in the Pacific Ocean.

National Geographic and especially Emory Kristof – the fine *Geographic* photographer I'd met in 1974 during Project Famous. Before long, each time we went to sea, we had not only color film, but an on-board film-processing van. For a time Emory also came to share my dream of finding the *Titanic*.

Once I'd completed my Ph.D., my position at Woods Hole became somewhat more secure. But I was still viewed as an upstart by many of my older and more established colleagues and my interest in finding the *Titanic* was looked upon by some as unscientific and inappropriate for someone working at an institution devoted primarily to pure science. Nonetheless, my desire to locate the sunken ship continued to grow even as I continued to add to my scientific credentials.

From 1974 until 1977, none of my *Titanic* schemes got very far off the ground. Looking back now, I'd have to say that 1977 was a pivotal year in my *Titanic* quest. It was the year of the *Alcoa Seaprobe* misadventure and the year I met Bill Tantum of the *Titanic* Historical Society.

As word circulated that I was interested in finding the *Titanic*, people began to come out of the woodwork. There was an outfit called Big Events which wrote to me in 1977. This company knew how to turn a publicity gimmick into a profit. One of their big successes had been buying up old cables from the Golden Gate Bridge, chopping them into small pieces, and selling them as souvenirs. I soon discovered that their goal for the *Titanic* was to turn her into paperweights. Our preliminary negotiations didn't last long. But before they were over, Big Events had introduced me to Bill Tantum – whom they were also trying to involve in their project.

When I met him, William H. Tantum IV was known as "Mr. *Titanic*" to buffs all over North America. As his wife Anne puts it now, "He really lived and died for the *Titanic*." In fact, Bill had first become interested in the ship in 1937 at the tender age of seven when he took a vacation cruise with his father on the Canadian Pacific steamer, *Duchess of Athol*. During that voyage, the passenger ship collided with the Danish collier *Maine*, which sank. Fortunately the *Duchess* sustained only minor damage, but the mishap led the passengers to talk about earlier steamship tragedies. And, for the first time, young Bill heard the names *Empress of Ireland*, (sunk in the St. Lawrence in 1914 with great loss of life), the *Lusitania* (sunk off the coast of Ireland in 1915, also with great loss of life), and the *Titanic*.

I doubt few alive knew more about the *Titanic*. Gradually, largely through his influence, the ship became much more than something to find in deep water. It became a fascinating chapter in human history. He let me browse through his collection of books and memorabilia – and he talked. Bill loved to talk and I used to love to sit and listen to him. He knew the *Titanic* story cold. And he knew its heart. As I listened to Bill, I began to understand the full dimensions of the tragedy and to acquire some of his passion for the ship. As he recreated the *Titanic*'s final hours, she began to take on a personality – to develop a soul. Pretty soon I could picture Captain Smith joking with the wireless operators as the ship was sinking or visualize Colonel Gracie huffing and puffing along the sloping Boat Deck in a vain but gallant search for the missing Mrs. Candee.

(Top) *Our deep-towed sled ANGUS (Acoustically Navigated Geological Underwater Survey) in the late '70s.*

(Middle) *Bill Tantum and I giving a presentation to a potential sponsor of our* Titanic *expedition.*

(Above) *Finding and filming the* Britannic, *one of the* Titanic*'s sister ships, was perhaps the highlight of Bill Tantum's life.*

Bill was a born comedian and a wonderful morale booster. He was always making you laugh until you cried, always had a new joke or a funny story to tell – even though he himself was in poor health and had been for many years. When I met him, he'd been working with Jacques Cousteau finding the *Britannic*, the *Titanic*'s short-lived sister vessel, which had been converted to a hospital ship and sunk by a German torpedo or mine in the Aegean in 1916.

Over the next few years until he died, he was my friend and cheerleader. When I got depressed or discouraged, he always seemed to be on the other end of the phone with words of encouragement. He never lost faith in me. Today, his wife Anne swears that from the first time we met he was sure I would be the one to find the *Titanic*. There were certainly many times I myself doubted it. And his support was very important – especially in the fall of 1977, when my dream seemed to have crashed permanently on the ocean floor.

In the spring of 1977, I started to negotiate with Alcoa Aluminum regarding the use of their advanced salvage ship the *Alcoa Seaprobe* to search for the *Titanic*. But Alcoa was one step ahead of me. Negotiations were already under way to give the ship to Woods Hole. Even though these negotiations eventually fizzled out, the news galvanized my plans. I began to study the ship in detail.

The *Seaprobe*, brainchild of Scripps' ocean engineer Willard Bascom, was essentially a drill ship – with a big drilling derrick placed amidships – which used a conventional drill pipe, not to drill, but to lower a heavy pod down to the bottom of the ocean. The pod was a rectangular box that contained various sensing instruments for conducting a search, including a side-looking sonar and both video and still cameras. The pod on the pipe had to be lowered in sections 60 feet long. Once one section had been lowered, the next one had to be screwed in place and the whole pipe lowered until another section could be attached – an annoyingly slow process. A wire strapped to the pipe communicated between the pod and the surface.

When something was found on the bottom, the pod was raised and replaced with a claw which was then lowered back down to grapple the object and laboriously raise it again to the surface, 60 feet at a time. The drill pipe was capable of a quarter of a million pounds of lift.

The ship and its rig represented a bold step forward in deep-sea technology, but it was far from ideal for my purposes. What I really needed was a system towed on a flexible cable that could be raised and lowered with relative ease, but the *Seaprobe* would have to do. It was the best thing then available. In the meantime, I would simply create a prototype of my future deep-towed video vehicle and put it in the pod on the end of the drill pipe.

I had to convince Woods Hole to support my venture. I argued that if *Seaprobe* found the *Titanic* our Institution would emerge in a relatively short period of time with the most advanced deep-sea search and mapping system in the world, a system that could then be used for scientific work. Dr. Paul Fye, then director, was sympathetic and, while the Institution's directorate was split, I was at least given the green light for a rigorous series of sea trials. Officially, these were to evaluate the potential value of the *Seaprobe* to the Institution. They would also prove whether I had what I needed for the *Titanic*.

I began borrowing sophisticated equipment: from Westinghouse, a

(Top) *The* Seaprobe *with its tall drilling derrick.*

(Above) *We lower the* Seaprobe *pod into the "moon pool" in preparation for our 1977 sea trials.*

side-scan sonar (a sonar we would attach to the pod and that could acoustically "see" objects on both sides); from the Naval Research Lab (NRL), a deep-towed magnetometer (an instrument towed on a long cable near the ocean floor that would measure the magnetic field of any object picked up by the sonar, allowing us to disqualify immediately anything the sonar found that wasn't made of metal); from the Navy, the LIBEC imaging system (a sophisticated black-and-white underwater still-camera system), developed by NRL's Bucky Buchanan; from Benthos, underwater cameras; and from *National Geographic*, additional filming equipment. The cameras and sonar would be mounted in the pod, the magnetometer on a boom. At the same time, I began approaching potential sponsors for the *Titanic* project, including Alcoa itself.

On the historical front, Bill Tantum and I began to tackle in earnest the problem of where the *Titanic* was really located and to speculate on what condition she would likely be in. If our sea trials were successful, I hoped that sometime in 1978 I could go after the ship for real. So Bill and I reviewed the historical data base and then I developed a search plan. I concluded that the *Titanic* was inside an area of 100 square nautical miles and estimated that the search would take 10-12 days. *Years* would have been more like it.

The basic historical facts were not in dispute. The *Titanic*'s official CQD or distress position was 41° 46'N, 50° 14'W, worked out by Fourth Officer Boxhall, who was generally considered to be an excellent navigator. But there was good evidence to suggest Boxhall was wrong. Captain Rostron on the *Carpathia*, steaming at full speed from the southeast in response to the *Titanic*'s distress call, reached the lifeboats well before he should have, which suggested the sinking was southeast of the official position.

In light of the variables, it would not have been all that surprising if Boxhall had made a mistake. His position was reached by dead reckoning – estimating the distance traveled from the last reliable navigational fix at sunset by simply extrapolating from estimated speed and direction of travel. But celestial navigation was itself notoriously inaccurate and dead reckoning only added to the imprecision. Furthermore, Boxhall knew nothing about the ocean currents, and if the ship had been traveling slightly more slowly than he thought, his final position could easily be ten miles off – possibly even more.

We were confident the *Titanic* wasn't west of the CQD position, but we had to come up with a search area big enough to be sure the wreck was somewhere inside it. As it turned out, the area I came up with in 1977 was virtually the same as the primary search area we used in 1985. In fact, Bill Tantum had figured out where the *Titanic* ought to be and the spot he'd marked on my map was remarkably close to where we actually found her. His guess was 50° 01'W, 41° 40'N, about three and a half miles west and slightly south of the wreck.

By the beginning of October 1977, everything was ready for our sea trials. Sadly, Bill Tantum's failing health prevented him from going on the trip but Emory Kristof was aboard – by now a familiar face on our expeditions – assigned by *National Geographic* to work with us on developing our deep-sea photography.

The *Seaprobe* may not have been the ideal ship for the job, but it appealed strongly to my romantic side – the Captain Nemo in my

The Seaprobe*'s derrick at night. In the foreground is the storage area for 3,000 feet of pipe.*

make-up. There was a big hole in the center of the vessel for the drill pipe to be lowered through and a tall derrick dominating the super-structure. At the base of the derrick – above the huge, cold, cavernous room where technicians worked on the pod – roughnecks assembled or disassembled the pipe during raisings and lowerings, while the water in the big salt "moon pool" sloshed about. To one side, behind plate glass giving a panoramic view of this noisy scene of clanking machinery and cursing humanity, was the control center – all clean and quiet, warm and bright, and filled with gleaming racks of science equipment. That was where Captain Nemo lived. I loved it.

The *Alcoa Seaprobe* set sail from Woods Hole right on schedule – just like the *Titanic* on her maiden voyage. And like the *Titanic*, a few days out of port, disaster struck. The drill crew had worked hard all during the preceding day lowering our vehicle pod with its expensive equipment 60 feet at a time, 3000 feet into the sea. Finally, we were only 60 feet above the ocean floor and the exhausted drill crew turned in for the night, while I prepared for the long hours needed to test our borrowed Westinghouse sonar. None of us knew as night descended that a fatal mistake had been made. Just before we sailed, our drilling superintendent had walked off the job and the remaining crew was unaware of a special reinforced section of pipe that was meant to be wedged into place during any towing operation.

At about two in the morning, after practically everyone on board had gone to bed, I was working in the control center with a skeleton crew of three, conducting a final sonar run in preparation for our first camera tests of the pod the next day. We were in that state of dream-like concentration that happens late at night when distractions are few. Except for the pinging of the sonar, only occasional scraps of conversation broke the silence.

Suddenly, there was a thunderous crash directly over our heads – it seemed as if the world was coming to an end. We rushed out of the room to be confronted by a grisly scene of disaster. The drill pipe had broken, and the huge counterweight perched high in the drilling derrick had dropped like a bomb over our heads. Three thousand feet of pipe weighing about 61,000 pounds plunged toward the ocean floor

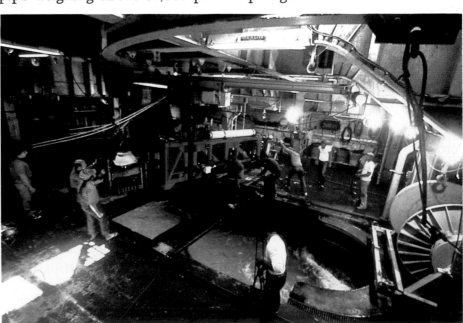

An overhead view of the "moon pool" through which our expensive equipment went crashing to the bottom.

with enough impact to bury our vehicle full of expensive equipment forever. The severed communication cable dangling from the derrick cracked like a whiplash, spewing dangerous sparks. Someone ran to switch off the power; others went to peer down into the empty "moon pool" – as if they expected to see some sign of the vanished pipe. Finally the disaster began to sink in: in one stroke our mission was destroyed. It was not only a terrible setback, but an enormous blow both to my reputation and my self-confidence.

I returned to Woods Hole with none of the borrowed hardware, apart from the magnetometer. Fortunately, Alcoa had an insurance policy that covered the lost $600,000 of borrowed equipment. But next time it would certainly be much harder to borrow things so easily. I'd been riding high, always with the feeling that luck was smiling on me, overstepping my bounds – and suddenly I was brought back down to earth.

But I wasn't about to give up on the *Titanic* because of one major setback. Even if I'd had any thoughts about abandoning my quest, Bill Tantum wouldn't have let me hear the end of it. He was even more determined than me that the *Titanic* would be found. Shortly after the *Seaprobe* debacle, he introduced me to a British filmmaker named Alan Ravenscroft, who was interested in making a documentary about the discovery, having already made a film about the *Titanic* tragedy. With the help of *National Geographic* executives and other friends, I began contacting a whole new group of potential funders, including the BBC, the major U.S. television networks, and Roy Disney.

This drawing was done in 1978 to show Roy Disney how we would explore the Titanic. *The underwater robot in the picture is not unlike the* Jason Junior *robotic vehicle we would eventually use in 1986.*

In the aftermath of the *Seaprobe* accident, Woods Hole began to distance itself from my *Titanic* project. In retrospect, I can see that this was understandable, but I felt abandoned. Essentially, they told me not to actively pursue the *Titanic* under their banner. Given the entrepreneurial partnership between Woods Hole and its scientists, I was in a bind. I was accustomed to raising money for my projects with the prestige and clout of the Institution behind me. Now this routine support was being denied.

I'm sure they assumed I'd simply fold up my tent and go back to basic science (something I'd never abandoned). Instead, I formed a company in partnership with Bill Tantum, Emory Kristof, and Alan Ravenscroft. It was called Seaonics International and it had a simple purpose: to raise money to build deep-towed visual-imaging vehicles and find the *Titanic*. Once I had the financial backing, I figured I could come back to Woods Hole management and present them with a fait accompli. Understandably, Woods Hole's new director John Steele wasn't too happy about this.

By May of 1978, I'd been turned down by all my major funding prospects except Roy Disney. He'd actually come out to Woods Hole and seemed genuinely impressed and interested. Then at the beginning of June, I got his decision: "Because of the enormous capital investment which you require immediately, it is simply not feasible for us to become involved." (We were asking for $1.5 million.) It was as if the *Seaprobe* pod had crashed to the ocean floor once more. I'll admit I was asking for a lot. I wanted someone to pay for the development of my underwater eyes and hands as well as funding the cost of the search expedition itself.

In 1979, with the *Titanic* still simmering, but definitely on the back burner, Emory Kristof and I had an opportunity to further develop

advanced imaging systems underwater. Emory and his *National Geographic* colleagues, Pete Petrone and Al Chandler, had been instrumental in helping to develop new cameras and to design the color-film lab that now processed our ANGUS pictures right on board ship. Now, as we returned to the Galápagos Rift for another look at the deep-sea life we'd discovered in 1977, we brought with us the latest in solid-state imaging devices produced in the highly competitive world of television technology. We hoped this would give us high-contrast video pictures at great depth.

This pocket-size television camera was mounted outside *Alvin* on its movable arm used for picking up samples. And this time when we visited the hydrothermal vents, we were able to come back with spectacular color video footage that was the highlight of a *National Geographic* television special called *Dive to the Edge of Creation*. Even more memorable, that trip was the first time scientists in *Alvin* turned their backs to the viewports and watched the television monitors instead for a better view. I could now imagine the day when we would replace *Alvin* altogether with remote-controlled eyes in the deep.

(Opposite) A "black smoker" belching fluids of 650°F or more.

During the years after the *Seaprobe* disaster, I continued to promote the *Titanic* project through Seaonics International with all the time and energy I could muster, but I was running out of steam. At one point, Seaonics was approached by a Texas oil millionaire named Jack Grimm who wanted to back a *Titanic* expedition. Emory Kristof negotiated with him briefly, but neither of us liked Grimm's style and the negotiations never got far. We'd had our fill of hustlers and promoters. Bill Tantum's enthusiasm never faded, but his health was finally giving out. And it seemed that my dream was dying with him. Then I got the news that Jack Grimm had teamed up with scientists at Scripps and Lamont-Doherty and that in the summer of 1980 they were going out to find the *Titanic*. The legendary Dr. Fred Spiess, whom I had come to regard as a sort of nemesis, would be in charge.

That pretty much knocked the wind out of me. Well, I thought, Fred could have the *Titanic*. It was time for me to attend to my own career. If I was finally going to get tenure, I had to get back to my writing. In June of 1979, I packed up my family and moved to California's Stanford University on sabbatical. It was a good place to work – and a good place to hide while I watched my dream realized by others. I had no doubt Fred Spiess and Bill Ryan of Lamont would find the ship and I didn't want to be anywhere close by when they did. I'm a fiercely competitive person and it looked like I'd just lost a race I'd fought very hard to win.

A year later, in early June of 1980, Bill Tantum died. Right up to the end, he'd continued to live and breathe the *Titanic* and the other great ships he loved so much. Only three weeks before the stroke that killed him, he'd traveled to Rimouski, Quebec, to speak at the opening of the *Empress of Ireland* museum. And apparently right to the end, he believed I'd find the *Titanic*. He had more faith than I did.

longitude

60°   40°   20°   0°

Southampton
Queenstown
Newfoundland   Cherbourg
60°
50°
40°
New York

latitude

552

70

194

259

380

361

St. Lawrence

1128

566

1633

1949

Anticosti I.

814   380

532

410

290

Halifax

Sable I.

Belle I.

Newfoundland

St. John's

310

303   292

220

2990

2194
Orphan
Knoll

FLEMISH
CAP

183

1862

3240

3300

3800

3322

3516

3400

3825

970

155   1346

327

179

2776

2120

690

1520

1530

2130

2842

3910

EIRIK   DRIFT

GLORIA   DRIFT

Northwest   Atlantic   Mid-Ocean   Canyon

3210

4387

4212

4410

4110

4571

4663

1224   2350   -3090
Milne
1919

GRAND BANKS

Newfoundland Seamounts

5139

FARADA

OCEANOGRAPHER

BROWNS BANK

GEORGES
BANK

HIAN MOUNTAINS

Hudson

Hudson

275

Boston

New London

New York

Washington

Norfolk

The Gully

4840

LAURENTIAN CONE   3594

NEWFOUNDLAND   RIDGE   4910

SOHM   ABYSSAL   PLAIN

5396   5221

5703

3290

5212

Heezen
Canyon

3730

1464   Mid-Ocean   Canyon

Kelvin   San Pablo

Rehoboth

CORNER   RIDGE

Corner
Seamounts

4916

Knauss

Caryn

Hudson Canyon

5011

2522
Nashville

280   Mull

4455   5536

2848

Hatteras Canyon

Blake Plateau

HUDSON DRIFT   3396

GULF STREAM DRIFT

BERMUDA   RISE

4950   4620

Bermuda

Hog High

5614

183

2926

5436

4847

CAICOS DRIFT

HATTERAS   ABYSSAL   PLAIN

570   Vema Gap   NARES   ABYSSAL   PLAIN   5907   5970

ANTILLES   DRIFT

3969

4608

90

Miami

Islands

TRENCH

1625

JAMAICA
PLATEAU

Jamaica

Cuba

Hispaniola

Puerto Rico

BEATA RIDGE

5565

4205   2225

Aruba Gap

COLOMBIA A.P.

Maracaibo

Barranquilla

Panama

MAGDALENA CONE

4941

5058

5486

AVES   RIDGE

Guadaloupe

Martinique

Barbados

1905

Caracas   Trinidad

Orinoco

20

DEMERARA
PLATEAU

AMAZON CONE   P.

5505

5200

5907

ZAMBIA   AB

5104

6640

5350

1938

1367

DEMERARA ABYSSAL PLAIN

ERACTU

CHAPTER 4
Watching From The Sidelines

HEN JACK GRIMM'S 1980 *TITANIC* EXPEDITION SET SAIL ABOARD THE *H.J.W. Fay* from Port Everglades, Florida, on July 14, 1980, I was on the other side of the world. Collaborating once again with fine French oceanographers, I was aboard the oceanographic research ship *Le Suroit* near Easter Island and Pitcairn Island in the southern Pacific. It didn't escape my notice that nearby Pitcairn Island was where mutineers from HMS *Bounty* had escaped to hide out. I felt as though I'd done the same thing.

Jack Grimm, the brash Texas oilman known as Cadillac Jack for his extensive collection of vintage cars, had certainly gotten plenty of publicity. He'd pre-sold media rights to the story and was talking about salvaging valuable artifacts from the wreck, some of which he would consider donating to the Smithsonian Institution. The way he carried on you'd have thought he'd already found the *Titanic*.

Grimm was a curious combination of hard-nosed business acumen and naive schoolboy romanticism, a man of mercurial disposition given to quixotic quests. He had previously backed a number of eccentric enterprises including looking for a "hole" in the North Pole, Noah's Ark in Turkey, Scotland's Loch Ness Monster, and even the Abominable Snowman of Tibet. He was a man not satisfied with simply making money. He wanted to be remembered in the history books. This time, since he was looking for something that definitely existed, he had a much better chance of success.

Grimm was a risk taker, but he was certainly no fool. To lead his first *Titanic* expedition he hired Fred Spiess and Bill Ryan, two of the top oceanographers in the world, both of them superb scientists and noble adversaries. Spiess, a geophysicist, was the natural choice as chief scientist since he knew as much as anyone in the world about towing sidescan sonars over the ocean floor. He agreed to take part because a successful *Titanic* expedition would be a big boost to the cause of sonar technology – leading to a higher profile and more funding. Ryan's main interest was in developing and eventually owning an advanced undersea mapping technology. Thus the expedition was suited to their respective scientific agendas. And, as well, both men were attracted to the challenge of the search.

When I was studying to become an oceanographer, Fred Spiess was already at the height of a scientific career that had put him in the forefront of underwater science. A distinguished U.S. submariner in World War Two, he'd subsequently earned his Ph.D. in nuclear physics, but then joined the Scripps Institute of Oceanography to get back to his first love, the ocean. He'd been there since 1952, since 1958 as head of the Marine Physical Laboratory, and he was in the forefront of developing technology to improve scientists' ability to accurately detect what is

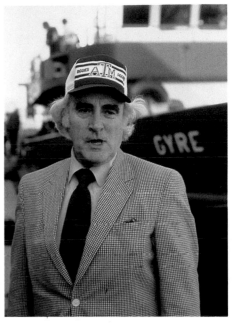

(Above) Jack Grimm stands on the dock in Boston after his second expedition in 1981.

(Opposite, inset, top) The path of the Titanic *from Southampton to the site of its distress position. (Opposite) This map of the ocean floor shows the underwater terrain in the area off the Grand Banks of Newfoundland where the* Titanic *sank. The approximate area of the sinking is marked on the map.*

on the sea floor using sonar. He had invented among many other things a partly submersible platform called FLIP for use in studying the way sound waves bent underwater. The long thin cylindrical vessel was towed into place and then its ballast tanks flooded, causing it to "flip" into a vertical position from which the scientists inside did their work. And over the years he'd also helped the Navy find a number of sunken wrecks.

The oceanographic community is small and rather close-knit. As I worked at Woods Hole, I'd gotten to know Fred Spiess and a friendly rivalry had developed between me and this man about the age of my father. I'd been turned down by Spiess when I had applied to the Scripps graduate program in the mid-sixties, and I still wanted to prove he'd made the wrong decision. We'd been on joint expeditions, including the 1979 trip to the East Pacific Rise that had found the black smokers, and we'd talked informally over the years about combining forces to go after the *Titanic*. But I'd never been able to come up with the money.

Bill Ryan, of the Lamont-Doherty Geological Observatory in New York, had actually worked at Woods Hole early in his career and had since done important research that contributed to our understanding of the formation of submarine canyons and active geological processes in the deep sea. He is now one of the leading mappers of the deep ocean. Like Spiess, Ryan is a dedicated scientist with a strong interest in exploration technology.

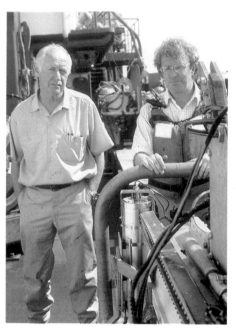

Fred Spiess of the Scripps Institute of Oceanography (left) and Bill Ryan of the Lamont-Doherty Geological Observatory.

Grimm's 1980 expedition was plagued by many problems – the most serious of which stemmed from the fact that he was not using proven Scripps technology, the Deep Tow. This was a deep-towed near-range side-scan sonar, much like the one the French would use in the first part of our 1985 expedition, which Spiess had developed in the early sixties. Over the years, he had refined it into a highly reliable mapping and search vehicle. But by early 1980, when the expedition was getting off the ground, Deep Tow had already been committed elsewhere for the summer – and it was still the only sonar around that could do the job. Instead, Bill Ryan convinced Grimm to fund the development of the *Sea MARC I* – an intermediate-range sonar for large-area mapping – designed to explore geological features like submarine landslides and canyon systems.

Unfortunately, *Sea MARC* was less than ideal for looking for the *Titanic*. In principle, it worked like all deep-towed side-looking sonars. As it was trailed 656 feet above the seafloor at the end of a long cable, it shone a "flashlight" out to either side, but instead of light waves its illumination was produced by means of sound waves. Any object caught by the flashlight's beam cast a shadow and its characteristics were recorded when the sound waves bounced off the object and back to the vehicle.

Sea MARC's great advantage for a search of this sort was that it would cut a swath one-and-a-half to three miles wide along the ocean floor, two-and-a-half to five times the width of the Scripps sonar – so it could cover much more ground in the short time available. Its disadvantage was that its images would not be as high-resolution as Deep Tow's even though it was designed to be able to pick out a *Titanic*-sized object right to the edges of its range. But if bad weather was encountered, *Sea MARC*'s sonar records would be even fuzzier, as surface motion reduces the effectiveness of any deep-towed vehicle. Because it was covering such a wide area, a large object might therefore be lost in the "shadows" of more complex bottom terrain. To make things even dicier, Ryan would still be working out the kinks of this new and untested piece of equipment, even while the search was being conducted. In sum, the *Sea MARC* might pass directly over the *Titanic* and not even see her.

The expedition was scheduled to reach the search area in late July. That gave Ryan roughly three months to design and build *Sea MARC* and work out any problems. Not surprisingly, when the ship left Florida they were still working on the equipment. It had its first test on the way out to the site, and last-minute hiccoughs led to a time-consuming delay in Bermuda. But, miraculously, Bill had it all working for the search, despite numerous operational wrinkles still to be ironed out.

Before the ship left port, Grimm did his best to turn the expedition into a publicity carnival. He arranged for a monkey by the name of Titan to go on the trip. According to William Hoffman, who wrote *Beyond Reach*, an account of Grimm's second expedition, "The monkey had been taught to point at a spot on the map indicating where the *Titanic* was. Grimm believed this was a remarkable accomplishment that would add immeasurably to the movie he was making out of the search. The scientists, especially the illustrious Dr. Spiess, thought the idea bizarre, insane, and circus-like, which could only detract from and hold up to ridicule what they regarded as a very serious endeavor. They laid down the law: 'It's either us or the monkey.' 'Fire the scientists,' was Grimm's reply. Saner heads prevailed. The monkey was left behind."

In 1980, they did no better than the monkey would have. Before setting out, the scientists had only concentrated on preparing for the scientific aspect of the expedition, while Grimm looked after the historical research. As Bill Ryan recalls it, they set out with only one working hypothesis: that the *Titanic* had sunk east of the ice barrier that the *Californian* had stopped in for the night. When the scientists discovered this lack of historical preparation, they hastily attempted to rectify matters on the way out to the site.

Sea MARC I *being recovered. Bill Ryan stands on the extreme right.*

Their basic search strategy was to first investigate the area in the vicinity of the *Titanic*'s distress or CQD position. If they found nothing there, they would survey a much larger area concentrating on a rectangle just east of the CQD position bounded by 41°40'N to 41°50'N and 50°00'W to 50°10'W. This region is bisected from northeast to southwest by a submarine valley with many tributaries, which the scientists christened *Titanic* Canyon.

Following their plan, the *Titanic*'s official distress position was investigated and nothing was found. Then they began to run a series of north-south lines, which surveyed wide swaths of the ocean floor with the *Sea* MARC side-looking sonar, carefully overlapping one line with the next. This technique is known as "mowing the lawn," a tedious and relentless back-and-forth process. In the meantime, the weather was getting worse and the *Fay* proved less than adequate for the task. On a number of occasions time was lost because she could only make way down wind and was going too fast to trail the *Sea* MARC at the right depth. According to Fred Spiess 30 to 50 percent of the time on site in 1980 was wasted due to either bad weather or equipment problems.

On August 2, only a day and a half into the search, disaster struck. The *Sea* MARC's fiberglass tailfin ripped off during a high-speed turn, taking the magnetometer to the depths with it. The loss of the magnetometer – which would have shown up any magnetic signature characteristic of large metal objects like a steel-hulled ship – combined with *Sea* MARC's teething pains, made the remainder of the 1980 expedition something like searching in the dark with one eye closed and the other one squinting. However, Ryan's sonar was soon repaired and went on to survey an area of roughly 500 nautical square miles and to identify 14 widely scattered sonar targets – including several that corresponded in size to the *Titanic*'s hull. Had the magnetometer been working, however, most if not all of those targets could have been eliminated as not being metallic.

Throughout the 1980 search, Spiess and Ryan were not only dogged by bad weather and equipment problems, but also by Grimm's public-relations pronouncements on shore. At one point, he actually led the press to believe that the *Titanic* had been found. When those on board the *Fay* heard the news report there was laughter and incredulity. Naturally, when they sailed into Boston on August 21, Grimm wanted the scientists to back up his claim. After the *Fay* docked there was something of a confrontation in the ship's lab. Grimm wanted the scientists to say that they'd found the ship – that one of those 14 sonar targets was the *Titanic*. As careful professionals Spiess and Ryan were having none of this. There was a long tense argument at the end of which the wording of a non-committal press communique was agreed to. All Grimm had to show for his money were some questionable maybes.

Jack Grimm's second *Titanic* expedition departed from Woods Hole on June 28, 1981, and there were crowds of people to see off his ship, the R/V *Gyre*. Although Woods Hole was the port of departure, it wasn't meant as a deliberate snub (it was simply that the *Gyre*'s preceding charter was held by Woods Hole scientists) but it felt as though Grimm was rubbing salt in the wound of my disappointment. And in 1981, he seemed assured of success.

This time, Grimm himself was on board along with both Fred Spiess and Bill Ryan, but now the searching sonar would be the Scripps Deep

The R.V. Gyre *leaving Woods Hole Harbor on June 28, 1981.*

Tow. (Ryan also brought with him an underwater imaging unit, the Deep Sea Color Video System, which would be used to photograph the wreck. He had deployed it only once in 1980 – on the way home after the search – and was anxious to try it on the ship itself.) The *Gyre* was still not ideal for the job, but this time they had the right equipment. The trouble was they would again spend most of their time looking in the wrong place.

After 1980, Grimm and the scientists had been more thorough about their historical homework. And this homework led them to the correct ultimate conclusion. They hypothesized that Fourth Officer Boxhall had made a mistake in calculating the distress position because he'd failed to properly take into account the retarding of the ship's local time as it moved west. This, they thought, could mean the real position was as much as eight miles further east. Indeed, from the position of the ice floe, as reported by the *Californian* and later the *Mount Temple*, they concluded that the *Titanic* might be as far east as 50°03'W. They pondered the speed at which the *Carpathia* had arrived on the scene and figured that the lifeboats could not have been further north than 40°45'N. They thought the *Titanic* hit the iceberg no further eastward than longitude 50°00'W and that she could have drifted a maximum of four miles before sinking.

Their final conclusion, once they'd analyzed the data, was that there was a "high probability" the *Titanic* wasn't west of longitude 50°20'W (the *Titanic*'s CQD position was 50°14'W) and that it wasn't east of 49°55'W. In addition, they figured that the ship couldn't be north of 41°55'N or south of 41°35'N.

As it turned out, the *Titanic* was within this rectangle – barely. And in 1981, the searchers again came close. But this time they were too busy going over old ground. If they'd followed their own conclusions and searched thoroughly east of 50°W, they would undoubtedly have found the ship. As it was, Deep Tow passed within a mile and a half of the wreck, a distance well outside the range of its sonar.

Hoffman provides a nice summing-up of the two fundamental assumptions underlying Grimm's 1981 search strategy: "Because of the extensive search conducted in 1980 and location of fourteen possible targets, the 1981 search operated on the assumption that the *Titanic* was more or less intact but acoustically obscured by nearby geological features." In other words, they thought they hadn't found her in 1980 because she was hidden in the shadow of some natural feature. This time, the more precise images of the Deep Tow would see into all these shadows and find the ship. Hoffman adds, "The scientists knew fairly well where the *Titanic* had to be, unless the ship's navigation was so poor that her SOS position was in error by more than ten miles. It seemed impossible since that implied corresponding errors for other ships as well." Both assumptions were wrong. And they led Grimm to spend most of his time investigating *Titanic* Canyon and its tributaries, the underwater feature that would mesmerize us as well in 1985.

Thus, instead of exploring new territory to the east of 50° W (where the *Carpathia* said it picked up the lifeboats), the 1981 expedition spent its whole time at sea investigating a smaller area within the 500 nautical square miles Sea MARC had searched the previous year and taking a closer look at those tantalizing 14 targets. Spiess undoubtedly felt that his Deep Tow would find the *Titanic* where Sea MARC had

(Above) Deployment of Lamont's Deep Sea Color Video System which Grimm hoped would photograph the wreck.

(Below) Fred Spiess plans transponder positions, while film producer Mike Harris looks on.

already looked.

Once again bad weather hampered the search, but the Deep Tow did a thorough job of covering *Sea MARC*'s tracks. One by one the sonar targets were eliminated – natural features every one.

After three weeks, they had not spotted even a sign of debris and Grimm was growing desperate. As the final hours of their time on site approached, the ship's winch broke, requiring recovery of the Deep Tow and apparently scotching further search efforts. While the winch was being frantically repaired, Grimm managed to wheedle the ship's owners into giving him ten more hours on site before the *Gyre* had to head home. By this time, the Deep Tow transponders – the underwater acoustic beacons that anchor its navigation – had been recovered. But Ryan was willing to put his video vehicle in the water for an eleventh-hour effort.

The Deep Sea Color Video System wasn't designed as a search instrument and Ryan knew the odds were one in a billion, but he figured it was a great opportunity to test his still-new equipment under difficult conditions. So they started by taking one last run down *Titanic* Canyon and then went east until it was time to head home.

This is a part of the story I'm particularly fond of because Ryan's camera vehicle was a piece of video hardware, not a sonar. So it was a visual search that found Grimm's "propeller." The Deep Sea Color Video doesn't show high-quality images in real time. What you see is a fuzzy black-and-white image on the shipboard TV screen while the high-quality color video is recorded and stored down below and can't be viewed until the vehicle is recovered. The vehicle is equipped with a microphone. So you get a color movie with underwater sound.

It wasn't until the *Gyre* was steaming back to Boston, as the crew gathered to watch the footage, that Grimm, Spiess, and Ryan could see clearly what Ryan's vehicle had seen. The surprise came in the last 30 minutes of the video – a point at which the ship had left *Titanic* Canyon and was moving east toward the area where the lifeboats had been picked up. As Hoffman describes it, "From a sea of empty life, just rushing water, stunningly it was there. It looked to be the twenty-six tons a *Titanic* propeller would weigh. The television coverage was so impressive because what was captured appeared suddenly, a colossus right before the eyes, and then it was gone." Accompanying this image was a metallic scraping sound picked up by the microphone. This could have been the frame of the vehicle hitting a large rock formation – or hitting the metal hull of the *Titanic*'s stern looming above. (Since the video vehicle lacked a magnetometer, there was no way of knowing.) But the camera showed no image of what it was scraping against, only the "propeller," which looked as if it was suspended in the water from above.

Spiess and Ryan of course balked at positive identification. The pictures weren't clear enough and there was no magnetic reading to reinforce the visual image. In fact, the area had been covered by the *Sea MARC* sonar in 1980 and by Deep Tow plus magnetometer in 1981, with no indication of the ship. But the professional sailors on board, including the ship's captain (and many who saw the video later) all agreed the fuzzy television image looked like a propeller and that it was the right size and general shape. The scientists remained dubious, but Grimm was completely convinced and told the world he'd found the *Titanic*.

The media dutifully reported his claim and the networks aired his

The Scripps Deep Tow, Fred Spiess' pioneering deep-towed side-looking sonar, being prepared for a launch.

video footage, but with mounting scepticism. Like the boy who cried wolf, Grimm was beginning to lose his credibility. For the second year, he was convinced he had found the wreck, but his scientists weren't. It wasn't long before the whole subject disappeared from the news pages.

It took Jack Grimm two years to raise the funds to take another look at his "propeller." This time, he would have only a handful of days on the site – but he figured that was all he needed. He believed it was simply a question of sailing out to his "propeller" and filming it attached to the hull of the *Titanic*. His expedition had been organized on short notice and Fred Spiess was committed to other projects, so only Bill Ryan was with Grimm aboard the R/V *Robert D. Conrad* when it departed from Halifax in July of 1983. By the time they reached the "propeller" position, the weather was turning from bad to worse – 30- to 40-knot winds and 15- to 30-foot seas.

Their plan was to check out the "propeller" with Ryan's sonar and, if that didn't work out, to continue their search to the east – east of 50°00'W, into an area they hadn't looked in since 1980 – and then into virgin territory. But the sonar showed nothing even close to the *Titanic*'s proportions at the "propeller" site, and the weather was deteriorating further.

In the time remaining, Ryan began his eastward search, hoping the weather would permit him to put in two north-south swaths that would extend the *Sea MARC* coverage about six miles to the east. At the end of a long day, he went to bed, assuming that when he awoke the next morning a lot of new territory would have been covered. But while he was asleep, Grimm ordered the watch to turn the ship around to take one more pass over his "propeller": he just couldn't believe the *Titanic* wasn't there. By the time that pass was complete, the weather had worsened and gale force winds made further sonar search impossible. A couple of last-ditch out-of-control camera runs over the "propeller" site yielded nothing and Grimm headed home knowing only that if a propeller was down there, it wasn't attached to any wreck.

Jack Grimm had been both foolish and, contrary to his reputation, unlucky. According to Bill Ryan, over the course of all three expeditions – more than 40 days on site – Grimm enjoyed only one day with winds of less than force 4 (13-18 mph).

Jack Grimm's three expeditions didn't find the *Titanic*, but they were of some use to underwater science. Bill Ryan developed and tested his large-area mapping sonar and showed some of the potential of visual imaging in the deep ocean. In fact, Ryan's *Sea MARC* actually passed within range of the *Titanic* several times. However, the *Titanic* did not stand out on the sonar record due to the fact the sonar was not working properly. Spiess and his Deep Tow gathered the most precise data yet on the seafloor in the area, including *Titanic* Canyon.

I think Grimm's failure can be ascribed to four basic problems. First, he didn't put enough faith in the scientists he'd hired. Second, he didn't go out with a thorough enough idea of where he should be looking. Third, he didn't stick to a basic search strategy, but kept going back to "targets" that fascinated him. Fourth, he wasn't at sea long enough on any one occasion to expand his search area once he didn't find the ship where he thought it should be. So, against all odds, the *Titanic* was still waiting to be found. I would soon be in a position to again take up the challenge myself.

(Top) *Jack Grimm at his 1981 press conference in Boston.*

(Above) *A mosaic of Grimm's "propeller." This image convinced many of the sailors on board the* Gyre *that the* Titanic – *or at least a piece of it – had been found.*

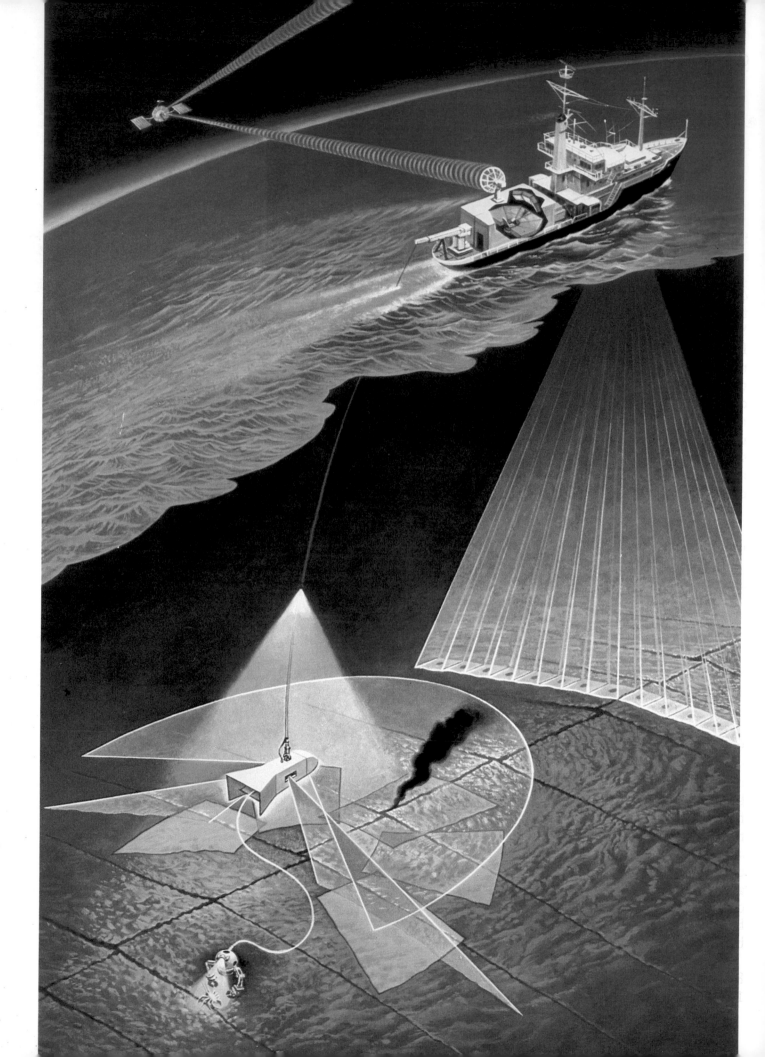

CHAPTER 5
Jason And The Argonauts

IN 1980, WITH BILL TANTUM'S DEATH AND JACK GRIMM OFF LOOKING FOR THE *Titanic*, I had turned to the U.S. Navy to fund the development of the deep-sea visual imaging technology I'd dreamed about – a dream which now carried the name *Argo/Jason*. After my year at Stanford – and the publication of several papers on hydrothermal vents – Woods Hole had granted me tenure. Now secure in the knowledge the Institution couldn't fire me as long as I raised enough money to sponsor my research, I could concentrate on bringing to fruition the concept that I'd been refining over the years. *Argo/Jason* was to be a remotely controlled deep-towed deep-sea video vehicle combined with a swimming robot on a long cable-leash. I had chosen the name *Argo* as a reference to Jason and his mythological ship the *Argo* which sailed in search of the Golden Fleece in the ancient Greek legend. It seemed an appropriate title for what I hoped would become the cutting edge in deep-sea research.

That fall, I concluded that the Office of Naval Research (ONR) was the best bet to back my vision. ONR has a tradition of taking chances on individual people as much as research programs. I also knew the Navy had until now overlooked the importance of visual imaging underwater and that my approach held great promise, not only for research and exploration, but for use in submarine warfare.

Needless to say, the Navy was interested.

As I conceived it then, *Argo* was to be an unmanned submersible loaded with video cameras towed above the ocean bottom at the end of a long fiber-optic cable by a mother ship cruising along at one or two knots. The ship's terrain-mapping, multiple-beam sonar would pave the way for *Argo* – surveying the area and digitizing the gathered data to produce a three-dimensional map. *Argo* itself would have two sonar systems – a forward-looking one to detect any obstacles in its path and a side-looking sonar to investigate bottom geology. It would also be equipped with five video cameras giving the operators, sitting comfortably in the control room on the surface, a panoramic view of the ocean floor. When the scientists spotted something interesting, they would then be able to activate the robot *Jason*, while *Argo* hovered stationary above the bottom. *Jason* would be attached to *Argo* on a tether and equipped with lights and stereo cameras and its own propulsion system, allowing it to roam into riskier places and gather specimens from the ocean floor or take close-up color images. Both *Argo*'s and *Jason*'s high-resolution images would also be available for instant transmission by satellite anywhere in the world.

After my return to Woods Hole, I continued to work with Emory Kristof on developing underwater photographing technology. In early 1981, testing a prototype SIT camera near the Caribbean island of St.

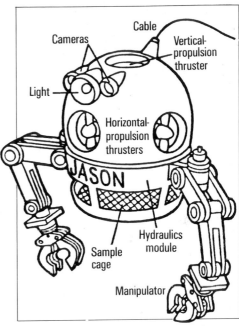

(Above) A 1981 drawing of Jason *during its early conceptual stages.*

(Opposite) The Argo/Jason *system as I conceived it in 1981. The pink arc indicates the area covered by* Argo's *forward-looking sonar; the pink triangles show the range of the side-looking sonar; and the green trapezoids show the view provided to those at the surface by* Argo's *five cameras.*

Croix, we took the largest underwater images ever seen, three-quarters of an acre in size. (SIT stands for Silicon Intensified Target; the technology was originally developed for sniper scopes used in the Vietnam War. It magnifies available natural light 10,000 times, making it possible to literally see in the dark.) The Navy was impressed with our results, but not with the fact we were unable to explain how we achieved them. Up until this point we'd proceeded largely by intuition. Now, in order to maintain Navy funding, I would have to come up with a much more scientific approach to the problem.

While Emory went on to other photographic pursuits, I now turned to the group of imaging engineers I had been gathering at Woods Hole – the nucleus of my newly formed Deep Submergence Laboratory (DSL). These were the modern equivalent of Jason's mythological Argonauts who would help me in my quest to find the Golden Fleece – the *Titanic*. They were eager to take over where Emory had left off and, unlike Emory and me, they were schooled in the complexities of imaging technology and electrical engineering – which meant they could explain exactly what they were doing. Their work was deeply rooted in physics and mathematics; they were up on robotics and control theory; and they would develop *Argo* and *Jason* step by step, testing it every inch of the way. My Navy sponsors felt much more at ease with this traditional approach.

Stu Harris (right) working on Argo *with James Saint (center) and Emile Bergeron (left).*

The genesis of DSL was the ANGUS group which I had formed and led during the latter half of the 1970s while I continued to dive in *Alvin*. At one stage, I'd spent more time in *Alvin* than any other scientist as well as more time on the deep-ocean floor than any other researcher using deep submersibles. If I was going to challenge the future of manned submersibles in the deep sea, at least I couldn't be accused of doing so from a position of ignorance.

My philosophy in building DSL was to create a family atmosphere similar to the one I'd experienced as part of the Alvin Group in the early seventies. In carrying out this philosophy the essential rule is that the team does the hiring and firing, not you. In this way they feel responsible for the strengths or shortcomings of an individual member.

One of the key people we hired for DSL was Stu Harris, the man who would be *Argo*'s chief designer. With a master's degree in electrical engineering and a strong background in visual-imaging systems, Stu was ideal for the role. The first person he picked to join the *Argo* team was Bob Squires, an expert in video-imaging software. A later addition to Stu's team was Tom Dettweiler, an excellent seagoing engineer who had already worked with a deep-towed vehicle system similar in many ways to *Argo* and had at-sea expertise in side-scan sonars and television search systems.

If the *Argo* team in some ways represented the brains of the Deep Submergence Lab, then the "techies" were its soul. Of these, the most vivid character was (and is) Earl Young, a crusty veteran of my ANGUS team, an irascible old salt and a superb seaman. Earl is a true intuitive techie – he feels his way to the heart of a problem and then fixes things with a hammer and hack saw. Many times, when the engineers on board are seasick or shaking their heads over a design problem, Earl and his buddies Emile Bergeron and Tom Crook are out on the rolling and freezing deck in the middle of the night, working coolly under fire and getting the job done.

The building years were 1980 to 1984 – both of a team and a new deep-sea exploration vehicle. By the time Jack Grimm came home empty-handed in the summer of 1983, the Deep Submergence Laboratory was at full strength and *Argo* was becoming a reality. (*Jason* was then still on the drawing board.) It now seemed a perfectly logical suggestion to test *Argo* in the area where the *Titanic* went down, or better, on the hull of the *Titanic* itself, a very deep wreck no one had yet photographed.

After all the years of dreaming of going to look for the ship, coming achingly close, then seeing my hopes dashed, it suddenly all came together. Early in 1984, the Navy agreed to fund a three-week test for the summer of 1985. I knew it would be a race, but I knew we would have *Argo* ready in time.

I had dreamed for so long of having a clear shot at the *Titanic* that it was hard to believe I was finally going to get one. Put a ship under me, I had said, and put my team and equipment on it, and the rest would be easy. I knew my team was the best, but 100 square miles of rugged

The *Argo* System

(Right) A side view of Argo *beginning a descent. It weighs 2 tons and is 15 feet long, 3.5 feet tall, and 3.5 feet wide.*

(Below) A schematic drawing of Argo *showing the placement of its internal components.*

(Right) A still photo of the video image Argo *sends from the ocean floor to a monitor screen in the control van on the surface ship's deck. This photograph is of a lava flow near the East Pacific Rise.*

(Above) A diagram of Argo's *photographic "footprint," showing the area covered by the sled's three cameras. The small rectangle in the center shows the zoom capacity of the telephoto lens.*

deep-sea terrain is a big piece of real estate and three weeks just didn't seem enough time to insure that I'd find the ship. (Grimm had several weeks and had failed to find it.) So as soon as I knew our 1985 expedition had been approved, I hopped on an airplane to Paris and the headquarters of IFREMER, the French National Institute of Oceanography. The French could almost always be counted on to join ranks with us, particularly when high technology was involved. Besides, having worked so well with them in the past, and knowing their predilection for underwater adventure, I was sure they'd want to get in on the action.

With the election of the Mitterand government there had been changes in IFREMER's top management – most notably a new director, Yves Sillard, who'd been involved in the French space program. But I still had friends in court. I'd known IFREMER's number-two man, Claude Riffaud, since the planning for Project Famous, which he had supervised from the French side. Jean Jarry, an engineer with whom I'd worked closely during the Famous expedition, had moved out of field operations at Brest into a position of responsibilty at head office. He was also bound to be interested. Then there was Jean-Louis Michel, another compatriot from Project Famous days, still working as a field engineer. Jean-Louis now had a fancy new side-looking sonar called SAR (for *sonar acoustique remorqué*) that was as good or better than the Scripps Deep Tow.

When I arrived in Paris, Claude Riffaud hosted a dinner at his apartment for Sillard and Jarry (Jean-Louis was in Brest). In a relaxed atmosphere of wine and good food, I explained my plan to find the *Titanic* and then film it with *Argo* and ANGUS. Was IFREMER willing to participate in a co-expedition? With our combined resources – which meant both more time and more technology – I was sure we would find the ship. For Sillard's benefit I compared the search for the *Titanic* to landing on the moon. It would be a great moment in the history of international scientific cooperation and a glorious scientific accomplishment. By the time dinner was over, I was sure IFREMER would go along. And indeed they did.

Jean Jarry would be the French project leader. Jean-Louis Michel – who would co-lead the expedition at sea with me – and I began to formulate a plan. The lion's share of the spadework would be done by the French, because my part of the expedition was not officially to look for the *Titanic* but to test a new piece of equipment, *Argo*. While I would be going out under the Woods Hole banner, the Institution was not backing me officially in any way. By contrast, the *Titanic* was an official goal for IFREMER, who saw it not only as a chance to demonstrate their equipment and expertise but as a potential source of revenue. There would undoubtedly be books and documentary films that would result if the ship were found.

The French agreed to recheck the weather patterns in the area to determine the optimum schedule: we knew the North Atlantic weather was unpredictable at the best of times and had badly hampered Grimm's expeditions. One of my major jobs was to research the nature of the bottom topography, especially any canyons that would make our efforts more difficult. (Canyons provide confusing echoes and large objects can get lost in this noise.) We already knew that water conditions at the *Titanic*'s depth were suitable for a visual search. (Years before, Bill Tantum had arranged to have the International Ice Patrol take

Jean Jarry, the French project leader.

Emory Kristof and two photographers out to check the bottom water.) Then there was the perennial question of where to search. Three previous attempts had been made by fine scientists using excellent equipment, but they had failed.

Bill Ryan at Lamont kindly showed Jean-Louis the *Sea MARC* records from 1980, but Fred Spiess was unwilling to release the 1981 Deep-Tow data without Grimm's approval. Although we doubted the Deep Tow had missed anything, there was still that possibility. After all, the sea bottom in the area was complicated, especially around *Titanic* Canyon. And there was no guarantee the ship was still in one big piece, as Spiess and Ryan had assumed. Lacking the Deep-Tow records, and seeing the poor quality of much of the *Sea MARC* data, we concluded we would have to go over the area covered by Spiess and Ryan just to be sure.

I concentrated my limited resources on finishing *Argo*, while IFREMER put money and man-hours into further historical research. Jean-Louis and I read and reread the various accounts of the disaster and pondered the conflicting information that has come down to us about the events before and after the sinking. When we had finished, we had come up with a 100 nautical-square-mile primary search area and a secondary search area of an additional 150 nautical square miles (which included part of the primary search area) mostly to the east. We were convinced that within this area the *Titanic* would be found.

At the Deep Submergence Laboratory, the spring of 1985 was a blur of action. As so often happens when you've got a tough deadline, things came down to the wire. Suppliers were late delivering key components. And I had to know the whole thing was working properly before we set out. The ship we would be using, the *Knorr*, was departing Woods Hole on another scientific expedition on June 17. *Argo* had to be ready by then.

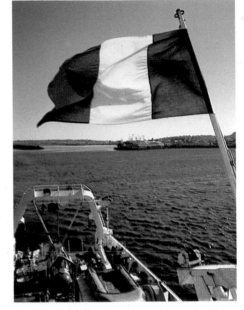

The French flag flies proudly over the fantail of Le Suroit.

Over the next five weeks the DSL Argonauts worked overtime – nights and weekends – as our deadline rapidly approached. The team spirit seldom waned; wives and children came to keep us company and held informal barbecues while we fine-tuned *Argo*, making last-minute adjustments to the telemetry system. At last everything was ready – except for the tow cable which hadn't yet arrived. It would have to be shipped air freight to the Azores where our team would board the *Knorr* in early August. If the cable didn't make it, *Argo* would be useless.

Our expedition plan called for a two-phase operation. During phase one (approximately four weeks on site) the French ship *Le Suroit*, led by Jean-Louis Michel, would find the *Titanic* by conducting a systematic search of the selected area using his newly developed deep-towed SAR sonar. In phase two (about 12 days on site), aboard the American ship *Knorr*, we would use *Argo* to visually inspect the various sonar targets SAR had picked up. The one that turned out to be the *Titanic* would be documented with *Argo* and with ANGUS, our veteran underwater still-camera vehicle that had by now taken hundreds of thousands of pictures in the ocean depths.

On June 24, 1985, *Le Suroit* set out from Brest, France. After a short stopover in the Azores, it then headed for the area where the *Titanic* went down. I would join the ship about halfway through the first phase of the expedition. I prayed the French wouldn't find the *Titanic* before I got there.

The sea was calm as Le Suroit *steamed out of St. Pierre to begin the second phase of the French sonar search.*

CHAPTER 6

Discovery

IN THE GRIM STRETCH OF THE NORTHWEST ATLANTIC WHERE THE *TITANIC* foundered, there is only a handful of weeks when the elements are likely to be kind. This prime summer "weather window" lasts from about mid-July to mid-September, but even in mid-summer terrible storms are possible – as Jack Grimm had the misfortune to find out. We knew that our decision to stretch these limits, and begin the search in late June, was a risky one. But given the size of the area we planned to search, it was a necessary gamble. Subtracting the time required to get to and from the search area – first for the French ship *Le Suroit*, then for the American ship *Knorr* – we would have barely five weeks to accomplish our mission. Five weeks not only to find the *Titanic*, but to bring back a detailed photographic record of the wreck for the waiting world. The 1985 *Titanic* expedition promised to be a constant fight against time and nature.

On paper, the search seemed simple. Our strategy was set, our equipment was in place and operational, and, as I'd always said, finding the *Titanic* should be easier than actually getting her on film. Jack Grimm, Fred Spiess, and Bill Ryan hadn't found the task so simple, however; neither would Jean-Louis Michel aboard the French research vessel *Le Suroit*.

Jean-Louis and his French crew arrived on site July 5 to begin the first part of the sonar search. Meanwhile, I was busy off the Pacific coast of Mexico, doing a series of dives in *Alvin* and conducting preliminary tests on *Jason Junior*, a prototype of the *Jason* robot that would eventually become part of the *Argo* system. Finally, on July 22, I arrived on the French island of St. Pierre, just south of Newfoundland in the Gulf of St. Lawrence, where, after two weeks of searching, *Le Suroit* had come to resupply.

So far the French had found nothing. They had covered a fair bit of ground, but had been hampered by a stronger than expected current. The expedition had barely begun and we were already behind schedule.

With me as I boarded the French ship were three other Americans who comprised the documentation team that would immortalize our mission if it became a success. Bill Lange, the youngest of the three, was from Woods Hole. Eager to learn and excited to be on the trip, he would be a combination of aide de camp and apprentice to the two veterans, Ralph White, whom I had hired to help document the expedition on 16 mm film, and my old partner Emory Kristof, the *National Geographic*'s renowned still photographer. (The *National Geographic* was helping to pay for the documentation of our expedition and would be the first to publish an in-depth story on our search – if it was successful.)

I'd wanted Emory on the trip not just because he's one of the best,

Our documentary photographer Emory Kristof, astride SAR, does his impression of Slim Pickens in the movie Dr. Strangelove.

which he is, and someone I'd worked with many times before, but because I felt he'd earned a piece of the discovery. Given our previous *Titanic* collaboration, it seemed only right that he should be present when our mutual dream was finally fulfilled.

Ralph and Emory are the journalistic equivalent of a SWAT team – photographic hit men who move swiftly into action the moment they're needed. They are the sort of people you want in the trenches during the heat of battle, but until the battle was joined they didn't have much to do except sit and wait.

When we walked on board *Le Suroit*, we entered a foreign country. I, at least, had spent a good deal of time aboard French ships over the years; and Jean-Louis Michel and I were good friends. But for Kristof, White, and Lange, it must have seemed as though they had landed on another planet. None of them spoke French and they were consigned to quarters in a separate container on the stern. As a result, they kept pretty much to themselves, playing cards, listening to music, reading – and waiting. Waiting for something to happen.

The first thing that strikes you on board a French oceanographic vessel is the importance of food. The smell of food is everywhere, the rich odors of meat and garlic pervade the ship, and mealtimes are the central and rather formal ritual of shipboard existence. Apparently as much as a third of a total expedition budget is spent on food. It was certainly all very civilized, but the general atmosphere was too restricted for my liking.

Le Suroit was also very cramped. With about 50 people on board, it was almost impossible to find a private space, particularly in bad weather. She's a small ship and she was simply jammed with equipment and people. I was forever banging my head or my knees and it was all I could do to get four feet of work space. Even the sleeping accommodations were crowded and the bathroom facilities inadequate. It was like living in a floating college dorm.

Thank God for Jean-Louis. Having spent a year at Woods Hole, he now spoke quite fluent English – with a charming Maurice Chevalier accent – and he was an old and good friend. With him on board, it made it easier for me to ignore the cramped formality of this foreign

In the crowded top lab aboard Le Suroit, *control center for the French phase of our mission, Jean-Louis Michel leans over the navigation center to discuss tracking with one of the expedition's navigators.*

ship and concentrate on the task at hand: finding the *Titanic*. Over the next three weeks, we spent a great deal of time together.

As *Le Suroit* put out to sea, I must confess I was having some mixed feelings. I was hoping the French would find the *Titanic* and I was hoping they wouldn't. If they failed, that would leave very little time for the American phase of the expedition to both locate the wreck and photograph it. But it was only human for me to want to be the one to find the ship. This is not to say that Jean-Louis and I didn't share the power and the responsibility of command. We were a team and he consulted me on every decision he made, but as long as we were on a French ship Jean-Louis had the final word. Later, our roles would be reversed.

Jean-Louis and I had always worked together well, something that may seem surprising to outsiders because we couldn't be more different. He is a very quiet person, very private, and very serious, the epitome of the professional engineer – dedicated, meticulous, and methodical to the point of stubbornness, extremely cautious, and with a quiet sense of humor. He's also cool under pressure. Really, he's a gentle man in the best sense – and very proud to be French, very proud of the accomplishments of French oceanography.

Jean-Louis and his baby, SAR.

By contrast, I'm always joking around; sometimes this gets me into trouble or I make a fool of myself. But the main difference is that whereas Jean-Louis is careful and conservative, I'm a risk taker. I'm always cutting corners, making imaginative leaps. Because we respect one another's strengths, which complement each other, we make a perfect combination. Together we take calculated risks: I dream up the risks and Jean-Louis does the calculating.

By the time *Le Suroit* arrived back in the area where the *Titanic* foundered, only 17 days remained to finish the sonar search. With good weather, it still might be possible. In order for his strategy to work, Jean-Louis had to know within 30 to 50 feet or so where his sonar SAR was as it was towed 12,500 feet beneath the support ship and only 600 feet above the ocean floor.

SAR was Jean-Louis' baby – he had designed and built it – and it was quite a beautiful child, resembling a spiffy red torpedo. Employing the latest in signal-processing technology, it was France's latest entry in the deep-towed, side-scan sonar business. Its shadow graphs, even better than those of the Scripps Deep Tow, were of such excellent quality that they resembled black-and-white photographs of the seafloor – visual pictures taken with sound waves. It was quite amazing. But for the search to work, SAR had to be towed with precision back and forth across the ocean floor so that nothing could escape its acute sense of hearing. It was the same laborious process, known as "mowing the lawn," that Spiess and Ryan had used.

The process was a bit like towing a kite on a two-and-a-half mile string. *Le Suroit*'s movements along the surface ultimately determined the path SAR followed. *Le Suroit*'s position could be plotted precisely with the help of an extensive net of acoustical transponders – rather like the sonic equivalent of a radio beacon – that had been positioned on the ocean floor at the beginning of the French search. Every ten seconds or so, *Le Suroit* would send out an acoustic signal from her "tow fish," a small instrument she towed just beneath the surface. When each transponder heard this signal, it would respond by sending out its own unique sound. SAR would also chime in at regular intervals and these alternating "conversations" with the fixed transponders, first from *Le Suroit* and then from the moving deep-towed vehicle, allowed those on board to know almost exactly where both *Le Suroit* and SAR were at any time.

When SAR showed up a possible target it would be cross-checked with the record produced by the magnetometer, which measured the magnetic field, towed behind the "torpedo." We expected to see numerous sonar targets in the search area that might look like the *Titanic*, but only the *Titanic* would also have the magnetic signature of a large metallic ship – or so we hoped.

In good weather, the kite flyer (*Le Suroit*) could keep the string taut and fly the kite (SAR) along a straight underwater path. But, as Jack Grimm had discovered, bad weather or strong currents at the surface made "mowing the lawn" much more difficult. Each swath cut by this acoustical lawnmower was about 1,000 meters wide. However, since a side-looking sonar towed close to the bottom casts a "shadow," it could well miss the *Titanic* if she were hidden in one of the canyons or gullies traversing the search area. That was why Spiess had gone over Ryan's 1980 *Sea MARC* coverage. And maybe that was why Deep Tow hadn't found the ship in 1981. To be as certain as possible that he too hadn't missed it, Jean-Louis had to run each new line slightly overlapping the first.

We picked up the search exactly where Jean-Louis had left off and for the first couple of days the weather held. We had a two-to-three-knot current to contend with, which made things slow enough. But then the weather turned and a series of storm fronts crossed over us, bouncing our ship around like a cork in a churning whirlpool. Having spent a great deal of my life in ships, I have always been amused when the weatherman reports that a "storm has gone harmlessly out to sea." I'd love to take one of those landbound meteorologists out on one of our tiny vessels to experience one of those "harmless" storms.

Life aboard *Le Suroit* became quite unpleasant during bad weather. The already cramped spaces became even more claustrophobic as we

(Below, right) Le Suroit's *magnetometer being launched.*

(Below) SAR *is launched from the fantail of* Le Suroit.

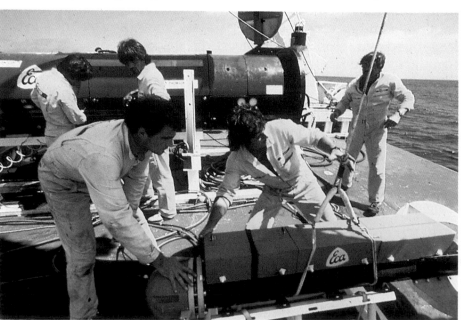

waited out a storm. Outside, the decks were awash with waves breaking over the sides, often getting us cold and wet. It was rough, tough thoroughly unpleasant seagoing, made worse by our impatience to get back to work.

Each time the weather worsened, Jean-Louis gallantly maintained the search until it simply became impossible to control SAR's path across the bottom, or to know where SAR was, or, worse, until we were in danger of losing the vehicle altogether. Then he was forced to recover his sonar and ride out the heavy seas, with more precious time lost. Grimm's bad luck seemed to have returned to curse the French, but Jean-Louis never lost his cool, never abandoned the search strategy he had decided on. If he was worried or depressed, he never showed it. He simply stuck grimly to the search plan, delicately tracking his underwater sonar kite back and forth across the ocean floor. This sort of searching becomes a mind-numbing experience. When bad weather is added, it becomes a physical and psychological endurance test.

Although by the end of the third week of the sonar search we hadn't yet found the *Titanic*, SAR had begun to tell a fascinating story, part of which might seriously affect our chance to find the ship, then film it. *Titanic* Canyon, which cut a diagonal through the eastern half of our search area, is a narrow but complex submarine valley with numerous tributaries producing a lot of false sonar targets and tantalizing magnetic anomalies (areas of higher than normal magnetism). In 1929, 17 years after the *Titanic* had sunk, the area 314 miles to the northwest had experienced a massive tremor known as the Grand Banks Earthquake which broke numerous transatlantic cables and triggered massive mudslides.

What if the mudslides had extended to the *Titanic* site and the ship was buried? We might be able to find evidence of her on the magnetometer, but we'd never know for sure if she were buried out of sight. Throughout the rest of our quest to find the lost ship, this thought would come back to haunt me: perhaps there was nothing there for us to find.

For the next week *Le Suroit* continued her patient sonar search, but as the first week gave way to the second and the second to the third – with

(Below, left) The intended French search area (our primary search quadrant).

(Below) The actual SAR coverage compared to the original search area.

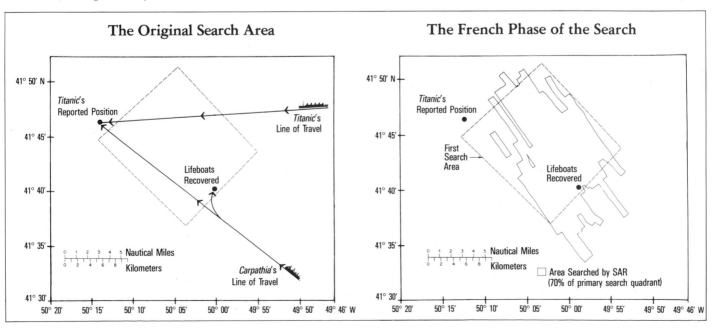

still nothing to show for our efforts – you could feel the sadness envelop the ship. SAR had performed magnificently in the face of considerable adversity, "mowing the lawn" over 70 percent of the search area Jean-Louis and I had initially decided on. The SAR data base was a work of technological art collected by a master in his trade and it had told us where the *Titanic* wasn't. But I could see that despite SAR's accomplishments Jean-Louis was deeply disappointed. He was a proud man and he had failed to corner our quarry. Now it would be up to an American ship and an American team to carry on our search.

On August 6, in the late morning, when it finally came time to recover SAR for good and head back to port, a hush seemed to fall over *Le Suroit*. The cramped and crowded ship suddenly seemed empty as people tried to find a quiet corner to reflect on failure. The day was gloomy, cool, and overcast and I remember walking out on the starboard side and back toward the fantail where SAR was moored, its work now done. I looked out at the choppy sea overcast with gray. Suddenly the sky cracked open, the sun's rays rifling down, and out of nowhere a beautiful rainbow arched in the distance. I may spend most of my time being a rational scientist, but as a sailor I'm also a little superstitious. Perhaps the rainbow was an omen of better things to come.

On August 12, four days and many connecting flights after leaving *Le Suroit* in St. Pierre, Jean-Louis and I arrived in Ponta Delgada, Azores, in the middle of the Atlantic. Waiting for us was the U.S. oceanographic research ship *Knorr* and the American science team from Woods Hole's Deep Submergence Laboratory. Emory Kristof and Ralph White would catch up with us before we sailed. And *Argo*'s crucial tow cable had arrived by air just in time.

After the cramped quarters and somewhat stifling formality of the French ship, walking on board *Knorr* was a little like going from a boarding school to a country club. *Knorr* has graceful lines, spacious quarters, and possesses a special cycloidal propulsion system that gives her maximum stability and maneuverability in bad weather. *Knorr*'s two cycloids are like giant egg beaters – one under the bow and one under the stern. As a result, the ship can go backward or forward with equal ease, turn on a dime, or hold an optimum stationary position in a heavy sea. She was the last word in seagoing technology.

Knorr may have seemed big beside *Le Suroit*, but she would have been dwarfed by the *Titanic*, which was almost four times *Knorr*'s length. In reality, she was anything but a country club, just the perfect ship for the job at hand – with one glaring exception. There was no suitable room on board to serve as a command center. I'd sailed on *Knorr* for 12 years and I knew that in her main lab I could never achieve the atmosphere of intense concentration I wanted during our search. The ship's main corridor runs through her center. During a voyage, the traffic down that corridor is constant and distracting.

As the end of the French phase of the expedition drew near, both Jean-Louis and I became increasingly discouraged.

Silhouettes of the Titanic, Le Suroit, *and the* Knorr *show their comparative sizes.*

Le Suroit

Knorr

R.M.S. *Titanic*

That was why, when I boarded the *Knorr* in the Azores, an alien object sat on her starboard afterdeck. It was a large rectangle, measuring 18 by 20 feet, composed of two portable shipping containers connected together like a mobile home. This was the *Argo*/ANGUS control van, mission control for the American phase of the expedition. Diagonally and aft across the deck from the van, on the port side, sat a third container – the photo-processing van where still photos would be developed. And sitting on the fantail, moored securely to the deck, were the white steel sleds of *Argo* and ANGUS, each about 15 feet long. Otherwise, the main piece of deck equipment was the take-up drum, just aft of the control van near the starboard rail. The cable ran from there up to the cable traction unit on the roof of the lab where an electric winch paid out the line or hauled it in. From the roof of the lab, the cable fed back across the fantail to an A-frame positioned over the starboard rail just aft of the take-up drum and thence down into the water.

The architects of the *Knorr* had presciently provided space for the van by shifting the ship's superstructure to the port side, leaving a big deck area to starboard. Even with all this stuff taking up space, there was still room for a game of touch football. Weather permitting, this fantail deck would become the social center aboard *Knorr*, the place where people would congregate off-duty to have a beer, talk, and relax, while still being able to follow any action on deck.

Walking from the fantail inside the superstructure, you entered the main lab, which we would mainly use for data-processing. If you continued down the main corridor that ran through the center of the ship, you'd pass the hospital, then the main dining galley, where the officers and science party ate. Beyond that was the kitchen and then the crew's galley.

The next two decks consisted mostly of sleeping quarters. The second deck also had a wet lab, a library, and a radio room. Forward on the third deck were the cabins for the chief scientist and the captain. On the fourth level was the bridge, the preserve of Captain Richard Bowen. I'd sailed with Captain Bowen before and knew him to be an excellent skipper. Richard is a laconic New Englander who runs his ship with a sure hand. I was glad he was on board.

(Top) The research vessel Knorr *at sea. (Above) The fantail of the* Knorr *showing ANGUS,* Argo *safely stowed under the tarpaulin, the launching crane, and other deck gear.*

Added to the perfect ship was the ideal team – old ANGUS hands like Earl Young, Emile Bergeron, Tom Crook, Steve Gegg, and Martin Bowen; and the *Argo* specialists including *Argo*'s designer, Stu Harris, and his engineers Tom Dettweiler and Bob Squires. They were backed up by navigators, data processors, and sonar operators making – with myself – 25 in all. This team was drawn mainly from the family that I had assembled at the Deep Submergence Laboratory. From past experience I knew this family would knit together well as the expedition progressed.

For the American phase of the search, Jean-Louis Michel would be joined by two other representatives of IFREMER, Jean Jarry and Bernard Pillaud. Jarry, now usually stuck in IFREMER's Paris head office, was looking forward to this brief return to the front lines. Bernard, a French Navy officer on loan to IFREMER, was experienced in the operation of cycloidal ships like *Knorr*. They would certainly bring added professionalism to our venture.

As we headed across the Atlantic, there was time to finally nail down our last-ditch search strategy – in the event a visual search of *Titanic*

Canyon (and the sonar targets identified by SAR and the Grimm expeditions) yielded no sign of the ship. The French had taken the traditional approach to underwater searches – sonar. Given the equipment at hand and my own background as a visual scientist, I intended to do something radically different – a visual search using *Argo*.

The new strategy was based on my long experience of looking for lost objects in the sea. Ever since 1964, when Woods Hole got into the diving business with *Alvin*, the phone had rung at least once a year with someone who wanted our help. The calls have run the gamut from the H-Bomb lost off Spain in that same year (which *Alvin* found), to the Korean Airlines jet shot down by the Soviets in 1984 (for which *Alvin* was unavailable). Although these were gloomy missions, they had taught us a tremendous amount about how objects behave as they plunge to the bottom of the deep sea.

Whatever the type of wreck, all experience some degree of fragmentation as they sink. In shallow water, where the fall is short, fragments land on the seafloor pretty well directly below where they sank. In deep water, however, where the fall to the bottom takes much longer, the ocean currents have an opportunity to disperse them: the heavier the object, the more direct its downward path; but the lightest fragments will fall slowly in the underwater currents like leaves blown from a tree. The result is a long comet of debris along the ocean bottom, with the heaviest objects at the "windward" end of the field. At normal ocean depths of about two and a half miles – the depth to which the *Titanic* sank – with average currents of slightly over one knot, we have found these debris fields to be typically a half mile to one mile in length or longer.

It was with this knowledge that I made what turned out to be a crucial decision. In the next phase of the search – if more searching was needed – we would look for the *Titanic*'s debris field, not the *Titanic*. With this as our target, a visual search made more sense than a sonar search, since a sonar cannot distinguish a small man-made object lying on the bottom from natural debris, but a camera can. I was betting that a camera would succeed where a sonar had failed.

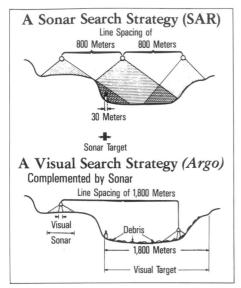

A Sonar Search Strategy (SAR)

A Visual Search Strategy (Argo)
Complemented by Sonar

(Above) In order to be sure they wouldn't miss something as small as the Titanic, *just over 30 meters (90 feet) wide, the French had to space their sonar lines approximately 800 meters (2,600 feet) apart. With* Argo, *because we were looking for any piece of a roughly mile-long plume of debris, we could space our visual lines 1,800 meters (6,000 feet) apart.*

The Transponder Net

The small "fish" or sonar receiver and transmitter towed below *Knorr* "talks" to the transponders and to *Argo* or ANGUS.

The Second Search Area

The expanded or secondary search area compared to the original or primary search area.

As we steamed out toward the search area, I met in my cabin with Jean-Louis and the other Frenchmen to discuss this new strategy. While a visual search was alien to their way of thinking, they could see it was the only way we could cover the remaining ground with *Argo* in the time available. We all knew that time was running out.

Jean-Louis and I now discussed expanding the original primary search area. We were both convinced that we had now searched further west than the *Titanic* could possibly have been. The secondary search area we'd identified was to the east of our initial one, but we now decided to extend it even further east than originally planned. Perhaps the *Titanic* had been traveling much more slowly than her captain thought. Perhaps the current that night was even stronger than we had calculated. The southern boundary of our new search area was simpler to come up with – the position where the lifeboats were found. These were in effect the lightest pieces of *Titanic* debris – they didn't sink at all, but simply drifted south with the current.

From the *Californian*'s logbook, we had been able to calculate the speed and direction of her drift that night. That ship had encountered the ice field at 10:32 p.m. on the evening of April 14, 1912, and had drifted until 6:00 a.m. the next morning, a distance of five nautical miles. Hence the current was 0.7 knots to the south-southeast. So the *Titanic* had to be north of where her lifeboats were found.

The current had also provided another crucial clue. If the lifeboats had drifted south, so must have the underwater debris. Therefore, the *Titanic* and her debris field should lie to the north of the lifeboats along a roughly north-south line extending approximately one mile in length and with the lightest debris at the southern end. This meant we would run our search pattern in east-west lines to intersect the debris field at right angles.

As we steamed out to the site aboard Knorr, *Jean-Louis Michel presented the SAR results from the first phase of the search. The chart behind him shows the SAR tracks crossing back and forth over* Titanic *Canyon.*

All that remained was to decide where in the expanded area to begin. Our analysis of the historical data gave us a bull's eye: a spot where the *Titanic* should be if all our assumptions were correct. But the one thing we knew for certain was that the *Titanic* wasn't in that exact spot (SAR had already checked there). And, in fact, one of the rules I always follow is never to start at the bull's eye. I always make a search area large enough so that the target must be inside it and then start at the edge. The obvious choice was to start at the southern end of the area near where the first of the *Titanic*'s lifeboats was picked up by the *Carpathia*.

Our strategy was now set. To save time, we would run our lines one mile apart. If we missed the wreck on the first set of passes, we would come back with runs halfway between our first set of lines, meaning we would have surveyed the bottom at half-mile intervals. In this way, we could cover ground much more quickly. But first, we would take one last look at *Titanic* Canyon and the various sonar targets to make sure Jean-Louis hadn't missed anything in its nooks and crannies.

Our decision to go back over the canyon, despite the fact that SAR had yielded nothing conclusive, was a combination of the canyon's geology and emotional pull. Grimm, Spiess, and Ryan had been drawn to the canyon, even obsessed by it, in part because it is by far the most dramatic underwater feature in the area and in part because canyons have a habit of collecting debris, something like a big vacuum cleaner. The vast landslide SAR had mapped had been stopped by the canyon, which acted like a moat into which the mud had flowed. If the wreck had settled somewhere in the canyon's vicinity, over the years some of its pieces might have flowed into the canyon. In that case, surely *Argo* would find some visual evidence of the *Titanic*.

As we neared *Titanic* Canyon, life on board the *Knorr* had settled into a fairly predictable routine. In contrast to *Le Suroit*, the atmosphere was informal and relaxed and meals were casual affairs. In their spare time, people were often seen reading the various *Titanic* books on board or watching one of two *Titanic* movies, *A Night to Remember* and *Raise the Titanic*, on the VCR. Some people played cards; others fished for squid or dolphin, or tried to catch occasional sharks that invariably trailed the ship.

At dusk, people would gather on the fantail to relax and unwind. They'd lounge in deck chairs and have a few of bottles of Sagres, a Portuguese beer bought in quantities in the Azores, and watch the sunset. When the weather was warm, people splashed in our ''swimming pool'' to take the heat off the day. (It was actually an enclosed area on the stern filled with water.) During these evening rituals, a casual observer would have had trouble guessing the seriousness of our mission or the high professionalism of those on board. But our real work was to come.

Early on the evening of August 24, we arrived in the vicinity of *Titanic* Canyon. We now had 12 days to go. Miraculously, the sea was flat calm. It was as if old King Neptune had said, ''Here it is, it's yours.'' What a contrast to the French phase, characterized throughout by gray choppy seas – when it hadn't been blowing a gale. Calm weather makes seasoned mariners nervous. It's like pitching a no-hitter in baseball. You don't talk about it, you just watch it happen. At sea, there's a superstition that whistling brings storms. That evening nobody was whistling aboard *Knorr*.

Satellites in orbit far above the earth gave us our position – so much more precise than the celestial fixes on which the *Titanic* and all other vessels depended back in 1912. I stood alone in the darkened chart room (the shades were pulled to eliminate glare) on the ship's bridge just aft of the helm, in the eerie glow of the red lights (used on all ships after dark because they don't affect night vision) and reflected once again on the *Titanic*'s endless fascination. Surely her remains lay somewhere within a few miles?

At 7 p.m. local time, Captain Bowen slowed *Knorr*'s mighty engines, declutched the aft cycloid, and reduced speed to four knots. The stern cycloid makes a lot of noise and we needed to be able to hear well underwater in order to pick up the signal from the acoustic transponder that *Le Suroit* had left behind. Over the next 18 hours, we worked steadily, and by early afternoon the next day, August 25, our transponder net had been meshed with our U.S. Navy map of the canyon. *Le Suroit*'s network and ours had become one. Now the hunt could begin in earnest.

People were pouring into the control van to man their stations. *Argo* was ready to dive. Whenever *Argo* was flying and the search was on, all shipboard operations were concentrated in our control van. Inside was a chart table and a desk set back from several banks of TV monitors. Every piece of information relevant to the search appeared on one of those screens. Every function related to the search could be carried out in that room.

I thought of the control van as the bridge of an imaginary submarine,

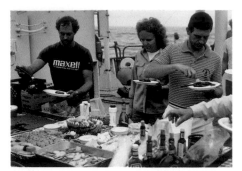

A picnic on the fantail. Left to right: Emile Bergeron, Cathy Offinger, and Bernard Pillaud.

its huge television monitors like windows into the sea. When I stepped into the van, I could dive to the bottom of the ocean with none of the peril and discomfort of real submarines like *Alvin* – and with no time limits. There is no question in my mind that *Argo* and its successors point the way to the future of underwater exploration.

From my position at the plotting table in the center of the van, I could observe every member of the seven-man crew of each successive watch during *Argo* operations. (ANGUS, having fewer instruments, operated with a much smaller contingent of three.) Because there were three watches, three different people were thus assigned to each of the seven jobs. Directly forward of me and to the left was the "flyer," the person operating the winch that controlled *Argo*'s cable. His responsibility was to fly *Argo* at an optimum distance from the bottom (altitude) and, above all, never to crash. My three flyers were my most experienced technicians, Earl Young, Martin Bowen, and Emile Bergeron.

In front of the flyer and slightly to the right sat the navigator. His (or her) job was to know where *Argo* and *Knorr* were at all times. The navigator had to be up on the most modern innovations in satellite navigation and on the magical black art of acoustic transponder navigation. My three trusty hands there were Steve Gegg, Tom Crook, and Cathy Offinger.

To the immediate right of the navigator sat the driver, the person actually steering the ship and controlling her speed. If we found the *Titanic*, that hot seat would belong to Captain Bowen, but during most of our straight-line search runs the job would be handled by a member of the regular watch. The steering mechanism reminded me of Pac-Man controls – two small levers with round black balls on top. One controlled the stern cycloid propeller and one the bow cycloid. For most of the expedition the three drivers were the watch leaders, Jean-Louis Michel, Jean Jarry, and Bernard Pillaud, who would mainly concentrate on driving the ship in tandem with the flyer. But if tactical decisions not covered by my instructions had to be made, they would make them – or wake me up to consult. When the driver and the flyer worked well together – and the best at it were Jean-Louis Michel and Earl Young – then we could cover the maximum amount of ground.

To the right of the driver was the work station for the *Argo* engineers – Stu Harris, Tom Dettweiler, or Bob Squires, who wrote *Argo*'s complex software. Stu, as *Argo*'s chief architect, was probably the most important member of our whole science team. If something went wrong, he'd be the one to figure out the problem, or find the right man to fix it. He's a steady anchor when tension rises, very good for morale. But he's a reluctant seagoer; throughout the whole cruise he wore a circular sea patch behind his ear, which steadily dispersed medicine through his pores to prevent seasickness.

Behind the *Argo* engineer sat our sonar operator. Lt. George Rey of the U.S. Navy was with us on a temporary duty assignment from the Submarine Development Group One, the Navy's center of expertise on deep submergence in San Diego, California. One of his two alternates was Terry Snyder from the Klein sonar company which had manufactured *Argo*'s side-scan. Between them these two had seen thousands of sonar blobs and smudges and had become masters at guessing what a shadow might be. The third sonar operator was Jim Saint, on loan from Colmek, the company in Utah which had manufactured *Argo*'s sensi-

Emile Bergeron in the van, flying Argo.

tive cameras and helped build its telemetry system.

The members of the documentation team also stood watch: Bill Lange, Emory Kristof, and Ralph White. They would document anything important that happened.

The final member of each watch, moving between work stations – mostly from navigator to *Argo* engineer to plotting table – was the data logger, either Sharon Callahan, Georgina Baker, or Lisa Schwarz. Their job was to maintain the "war" map resting on the chart table, a topographic map of the search area that already showed where SAR had been and also showed *Argo*'s proposed tracklines. As *Argo* inched along, the data loggers gathered information from the work stations and laid out on this map the actual sonar and visual coverage. In turn they gave the navigator and driver the tracking information as it was required.

The last member of the team was unattached to any particular watch but was often in the van. This was Dana Yoerger, a freshly minted Ph.D. in robotics from M.I.T., and the future father of *Jason*. He was along to smell and taste what the slogging was like in the trenches of oceanographic research. Since he wasn't needed on watch, he spent most of his time rewriting *Argo*'s tracking software, which was in desperate need of revision.

Whenever I walked into the control van, I could look at the map and see the order of battle at a glance. As chief scientist of the *Knorr* expedition, I didn't stand a watch, but I could almost always be found in mission control when not asleep. My job was to be where the action was whether at two in the morning or two in the afternoon: sleep would come when I got it. As long as the search was routine and no sign of wreckage appeared, I would have lots of time for rest and contemplation. When I was in the van, I'd be at the large chart table in the center of the room which gave me a bird's-eye view of things as they unfolded. Or I would circulate from work station to work station for a close-up view of one aspect of the search.

During the watch, there was usually music playing – everything from reggae to Ravel – and often the van would be filled with the smell of fresh buttered popcorn brought in from the galley. When the weather grew cold and wet, as it would later in the voyage, the van was a haven of warmth and camaraderie. You could always find a place to "hide" in the back – close to the action but out of the way. When it was hot, as it had been for much of the trip to date, the van's four air conditioners kept the temperature cool. The only real problem was the amount of cigarette smoke. As many as half the members of any watch were

Jean-Louis Michel and I plot the next Argo *run.*

smokers and sometimes the cloud got so dense that I had to ration cigarette time in order not to overload the air circulation system – and the lungs of the non-smokers.

On our first launch on the afternoon of August 25, Earl Young was flying *Argo*, wearing a hard-hat turned backwards on his head and cursing colorfully at the slightest irritant. Of the old salts aboard, Earl was the saltiest. Since I had first encountered him blithely working amidst dangerously high voltage at sea, he had taught me what New England seafarers were all about, tough types bred of several hundred years of hardship on the high seas. Although I'd long ago nicknamed him Grumpy for his unfailingly sour demeanor and constant critical commentary, I couldn't think of a better man to have at the controls. We'd been through quite a few wars together and he'd never once broken ranks, no matter how rough the seas, late the hours, or challenging the task.

Now I watched Earl as he got ready, clutching the winch controls and checking the altimeter which measured *Argo*'s height above the bottom, then glancing at the screen which would show the underwater scene viewed by *Argo*'s forward-looking camera. Should something suddenly appear on the screen, it was Grumpy's job to bail out fast, reeling in *Argo*'s 0.68-inch-thick cable quickly enough to lift the vehicle above any obstacle. He was a veteran of several crashes with *Argo*'s sibling, ANGUS, but now he had the advantage of real-time eyes underwater. He could see what he was doing with *Argo*, whereas ANGUS flies blind with only a down-looking sonar to guide it.

Now Earl jammed the control lever forward, paying out cable, and *Argo* began the first serious descent of its brief career. It had worked fine in test lowerings; but this one was for real. On Earl's right, Tom Crook, the navigator, watched his monitors to make sure *Argo* was in the right place. Tom is another Woods Hole old-timer – our all-time navigational expert at sea and a steady hand at the controls.

So far the launch was picture perfect. But no sooner had we begun to relax than Stu Harris, at the *Argo* work station, reported technical problems. Evidently a ground had shorted out *Argo*'s telemetry system – the television monitors in the van were washed with static. That meant *Argo* would have to return to the surface. . . .

A short time later, with the white sled back on deck outside the van, its engineers swarmed over it like worker bees pampering a queen. Within 22 minutes *Argo* was on its way back to the bottom. Everyone on board knew we hadn't a minute to waste.

The beginning of a highly technical expedition is always plagued with problems. When the expedition is also inaugurating a completely new piece of hardware like *Argo*, these problems tend to multiply. New or not, no instrument system as complex as this could have been immune to the steady pounding of waves against *Knorr*'s hull and the constant vibration caused by the engines during the long trip out from the Azores. As well, there's the ever-present salt and humidity which love to wreak havoc with electronics, laying down a corrosive layer of salt on our circuit boards. In expeditions such as this one, the question is not whether we will have equipment problems but when and how many.

One hour and 40 minutes later, *Argo*'s altimeters finally sensed

(Top) Argo *is launched and* *(above)* *begins its descent.*

bottom 100 feet below it. At the winch control, Earl now slowed *Argo*'s descent and the watch tensed for our first look at the bottom. A few minutes later, at 3:30 p.m., the sea floor came into view on our black-and-white monitors with *Argo* hovering at 50 feet. Bottom depth was 12,690 feet from the surface. The faint tracks of deep-sea slugs, or holothurians, appeared, etched in the mud. Otherwise nothing. . . .

For the next several hours, we explored a region a few miles to the east of the canyon, the watch team settling down into a routine set to the rhythm and tune of *Argo*'s instruments: pings sent out by the navigation system, *Argo*'s sonar, and the ship's echo sounder; the hard copy recorder singing out a line of data. The smell of buttered popcorn filled the van and the mood was one of relaxed concentration. After the long, slow trip out to the site, finally we were getting down to business.

With the help of the sonar, we investigated a number of "bomb craters" I knew from previous experience could have been made by the impact of heavy pieces of *Titanic* wreckage. Most of them were empty, but in one we saw a huge glacial boulder. It would be a wonderful irony, I mused, if this boulder had come loose from the very iceberg that had sunk our quarry, jogged loose by a titanic collision of ice and steel. Apart from these craters, the cameras revealed only a gently rolling countryside consisting of hills of muddy sediment.

Over the next two days, as the clock ticked relentlessly onward, we investigated the various sonar targets identified by the Grimm expeditions and by SAR. Jean-Louis and I knew we were groping at straws, but we felt we had to definitely eliminate all possible targets in the canyon and vicinity before starting a new search effort. Three of Grimm's sonar and magnetometer targets held particular interest. One was the "propeller" site. Another was one we nicknamed "Ryan's Madness" after Bill Ryan of Lamont, who had identified it. The third was dubbed "Spiess' Obsession" in honor of Fred Spiess. This one had really mesmerized him. During Grimm's 1981 expedition he'd come back to it again and again.

I didn't know it then, but Grimm had played a trick on us. The position of the "propeller" site we checked so carefully was wrong. Grimm had deliberately falsified its location on the map of the search area published in his book *Beyond Reach*. Furthermore, none of Grimm's legitimate sonar targets showed up anything of interest, just

A diagram showing Argo's *investigation of* Titanic *Canyon and vicinity. The main* Argo *coverage corresponds roughly to the axis of the canyon. Both Grimm's "propeller" site and a sonar target Fred Spiess kept coming back to are pinpointed.*

The *Argo* Search – Phase I

glacial droppings and canyon outcroppings. The canyon and its tributaries were clean – as far as SAR and *Argo* could determine.

In the process of touring the canyon itself, we had gone on a fascinating slalom ride, glimpsing beautifully worn outcrops of canyon fill as we zigzagged back and forth. The carved walls were reminiscent of the Grand Canyon, etched layers that told a long and complex story of deposition, erosion, and redeposition. Near the southern limit of our search, the canyon bottom became rough as numerous gullies cut into the slopes, reminding me of the badlands of South Dakota. Before we called it quits, we actually continued well south of the southern limit of our search area, guessing that over the years debris might have been transported far from the actual wreck. No such luck, but *Argo* had reached a major milestone, exceeding for the first time *Alvin*'s diving depth of 13,000 feet. New visual frontiers were opening to us now.

Never before had anyone shot the rapids of a submarine canyon in such comfort. Years before, I had explored similar underwater valleys off the coast of New England inside the cramped and cold quarters of our submarine *Alvin*. Now here I was sitting in a comfortable chair, drinking a Coke Classic and eating a warm piece of pie, with the strains of a Willy Nelson tape filling the van, while the submarine landscape rolled by. Now this was exploring.

By late morning on August 27, almost exactly two days after we began our tour of *Titanic* Canyon, *Argo* was back on the fantail having eliminated all possible sonar and magnetic targets from past expeditions. Nine days to go and the crunch had come. Suddenly the ocean was huge and self-doubt began to loom large. Was the *Titanic* really in our carefully plotted search area? If so, surely some evidence of her debris would have shown up in the canyon? Were we looking in the wrong place?

Deep down I had really believed we would find something in the canyon – some tiny piece of wreckage, some clue to the *Titanic*'s whereabouts. Now I began to feel a rising panic – and others on board seemed to be feeling it too: the tension increased and the atmosphere became almost frantic. This thing was harder to crack than we'd allowed ourselves to believe.

Jean-Louis, as usual, showed no sign he was worried. Perhaps it was easier for him because it wasn't his ship, but if we didn't find the

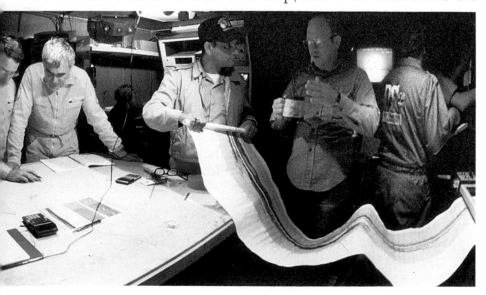

As each watch changes, those coming on duty are briefed by those about to leave. At the plotting table in the control van are (from left): Georgina Baker, Sharon Callahan, Jean-Louis Michel, and Jean Jarry. At right, Lt. George Rey and James Saint review the results of the latest shadow graph.

Titanic it would be a shared failure. Nonetheless, the visual search strategy was my brainchild. If it worked, I'd look pretty smart. If not . . . I'd take the lion's share of the blame.

At 1:40 p.m. in the afternoon of the 27th, after recovering, repairing, and relaunching a malfunctioning transponder, we were underway to the east into the unexplored waters of our expanded search area. A small wedge at the eastern edge of the primary search quadrant had been previously missed by SAR due to the current, so the new area slightly overlapped the old to include this missed portion. Hedging our bets, we left the *Titanic* Canyon transponder net in place. If we came up empty, we could always return to the canyon for one more try. It was still difficult to let go of the idea that the *Titanic* was in that canyon somewhere.

During our short ten-mile transit to the southeast, the *Knorr*'s engineering department made a number of repairs to *Argo*'s large winch system. I didn't want anything to hold us up, and during the last lowering we had noticed that the take-up drum, which stored *Argo*'s expensive conducting cable as it was winched in, was slowly shifting off its axis. If that continued uncorrected, we might lose *Argo* and with it all chance of finding the *Titanic*.

Launching a transponder at night.

By mid-afternoon, we were ready to position a new transponder network that would enable us to know where we were as we conducted this final search. With less than nine full days left, I decided on a shortcut. Instead of the three groups of three transponders that would ensure ideal navigation, I elected to put in only one group of three, forming a triangle in the middle of the remaining search quadrant. This would save a lot of time, but would make tracking poor to the north and south as distance from this net increased. The visual search strategy, which didn't require precise overlapping lines, permitted me to take this risk. I hoped it would work.

By 1:44 a.m. the next morning, August 28, we had surveyed the new transponder net into place and we were in position just south of where the *Carpathia* had retrieved the first lifeboats. We were ready to launch *Argo* into unknown waters.

As the little white sled with its jaunty tailfin slid beneath the gentle Atlantic swells, I contemplated what lay ahead. So far we had been blessed with almost perfect weather and in the darkness of the early morning hours it was cool, but calm. The area to be covered was about 100 square miles. This meant it would require ten to twelve east-west passes a mile apart. If all went well, I figured this process should take up five to six of our remaining eight-and-a-half days. If we didn't find the ship by then, there would be time for only a partial doubling back between these lines.

Two-and-a-half miles below us, the water was markedly clearer than in the canyon, making it possible to fly *Argo* at a higher altitude and for us to see farther out to the side. This extra width wasn't critical to our current mission, but it demonstrated how useful *Argo* would be on future scientific expeditions. What was important to us here was *Argo*'s ability to send continuous real-time television pictures of the ocean bottom to the van for instant analysis, playback, and response. The first thing *Argo* showed us, however, was a bottom of narrowly spaced sand ripples, large sand waves, and sand dunes. Jean-Louis, who was in the van for the lowering, remarked that it reminded him of a beach in Brittany – an empty beach, unfortunately.

By this point in our voyage, the three watches had each assumed a distinct personality and two of the three had already earned nicknames. Jean-Louis Michel's watch – midnight to 4 a.m. and noon to 4 p.m. – had christened itself with characteristic bravado the "The Watch of Quiet Excellence." They were also occasionally known as "Harris' Heroes," after Stu Harris, *Argo*'s technical wizard. Their excellence stemmed from the fact that taciturn Jean-Louis at the helm and grumpy Earl on the winch control had developed into the most competent team at getting the most out of *Argo*. Since Jean-Louis had relinquished overall command for the American portion of the expedition, I had made sure he had the best watch. For some reason, the midnight watch always seems to be the one where things happen.

In 12,500 feet of water, it was impossible to tow *Argo* at high speeds because of the water friction that built up around the long cable running up to the surface. At only 0.68 inches in diameter this cable may not seem like much, but over two and a half miles that adds up to a lot of surface area. The faster Jean-Louis or one of his French colleagues drove the boat, the more *Argo* had a tendency to "kite" higher in the water and out of viewing range. We had counteracted this to some degree by making *Argo* heavier. As a result it towed closely behind the ship – the cable all but vertical – making it much easier to maneuver ship and underwater sled in tandem, especially during the turn at the end of each pass. Having *Argo* almost straight below us also made it easier to know where the sled was. The problem was that a heavier *Argo* put more strain on the cable and the whole winch apparatus.

Towing *Argo* became a balancing act between maximizing speed over the bottom while not exceeding the highest viewing altitude. Jean-Louis and Earl performed the job like veteran tightrope walkers. As the kiting action began to lift *Argo* off the bottom, Earl would pay out more cable. As Earl ran out of cable, Jean-Louis would stall the ship's forward progress, either by using the forward cycloids or by bringing the bow slightly into the wind. As *Knorr* slowed and *Argo* began falling, Earl would take in cable to prevent the vehicle from crashing to the bottom. This went on, hour after hour, day after day.

It was an *Argo* mishap that earned the 8 a.m.-to-noon/8 p.m.-to-midnight watch its nickname, "The Crash Crew," and almost proved fatal to the entire expedition. After breakfast on August 28, we'd enjoyed another beautiful sunrise on the fantail as we neared the end of line number one. I was back in the control van as we prepared to execute what would become a routine maneuver – turning the ship to the north to begin the next line a mile away. Bernard Pillaud was driving the ship and Martin Bowen was on the winch controls. Martin, no relative of Captain Bowen, is the Deep Submergence Laboratory's specialist in remotely controlled robots, a marine biologist turned techie and an ANGUS veteran. He was the man who would drive *Jason Junior* on his maiden voyage the following year. For him, flying *Argo* was second nature.

A shorter tether would make the turn easier to execute, so Bernard stalled the ship, causing *Argo* to descend toward the bottom, and Martin began taking in cable. But he wasn't fast enough – *Argo* was heading for a crash landing. Instinctively, Martin threw the winch lever forward and the traction unit, perched on the deck over the main lab, began to send the cable toward the take-up drum 15 feet down on the

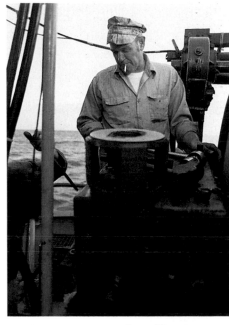

While we sailed east from Titanic Canyon *to begin our visual investigation of the expanded search area, electrician Harry Rougas made repairs to the winch system.*

starboard deck. He'd done the right thing, but the repairs just made to the take-up drum unexpectedly slowed down its turning. At this reduced speed of take-up, it couldn't keep pace with the amount of cable being fed to it. Martin glanced at the television screen (which monitored the cable as it runs from the traction unit to the take-up drum) only to see a large loop of cable forming – across the ship's main passageway. If someone were to walk down that passage as the loop went tight, it would cut him in half.

I was at the plotting table with my back to the work stations pondering the next line when I heard Martin yell. I spun around, took one look at Martin's face, and bolted out the door. Meanwhile Martin reversed the control lever to pay out *Argo* cable and take up the slack, but this only compounded the problem. As I emerged from the van, I watched helplessly as the now-limp cable jumped off the traction unit and started to wind around the winch axle. Then, as the axle began to eat the cable in half, it stalled, automatically shutting down the system. By the time I'd galloped up the ladder to the traction unit, I could see we had a disaster on our hands. The cable couldn't go forward or back and would soon be under enormous pressure. Only quick work would save *Argo*.

The stall had probably saved the cable from breaking, but back in the van Martin could no longer control *Argo*'s depth and the sled fell relentlessly toward the bottom. Out on the upper deck I could see that the winch axle had completely eaten through the cable's strong exterior armor; that meant if we speeded up the ship to kite *Argo* off the bottom, the cable would break and *Argo* would be lost for good. Our only hope was to let *Argo* crash and drag along the bottom while we desperately tried to solve our winch problem.

To make a bad situation worse, the ship was now at the very furthest point from our transponder net, making navigation shaky at best. Since we didn't have good tracking, we couldn't tell exactly where the ship was relative to *Argo*, which had now dug into the soft bottom and was acting like an anchor – on a very fragile chain. Any move in the wrong direction would increase tension and snap the damaged cable. I decided to let the ship drift while we attempted to salvage the situation. Fortunately, the seas were calm and the wind slight.

A close-up of the damaged cable wrapped around the axle of the traction unit.

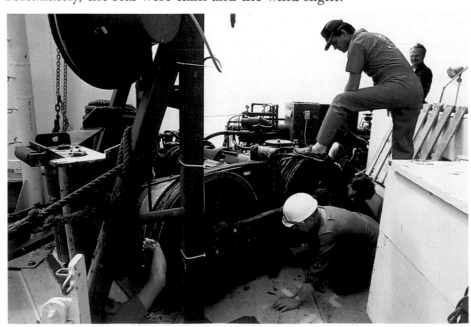

I grimly survey the damage while bosun Jerry Cotter begins the delicate task of rescuing Argo.

The cable's tension held at 17,000 pounds while Earl Young, *Knorr* bosun Jerry Cotter, the ship's deck crew and I went madly to work. If the tension increased to 20,000 pounds, the cable was in doubt; at 25,000, it would snap for sure; I had heard too many stories of cables parting under tension and dismembering or decapitating anyone in the way. Of all the things we did during the entire 1985 *Titanic* expedition, this was the most dangerous.

As we worked against the clock, everyone was on full alert. Occasionally, a terse comment or command punctuated the silence: ''I need a knife''; ''Get me line''; ''Watch the tension''; ''Be careful! Be careful!'' Covered in grease, our knuckles bleeding, we all knew this was a desperate race against time.

In a frantic 20 minutes, we rigged a scaffolding on the stern beneath the damaged piece of cable, spliced in an attach point below the damage, and transferred the tension to a temporary line we'd fastened to a post on the fantail deck. The damaged section was now free of tension and at last we could breathe a partial sigh of relief – *Argo* could now be recovered – but seemingly for the last time. Even if we could figure a way to fly *Argo* again, it would be blind – the cable's innards must by now have been irretrievably damaged.

Back in the control van, Bernard and Martin were taking it pretty hard. But the accident could have happened on any watch: no one had foreseen the problem that would result from the repairs to the take-up drum. Around me, the other members of the watch weren't talking; the van was uncomfortably silent. We were all a bit in shock, looking the end of our expedition square in the face after completing only one line of our visual search.

Then, like a clemency call from the governor moments before an execution, we were granted a reprieve. Stu Harris had joined us in the van and decided to turn *Argo*'s power back on to assess the damage. As *Knorr* increased speed, *Argo* broke free of the bottom. The television pictures were suddenly crystal clear! The cable armor had been cut, but the cable's innards were fine. Quickly, we studied the cable meter readings and the depth charts of the search area. A second reprieve: our search pattern would slowly but continuously move us into shallower

Martin Bowen feels pretty low after the near loss of Argo *as Jean Jarry checks the logbook.*

The mood in the van is tense as we wait for Stu Harris to test Argo's *damaged cable.*

water as we worked our way up the continental rise toward the Grand Banks. We wouldn't be able to pay out cable to maximize our speed, but we would be able to continue the search.

So that was how the 8-to-12 watch came to be known as "The Crash Crew." Since they were generally a pretty quiet group, the name stuck. Fortunately, however, they did nothing further during the search to warrant their nickname.

A little after midnight, in the early morning of August 29 as we were traveling the third line, words like "boring" began to enter the logs kept at the various work stations. The routine inside the van had become numbing, hour after hour of staring at video images of flat bottom mud, occasionally interrupted by a sea-slug track or a boulder crater. After an hour or so staring at a video monitor or sonar read-out, your eyes get sore, your mind begins to wander, you start to go squirrely and something has to give. Occasionally, I entered the van to discover the watch members out of their chairs and boogeying to loud reggae music. As the days wore on, people concocted some elaborate practical jokes to relieve the tedium.

The wildest watch, and the focus for much of these carryings on, was the 4 a.m. to 8 a.m. There's nothing like getting up in the middle of the night to start work, and from the beginning this watch had been a little bit crazy. One time, they marched into the van at four in the morning in a neat little line whistling the tune the dwarfs sang in *Snow White and The Seven Dwarfs* – "Hi-Ho, Hi-Ho, it's off to work we go." Stunts like this earned them their nickname, "The Zoo Crew."

Despite such antics, by August 30 as we reached the middle of line number five, morale was beginning to plummet. The navigator's log told the tale: "No GPS, no Loran, no satellites, no ACNAV [all references to determine positions], full speed against the wind, where are we? Tracking useless due to amount of thrust necessary to maintain course and speed." To boredom was now added a turn in the weather as wind and seas began to build. As we steamed north to begin line six, *Argo*'s cable got tangled in the second cable towing the small "fish" that talked to the transponders. Valuable time slipped away as the "fish" was recovered and the knots untied. Our concentration and dedication appeared to be slipping with only six days to go.

Not surprisingly, the first serious rumbles of discontent came from the most obstreperous watch, the Zoo Crew, and the epicenter was my old friend Emory Kristof. Understandably, Emory was getting impatient with the way things were going. And he was probably getting tired of being a watch flunkie. Emory likes to be a parachute commando, not a footsoldier. He and his sidekick Ralph White had lots of time to formulate their own theories about where the *Titanic* was and what it would look like on sonar, and indeed, for several days, new theories about where to look for the *Titanic* had been rattling around the control van. People who knew nothing about the *Titanic* before stepping on board *Knorr* had been reading the various historical accounts sitting on the plotting table and they had become instant armchair experts.

During the 4-8 watch on the evening of August 30, as the Zoo Crew conducted the sixth pass over the search area, Jean-Louis and I suddenly found ourselves faced with a minor rebellion in the ranks. *Argo*'s sonar

Launching the small "fish," sometimes nicknamed the pollywog, that communicated with our transponders and with ANGUS and Argo.

had found a target that seemed to correspond in size and signal intensity to the main wreckage of the *Titanic* – or so the Zoo Crew thought. Jean-Louis and I were quite certain it was nothing more than the crests of high sandwaves. We'd become quite familiar with how these looked on SAR's sonar and we were also quite familiar with how the *Titanic* should look on a shadow graph. We knew this definitely wasn't it.

But as morale dropped and boredom became unbearable, sonar targets began to grow in size and importance. Emory demanded rather forcefully that we abandon our carefully conceived search pattern and go check this one out. Others in the van seemed to think this was a good idea. But checking it out would take valuable time, time that might mean the difference between finding the *Titanic* and not.

What we were faced with was hardly a mutiny, but it was nonetheless a serious challenge to authority that might open a Pandora's box of other problems with every new sonar target growing in importance. There seems to be a point in almost every expedition when this happens and it was happening to us now. I knew that fast, decisive action was required.

Inside the van, the tension was rising. Seeing that the possibility for rational discussion had passed, I asked Jean-Louis to join me outside to discuss a plan of action. We stood outside on the fantail and talked it over. The early evening air was cool and the damp wind cut into our summer clothes – a sure sign the storm front was getting closer. We were more than halfway through the search area and still no visual sign of wreckage. Our own faith was at its lowest ebb. Perhaps we were wrong and Kristof and the gang were right.

Plotting our next Argo *line after the minor "mutiny".*

We shook off these doubts and agreed on a compromise we felt would nip the "mutiny" in the bud. We decided to double back and run a line between numbers five and six. (Our original plan was that if we didn't find the *Titanic* during our first series of passes we'd double back between the original lines – so this would be a line we might have to run regardless.) Then we'd continue with the search pattern exactly as planned.

Jean-Louis and I re-entered the van. Without saying anything, I walked over to the watch navigator Steve Gegg and gave him the new plan. That accomplished, and with no further words exchanged, Jean-Louis and I started to leave the van. At that moment, Emory approached with fire in his eyes and gruffly asked what I was going to do. "Ask the navigator," was my reply. I followed Jean-Louis out the door.

Line seven proved eventless. The mystery targets were indeed sand dunes. And that was the last hint of rebellion on board.

At lunchtime on August 31, after a minor delay to make some adjustments to *Argo*, we began the eighth pass. The weather was getting steadily worse and the sea beginning to build; it seemed to be only a matter of time before the storm hit. Evening came and still nothing. All was quiet in the ranks and I had begun to face defeat. In only five days we would have to head home. Alone in my cabin after dinner, I washed my face and stared into the mirror. The specially designed *Titanic* patch – a gift from Jean-Louis Michel – sewn on the breast of my blue jumpsuit stared back at me. Each member of the scientific party had proudly sewn on one of these as we had sailed out of the Azores. That now seemed light years away. Could it have been less than three weeks ago?

Whatever happened I knew I'd still be wearing the patch when we sailed into our home port at Woods Hole. Right then, however, I hoped our return would be under cover of darkness.

I went back to the control van, where the Crash Crew had just come on watch. Line nine was now in progress. Maybe Martin and Bernard would redeem their earlier humiliation and be the ones to spot the first sign of wreckage. But I doubted it. Wearily, I laid out the next line on the plotting table so navigator Cathy Offinger would know which course to follow when it came time to begin line ten. Our coverage of the new search area was now nearly complete. I noted that line nine would take us directly to the northeastern limit of previous SAR coverage, overlapping the portion they had missed – that sliver of bottom one mile wide and five miles long.

Bill Lange shouldering a video camera.

I stayed in the van until the midnight watch change. Jean-Louis and the other members of the Watch of Quiet Excellence came tumbling in, still rubbing their eyes and holding warm cups of coffee, breaking the quiet mood with a sudden infusion of noise and energy. With the changing of the guard seven separate and simultaneous conversations filled the command center as the outgoing member of each station reported status to his replacement. The pleasant hubbub was occasionally punctuated by calls coming in over the speakers hooked up to the bridge; all underscored with the never-ending background noise of printers printing and sonars pinging. Then, after ten or fifteen minutes, the old watch was gone and the new watch settled down to work. This was always the quietest time of all – before the music and gossip returned. So began the graveyard shift of September 1, 1985.

During his watch, Jean-Louis was to continue line nine until *Argo* crossed over into the area already covered by SAR and then head north one mile to begin line ten, which should happen not long before the watch changed at 4 a.m. Since the injury to *Argo*'s cable, Jean-Louis and Earl had maintained their reputation as the master flyers who covered more ground than the other watches – they had simply changed their style, speeding the ship up (and paying out the full length of undamaged cable) until *Argo* kited to maximum viewing height, then slowing it down again.

With Jean-Louis in charge and Harris' Heroes in the van, I knew *Argo* was in good hands. Now it was time for me to take a break. But before I left, I heard Billy Lange make his nightly forecast. The last couple of nights he'd taken to predicting exactly when the *Titanic* would be found. He'd pick a spot on the chart and estimate when *Argo* would be there. Tonight, he said, they would find the ship between 2 and 2:30. The *Titanic* sank at 2:20 a.m. Lange was getting superstitious, I thought, but I hoped against hope that tonight he would be right. As I left the van, "I Heard It Through the Grapevine" played softly on the stereo.

Back in my cabin, propped up in my bunk in warm flannel pajamas, I picked up Chuck Yeager's autobiography. As I began to read, my mind soon left the ocean depths and was soaring high into the stratosphere.

Unbeknownst to me, a drama was beginning to act itself out in the control van below. About 12 minutes before 1 a.m., Bill Lange turned to Stu Harris and said, "What are we going to do to keep ourselves awake tonight?" All they'd seen so far was more mud, endless miles of bland, featureless bottom. Stu didn't answer. His eyes were glued to the *Argo* monitor. He had seen a new kind of image. "There's something," he said simply, as he pointed to the TV screen. Suddenly, every member of the sleepy watch became alive and alert, but no one could believe that it wasn't just another false alarm, or a practical joke. Had Zoo Crew fever infected the Watch of Quiet Excellence?

But no. Stu switched *Argo*'s cameras from forward-looking camera to down-looking zoom and a few seconds later Stu chimed in excitedly, "It's coming in!" and then a few seconds later, Bill Lange exclaimed, "Wreckage!" And sure enough, there on the video screen were the unmistakable images of things man-made. A few seconds later, Stu added his exultant note: "Bingo!" and then the van echoed with a chorus: "Yeah!" followed by shrieks and war whoops.

Moments later, Lieutenant Rey on the sonar reported, "I'm getting a hard contact." For a few minutes there was nothing more to see save for a few small glacial boulders. Had they been seeing things after all? A discussion started as to whether they should go wake Ralph White so he could start filming. Then, at two minutes to one, more small definite debris fragments began to appear. They decided to go get Ralph.

After the long, tedious, fruitless search and yesterday's minor mutiny, no one wanted to drag me out of the sack on a false alarm. Nothing is more embarrassing than to become a member of the "I Saw A Flare Club." Bill Lange was the first to suggest that "Someone should go get Bob," but no one made a move. By four minutes past one, everyone in the van had become convinced something was up, but as all sorts of wreckage streamed past, no one wanted to leave. Now Stu Harris said, "Let's go get Bob," but still there were no volunteers. Ironically, the ship's cook, who had never before ventured into the van, now wandered in. He sure had picked a hell of a moment to take his first peek. The van crew immediately pressed him into service and sent him up to rouse me.

While the cook headed aft and up to my quarters, something new appeared amidst the unrecognizable wreckage passing by on the video screen. It was perfectly circular ... "a boiler?" someone mused. "It's a boiler!" Bill Lange sang out. Now there could be absolutely no doubt. But Jean-Louis still wouldn't believe what his eyes were telling him. He

The graveyard shift – the Watch of Quiet Excellence – goes quietly about its work. Bottom to top: Jean-Louis Michel, Tom Crook, and Steve Gegg.

opened the book containing a facsimile of the now-famous 1911 *Shipbuilder* article on the *Olympic* and the *Titanic* and turned to the page with the pictures of the boilers. He looked from page to screen and back again, repeating over and over, as if to convince himself, ''Yes, it *ees* a boiler.''

When the cook stuck his head through the door of my cabin, I was still busy breaking the sound barrier with Yeager. Finally, I'd gotten the *Titanic* out of my mind. ''The guys think you should come down to the van,'' he said. It took a couple of seconds for the import of his words to penetrate, then I sprang out of my bunk, Yeager's book flying, pulled on my jumpsuit over my pajamas, and practically knocked the cook out of the way in my haste to get to the van. I must have run the three decks down and aft in about 30 seconds.

When I burst into the van, Stu informed me that *Argo* had just passed over a massive ship's boiler. The initial elation in the room had subsided to a simmer, but was still ready to boil over again. Quickly, they replayed the tape and sure enough I saw the image of a big ship's boiler – *Titanic*'s. I didn't yelp or shout. In fact, for a few seconds, I didn't say anything. Then, totally at a loss for words, I simply kept repeating in a quiet but incredulous voice, ''God damn. God damn....''

I turned to Jean-Louis. The look in his eyes said everything. The *Titanic* had been found. We'd been right all along. Then he said softly, ''It was not luck. We earned it.''

Our hunt was almost over. Somewhere very near us lay the R.M.S. *Titanic*.

Around us the van again erupted in whoops and shouts. I went around and congratulated the members of the watch, shaking hands, patting people on the back. But in the midst of my elation, I began to realize the danger we were in. Larger and larger pieces of wreckage were now passing under *Argo* and Earl had to winch in to avoid hitting them. We didn't yet know where the main wreck was. If large pieces of it were intact, they would loom up quite suddenly – too suddenly for even Grumpy to avoid. I cautioned the watch, ''Be careful now about the altitude.'' But we were all so mesmerized by what we were seeing that it

(Top) This 1911 photograph of boilers being assembled in the shop helped identify the first image of a boiler face (above) that appeared on Argo's *monitor early on the morning of September 1, 1985.*

A scene of jubilation in the van: we toast our success with Portuguese wine in paper cups. Left to right: Martin Bowen, Stu Harris, Dana Yoerger, Bill Lange, Jean Jarry, myself, and Cathy Offinger.

was some minutes before I converted the warning into a command.

As the images on the video screen grew more and more vivid – large pieces of twisted hull plating, portholes, a piece of railing turned on its side – for the first time since I had started on this quest 12 years before, the full human impact of the *Titanic*'s terrifying tragedy began to sink in. Here at the bottom of the ocean lay not only the graveyard of a great ship, but the only fitting monument to the more than 1500 people who had perished when she went down. And we were the very first people in 73 years to come to this precise spot to pay our respects. Images from the night of the disaster – a story I now knew by heart – flashed through my mind with painful intensity.

At 1:13 a.m. – eight minutes after *Argo* passed over the boiler – I snapped out of my reverie and gave the order to raise *Argo* to its strobing altitude of 80 to 100 feet. I was being careful, but I didn't realize until later just how dangerous our situation was. Unwittingly, we were coming into the wreck at the worst spot. I would never have flown *Argo* through that place in the way that I did, knowing what I know now. It was like we were towing our sled through downtown Manhattan after World War Three. We were only about 12 feet above the *Titanic*'s deck.

Word had now spread through the ship and people were pouring into the van. The place was becoming a madhouse. With *Argo*'s running lights turned off, the newcomers saw, not a real-time image of the bottom, but a series of snapshots taken every eight seconds – a sort of disco effect. By 1:25, we had crossed the debris field and I decided to pull *Argo* up. In this northwestern corner of our new search area, the tracking was poor. I wanted to put in a new transponder net before surveying the wreckage in detail. Besides, bedlam had erupted in the van – it was time for celebration before getting back to work – and people had started to pass around paper cups of Mateus wine purchased in the Azores. At least the stuff was bubbly. It was the closest we came to champagne.

I won't soon forget that scene of triumph and jubilation. Emory Kristof clapped me on the back and then went back to snapping pictures. Ralph White filmed furiously away. Jean-Louis grinned

Dana Yoerger (left) and Lt. George Rey beaming over our success.

The *Argo* Search – Phase II

41° 50' N

SAR Coverage

Titanic's Reported Position

Second Search Area

41° 45'

Bow Section

Stern Section

First Search

41° 40'

Lifeboats Recovered

41° 35'

0 1 2 3 4 5 Nautical Miles
0 2 4 6 8 Kilometers

Argo Coverage (Camera and Sonar)

41° 30'

50° 20'   50° 15'   50° 10'   50° 05'   50° 00'   49° 55'   49° 50'   49° 46' W

Argo *tracks leading to the location of the* Titanic *are shown on this Phase II chart.*

broadly. Everybody was talking at once, congratulating each other, while trying to pay attention to the job at hand.

Then, at the height of this victory celebration, our mood suddenly crashed as if *Argo* had again hit bottom. Someone – I don't remember who – pointed up to the twin clocks, one with Zulu (Greenwich time) and one with local time on it, and said something like "Oh my God!" It was approaching 2 a.m. local time, very close to the exact hour of the *Titanic*'s sinking. That was all it took to break our mood. Here we were just catching our breaths at the peak of elation and suddenly we felt awkward, even sad. Part of our vulnerability may have been due to the fact that for the first time since the search had started we were without a purpose. All at once the professional was replaced by the human being. The van became quiet.

I said something like, "I don't know how you people feel, and I don't want to impose my feelings on you at all, but I know that in about 20 minutes I'm going out on the fantail. If anyone wants to join me, they're welcome. If not, that's okay." That was it. Then I walked out of the van.

I don't remember exactly what I did for the next 20 minutes. I just found a quiet corner to be alone with my thoughts. And I imagine a lot of others did the same. When I got to the fantail, quite a few people had gathered. I raised the Harland & Wolff flag, the emblem of the Belfast shipyard that had built the *Titanic*. I wasn't trying to be theatrical about it, it just seemed the right thing to do. The storm that had appeared to threaten us had passed by at a safe distance and the weather was beautiful: the sky was clear and filled with stars, the sea calm. Except for the moon, it was just like the night the *Titanic* went down. I spoke only a few words: "I really don't have much to say, but I thought we might just observe a few moments of silence."

It was one thing to have won – to have found the ship. It was another thing to be there. That was the spooky part. I could see the *Titanic* as she slipped nose first into the glassy water. Around me were the ghostly shapes of the lifeboats and the piercing shouts and screams of people freezing to death in the water.

Our little memorial service lasted five, maybe ten minutes. Then I just said, "Thank you all. Now, let's get back to work."

Lt. Rey raises the Harland & Wolff flag in preparation for our fantail memorial service.

We pause on the darkened deck to remember those who died when the Titanic *went down. Left to right: myself, Martin Bowen, Terry Snyder, and Cathy Offinger.*

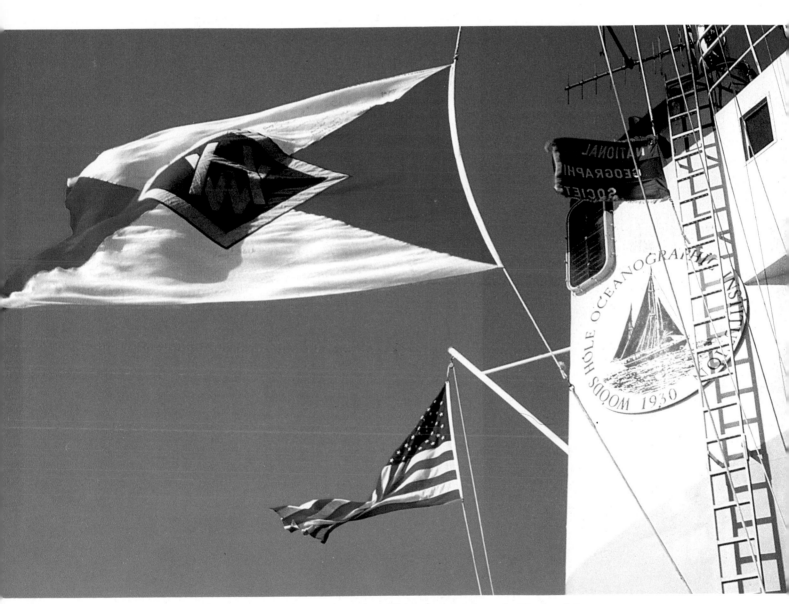

*The next morning, the Harland &
Wolff flag was still flying alongside the
Stars and Stripes.*

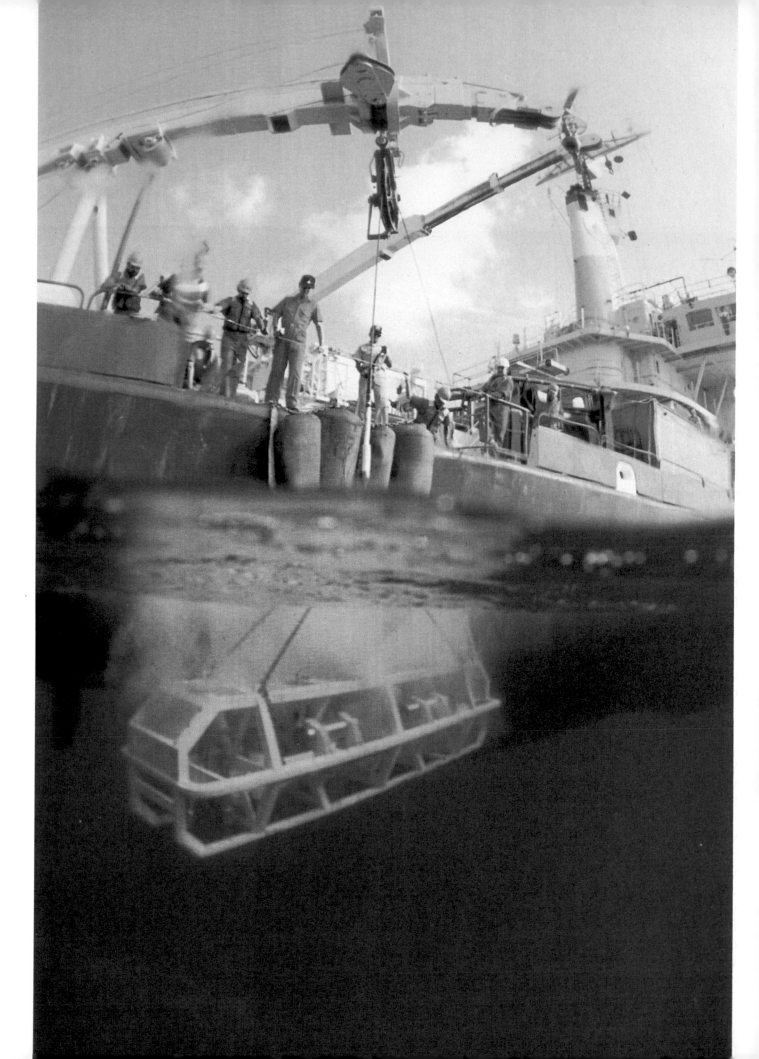

CHAPTER 7
Titanic Found

(Above) Jean-Louis and I plot our first Argo *run over the wreck.*

(Opposite) Argo *is launched.*

A S DAWN BROKE ON THE COOL, GRAY MORNING OF SUNDAY, SEPTEMBER 1, 1985, the *Knorr*'s radar told us our tiny vessel was surrounded by ships. Suddenly, a P-3 Orion submarine hunter thundered overhead, barely clearing the bridge as it tested its magnetometer on *Knorr*. Moments later, a fighter bomber sporting a big red Canadian maple leaf flew past. All at once the sea and sky were alive with ships and airplanes. Did everyone in the world know that we had found the *Titanic*? As it turned out we had landed by pure chance in the middle of a NATO exercise: our discovery was not yet known to the world – or was it?

When I called Woods Hole to give them the good news, I was met with a jolt. The guard who answered the phone informed me that the press had been calling all morning wanting details of our *Titanic* discovery. Apparently, there'd been a story in the Sunday London *Observer*. If that was true, then the paper had gone to press at about the time we'd found the ship. Impossible. Or had someone been eavesdropping on our radio conversations between the van and the bridge?

I didn't have time to ponder the matter. Although the weather was still fairly calm, I could smell a storm on the way. Sure enough, our satellite read-out had located an approaching storm front. We had barely four days before we were due to head back to Woods Hole and a North Atlantic gale could cut seriously into that time, or put a premature end to our expedition.

In the short space remaining, I planned to get as many pictures of the wreck as possible. I wanted to be able to show the waiting world what condition the *Titanic* was in after 73 years on the bottom. A million questions surged through my mind: would the ship be basically intact or broken into countless pieces? Was the rigging still in place, were the smokestacks still upright, the wooden decking preserved in deep salt water? And a darker thought, would we find any evidence of the people who'd perished with her? Pictures would give us the answers – first video runs with *Argo*, then more perilous passes with ANGUS to get full-color, close-up photographs.

The next 24 hours blurred into a controlled frenzy of activity. First, we launched more transponders, capturing the wreck firmly in our high-tech net. Then we mapped the debris field with *Argo*, avoiding the main wreckage and getting to know the lay of the land before we went in for a closer look. Ironically, *Knorr*'s old-fashioned echo sounder, which had been left running when the transponder net was surveyed into place, had located the main piece of the hull. With all this fancy equipment on board we had pin-pointed the location of the *Titanic* with a run-of-the-mill fathometer, no better than you'd find on an ordinary deep-water fishing trawler.

A much more bitter irony became apparent when Jean-Louis and I examined how close *Le Suroit* had come to finding the wreck. On one of his very first passes Jean-Louis had come within less than 3,300 feet of the *Titanic*. The ship lay on the eastern edge of the primary search area – in that narrow wedge Jean-Louis had missed due to the strong current. The hand of fate? If only Jean-Louis had been able to make his early lines a little straighter.... His misfortune and my luck were intertwined. I tried to cheer him up, reminding him that ours was a partnership and that the glory would be shared. But he was inconsolable. "Paris will look at it as my failure," he told me, then stoically returned to work, patiently plotting our *Argo* runs on the van chart table.

In the meantime, our reconnaissance runs over the debris field had taken too much time due to recurring tracking problems and I was beginning to feel desperate. But by early afternoon on September 2, as the storm drew closer and the winds began to build, I'd gathered enough information and screwed up enough courage to order our first *Argo* run over the major piece of wreckage we'd located. The risk I would be taking was brought forcibly home by the large profile of the *Titanic* that Jean-Louis had hung on the back wall of the van. It showed the ship's huge smokestacks and complex rigging, and was a constant reminder to me and everyone else of the dangers lurking below. If *Argo* got caught in wires or wreckage it would take a miracle to free it – likely we'd have to cut the cable and kiss a half-million dollars of new technology goodbye, not to mention the rest of the expedition.

Captain Bowen at the controls.

Despite the delays, *Argo* had now added to our knowledge of the wreck site. It had explored large parts of the debris field and seen one of the ship's giant cranes lying on its side, the boom badly bent. It had crossed over a region of massive wreckage in the vicinity of our boiler – a tangled pile of twisted bulkheads and upturned hull plating. But we still didn't know what condition this main part of the wreck would be in – that major section we had so far stayed clear of. We still believed the ship could be in one piece – all the wreckage we'd seen could have been emptied from the interior of the ship after boilers and other heavy material had crashed through. (Many survivor eyewitnesses had described loud crashing noises when the ship had turned on end.) There still seemed a strong likelihood that some smokestacks remained upright and some rigging was still in place.

As we maneuvered *Knorr* into position to make *Argo*'s first run across the main wreck, the word swiftly spread among the science party and a crowd began to gather in the back of the van. Not a word was spoken except for the terse dialogue between me and the watch crew. Appropriately, the *Titanic* discovery watch, Harris' Heroes, were at their posts, with Captain Bowen's expert hands at *Knorr*'s controls.

As *Argo* neared the bottom, I gave the first command: "Flyer, stop at an altitude of 50 meters." No one moved in the van. The only noise was the pinging of the sonar and the buzz of the printers.

"Roger that." Earl Young was all business today. The flatness of his tone disguised the tension he and I were feeling as he stared at *Argo*'s fathometer, bouncing an echo straight down off the bottom.

"Sonar, tell me when you see anything."

"Roger that," replied Lt. Rey, ready for battle. His paper print-out told him what *Argo*'s side-looking sonar saw to either side.

"*Argo* con, I want to begin the approach in high-altitude strobe mode."

"Roger that," Stu Harris returned softly. He was beginning to turn green from seasickness, but this was a moment he wasn't going to miss. Now his boy *Argo* could really show his stuff.

For our first approach, we would take as few chances as possible and come in at a safer high altitude. This meant using our high-power strobe flash, which concentrated our lighting energy into short, powerful bursts every ten seconds. In the flashes, *Argo* could see further than in the continuous television mode. So although *Argo*'s video cameras would be running continuously, our screen would only show snapshots every ten seconds.

Earl informed me we were at strobing altitude – safely above the stacks and masts – we hoped.

"Ship con, let's begin our first pass. Try to maintain speed over the bottom of less than .5 knots."

In the driver's seat, Captain Bowen was clearly enjoying himself. During the search, he'd been mostly on the outside, usually holed up in his cabin with not much to do. Now his skill at handling the ship made him essential to our discovery mission.

"Flyer, keep your eyes peeled for a sudden change in altitude. Let it come up. It should stop at an altitude of 30 to 35 meters." My voice remained calm, but my hands were beginning to shake. In a few moments we'd know the worst.

"Roger that." Earl was hard as nails.

At an altitude of 50 meters (164 feet), *Argo* was blind. It couldn't see bottom so neither could we. Our video monitors were filled with the glare of strobe lights bouncing off tiny objects in the water. Too much submarine fog meant backscatter for *Argo*'s headlights, so we had to depend on sonar – the fathometer pinging directly off the bottom. *Argo*'s fathometer would tell us when we crossed over the *Titanic*. Flying at 50 meters, we should be safely above it. Should be. If we weren't and if Earl couldn't bail out in time that would be the end of *Argo*, the end of our mission, possibly our last ever look at the *Titanic*. I held my breath. . . .

Earl: "The altimeter is beginning to flicker."

Rey: "I have a massive object off to starboard on sonar; we're about to cross it."

Earl: "Altimeter has just jumped; the altitude is now 25 meters."

Me: "Hold; don't take in cable."

Earl Young flying Argo.

A pilot fish examining Argo. *In the background can be seen one of the* Knorr's *unique cycloidal propellers.*

It was now or never.

Argo was passing directly over the main hull of the *Titanic* – the Golden Fleece was in our grasp at last. Not a word in the van, just 20 sets of lungs breathing as faint objects flashed on the video screens. If we'd miscalculated I'd know it soon.

It was time to risk a closer look, to take the plunge.

"Shift to real time mode. We're going down."

It was as if the crowd in the van, already holding its collective breath, inhaled further while, with the light touch of fingers on a keyboard, Stu Harris sent digital commands down to *Argo*'s onboard computer, ordering it to turn on its incandescent lights and to again act like a normal television camera with very sensitive eyes.

"Flyer, down five meters."

"Roger that."

We were now dropping below the stack level of the *Titanic*. If the stacks were there – worse still, if the masts and rigging were still intact – we were in big trouble.

On the video screen I could see the dim shape of a hull: "It's the side of the ship. She's upright."

Lt. Rey immediately chimed in his sonar report: "I have what appears to be stacks off to the starboard on sonar. We are below them."

"Roger that," I responded. "Keep your eyes peeled." As if I needed to remind them.

Suddenly, out of the gloom the Boat Deck of the ship came into view. We were on the port side looking at what appeared to be a stack opening – but the funnel was gone, the same forward funnel that had fallen into the water a few minutes before the ship sank, nearly hitting collapsible B to which a handful of survivors – including Second Officer Lightoller, Colonel Gracie, and Marconi Operator Bride – had been clinging for dear life. Miraculously, its wash had pushed them clear of the hull just in time.

As we crossed over the center axis of the ship, we could see the flattened rectangular outline of the bridge. Was this where Captain Smith had stood stoically to the end? Thank God the cables were gone now.

Then I saw it, just off to the starboard side of the bridge, the unmistakable image of a boat davit; and suddenly it hit me square in

My eyes are riveted on the monitor as we make our first Argo *run over the main wreck.*

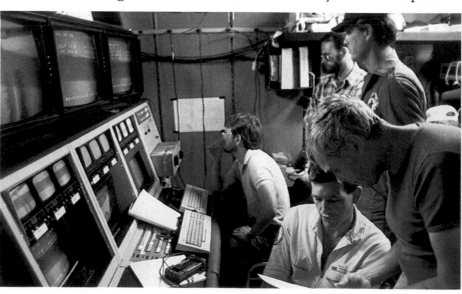

In the control van the team monitors the first crossing. Clockwise from left: Tom Dettweiler, Bob Squires, myself, Jean Jarry, and Bernard Pillaud.

the stomach. Empty davits: not enough lifeboats. How could such a mighty ship, the biggest and the best that money could build, not have had enough lifeboats for crew and passengers?

Before we knew it, *Argo* had safely passed out over the starboard bow railing and back into the featureless murk. All at once, the bottled-up excitement in the crowded van exploded. People were whooping, hugging, and dancing around while Jean-Louis and I stood quietly in the midst of this crazy throng pondering the significance of the moment. In a few brief minutes, what our joint team of engineers had accomplished rivaled or surpassed all our previous underwater exploits – from the investigation of the Mid-Ocean Ridge to the discovery of the black smokers. As the celebrations continued around us, Jean-Louis and I were almost in tears. Perhaps we were – I don't remember.

From start to finish our first look at the *Titanic* had lasted just under six minutes. But that first run taught us a lot. Had the expedition ended then and there it would have been a great success. We now knew that the *Titanic* was upright and that a major portion of the ship appeared to be intact. As eyewitnesses at the time of the sinking had reported, the number 1 funnel was gone. There was still no reason to think the ship was not in one piece. We also knew the bow was facing slightly east of north, and we had established a safe viewing altitude, information we could use to make subsequent video runs over the ship and later to make more dangerous close-up runs with ANGUS.

I was ready to go back at the bow, but first it was time to clear the van. I needed my team as rested as possible for the next 64 hours, so I addressed the crowd: "Hey, we've got too many people up. Your butts are going to be dragging when your watch comes up. Let's get some of you back in the rack. This is a 24-hour operation." With a bit of good-humored grumbling, the reserve troops left the van and headed off to get some shut-eye – if they could calm down enough to do it. I wouldn't have had a hope of falling asleep, and there was no way I was going to miss a single run over the *Titanic*. If we lost *Argo* in the wreckage, I was going to be the one to lose it.

During the rest of that afternoon and evening, we only managed two more *Argo* passes over the wreck, our work increasingly hampered by the rising winds and seas which gave *Knorr*'s cycloids all they could handle. On the second of these subsequent *Argo* runs, as we moved aft

(Top) Jean-Louis identifies parts of the Titanic *as we cross over the wreck.*

(Above and below) ANGUS *pictures of what we saw on* Argo's *monitor.* *(Above) Intact cranes in the Well Deck.* *(Below, left) A lonely lifeboat davit.* *(Below, right) The number 1 funnel opening.*

from the area of the number 2 funnel – we still thought the funnel itself could be there because of sonar image recorded on our first *Argo* approach – to where the stern half of the hull should have been, the deck began to plunge away from us and, as Earl lowered *Argo* to keep the hull in view, the video images faded into a confusing mass of twisted wreckage: turned-up windows, torn hull sections, razor-sharp edges of jagged steel. To our surprise and disappointment, the stern was gone. On the plotting table, we pinned a paper silhouette of the *Titanic* giving a plan, or overhead view, of the bow section, showing the wreck's compass orientation and its position in our transponder net. On the cut-out we marked everything we knew about the *Titanic* up to that point: where the ship's bridge was, the position of the Grand Staircase opening, the number 1 funnel opening.

At the end of that pass, the rising seas had made handling *Argo* too difficult – at one point we'd crashed the sled into the hull – and I ordered a recovery. It was near 11:30 p.m. on September 2, nearly 24 hours since I'd last seen a bed. As the storm was reaching its absolute peak, with winds gusting to 35 knots, *Argo*'s crew, dressed in bright yellow foul-weather gear, spilled out of the warm control van and onto a dark, cold, wet, windy deck, the bitter salt spray slapping their faces. The scene was enacted in the garish glare of the *Knorr*'s floodlights, giving the whole thing a nightmarish, surreal quality. As the wind howled across the rolling deck, the yellow figures moved to their assigned positions as the officer on the bridge maneuvered *Knorr*'s bow into the wind, using her tall superstructure as a partial wind break. But nothing could stop the pitching and heaving of the ship.

Meanwhile, the *Argo* crew hung the large halter of black water-filled bumpers out beyond the starboard railing, ready to receive the sled. As *Argo* broke through the surface, it began to swing wildly in a magnified version of *Knorr*'s heaving action. Now every second counted as ship's bosun Jerry Cotter shouted orders into the gale. The *Argo* crew – like bronco busters trying to put a saddle on a bucking horse – swiftly attached lines to the yawing sled. Then, at a sign from Jerry, the crane operator brought *Argo* toward the ship and crashing down into its rubber berth – tamed and docile at last.

Argo recovery could be extremely risky in high seas.

It was mid-morning of Tuesday, September 3, and I had run out of patience. For ten painful hours I had waited for the storm to abate. I'd even spent a few futile and frustrating hours trying to catch some sleep in my constantly pitching cabin, but to no avail. Finally, I'd decided that if we couldn't work with *Argo* then at least we could lower ANGUS and get some still pictures of the debris field. ANGUS had worked in rougher seas than these. Anyway, the fear of losing ANGUS would take our minds off the rotten weather.

Through the afternoon and into the late evening of September 3, ANGUS' still cameras snapped off thousands of color pictures of the debris field. A few hours later, when Martin Bowen had developed the film, we discovered we had amassed a somber visual collection of artifacts – a chamber pot here, a bedspring there, a tea cup over there, a silver serving platter, a multitude of wine bottles, even the white-painted headboard from a bed. And huge piles of unrecognizable wreckage.

By midnight, the storm front finally passed and the seas began to fall. Late that afternoon, we readied ourselves for our first ANGUS run over the main wreck. It was a nail-biter from start to finish – exhaustion and adrenalin competing for control of our weary bodies as Earl Young, Tom Crook, and Captain Bowen maneuvered our sightless ''dope on a rope'' back and forth over the *Titanic*'s decks. Each pass across the wreck was heart-stopping, not to mention stomach-turning. If slow maneuvers in a cycloidal ship in heavy seas don't make you sick, nothing will. Carefully, ever so carefully, Jean-Louis conducted *Knorr* and ANGUS through four more runs, each one lasting about 30 minutes. As the fifth and final run came to an end, night had fallen for the last time on our *Titanic* mission. I ordered ANGUS recovered. If these pictures didn't come out, there was still time for one last go.

I wondered for a moment what a passing ship would have thought of our antics. There we were, this tiny vessel in the middle of nowhere, spinning around in circles for no apparent reason like a cat chasing its tail. They would surely have thought we had all gone mad.

Six hours later, madness seemed all too real a possibility. All we had to show for ANGUS' first terrifying runs over the wreck were blurry images buried in a blue haze of backscatter. At least the cameras were working fine, but our passes had simply been too high, too cautious. I felt victory slipping away, my remaining energy seeping from my body.

Right then I wished I could have just given up and gone home. My leg was throbbing from a fall on the slippery deck and I felt miserable. We had found the *Titanic*; wasn't that good enough? Who said we had to bring home pretty pictures to please the press?

Somewhere within my exhausted body I found the resolve to continue. There was no way I was going to leave the *Titanic*'s resting place without trying one more time. We had until 7:30 a.m. when the remaining transponders would have to be recovered. Allowing one hour for lowering and one for recovering ANGUS, that meant a mere four and a half hours for our last attempt.

The final launching of ANGUS was a terror to behold. The wind and sea had picked up, again making it difficult to hold *Knorr*'s head to wind. As soon as ANGUS' steel frame was freed from its moorings, it swung wildly despite the best efforts of the six-man ANGUS team, each man on a line threaded through block and tackle and attached to a 6,000-pound wrecking ball. Earl crawled out on ANGUS' frame to acti-

This scale drawing shows the enormous distance between the Knorr *and the* Titanic *wreck.*

To Scale: approximately 13,000 feet

vate the cameras and strobes – a routine maneuver made hair-raising in such conditions. He had lashed himself securely to the ship, but, just in case, Martin Bowen was hanging onto his life-vest and Emile Bergeron onto Martin's. Then a bright flash lit up the sky as 1500 watts of energy exploded through ANGUS' twin strobes. Satisfied the cameras were working, Earl gave the thumb's down and ANGUS went crashing into the churning sea.

As we re-entered the control van and struggled out of our wet foul-weather gear, I could see that Jean-Louis had reached his physical limit. The look in his eyes told me that he wanted to keep fighting, but his eyelids simply refused to stay open. ''Get to bed,'' I told him, ''there's no need for both of us to stay up.'' Reluctantly, but gratefully, he left the van.

I had to lie down or I would fall down, but I couldn't afford to leave my post. So, crawling on my hands and knees, I began to clear a small area beneath the chart table. From my prone position I could still talk to Earl on the winch, Tom Crook on navigation, and Captain Bowen on the ship controls. For our last desperate attempt we were down to a three-man ANGUS team under my command.

Now, even Earl was silent – one of the rare times I've known him to be at a loss for words. We both knew that what we were about to attempt was even crazier than the dangerous ANGUS launch just completed. I figured we now had to get our cameras within 23 feet of *Titanic*'s decks, but with the sea rising again *Knorr* itself was now heaving up and down between 10 and 13 feet, and this motion would be transmitted down our 12,500 feet of cable to ANGUS. What the hell. If I was going to lose ANGUS, I couldn't think of a better time or place. I might as well wrap the silk scarf around my neck and recite the last rites of the kamikaze pilot.

By the time we reached approach depth almost all my strength was gone, so I draped myself over Earl's right shoulder and whispered commands in his ear. We certainly didn't look the part of a dashing suicide crew that night.

''Down to four meters,'' I croaked.

''Four meters?'' Earl's question mark implied, ''Are you crazy?''

''Four meters,'' I repeated.

For the next three hours hardly a word was spoken beyond whispered commands and quiet replies as we made pass after frighteningly close pass over the *Titanic*. The dim red glow of the night lights (which illuminated the van in tight moments like these) gave a ghoulish air to the stressed faces and bloodshot eyes of the ANGUS crew, already scruffy with four-day-old beards and haggard from lack of sleep. The usually imperturbable Earl Young gripped the winch controls so hard his knuckles were white and it seemed as if the metal lever was about to ooze between his fingers. Outside, the wind rattled the walls of the van as the storm blew itself out. Inside, time became a sort of trance-like blur from which we were finally jolted at 5:56 a.m. when a simple message boomed over the bridge intercom: ''You have to start up now.''

Time and money had run out. Scientists were waiting back home to take *Knorr* off on other scientific pursuits.

At 7:28 a.m., right on schedule, ANGUS was back on deck. There was no way I could sleep now, so I stood in the processing van and watched as Martin developed each 400-foot roll of film.

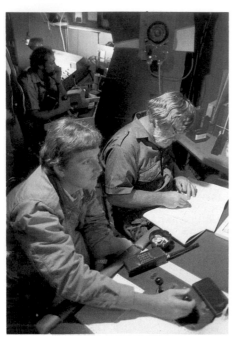

Captain Bowen driving and Tom Crook navigating as we pass ANGUS over the Titanic.

After several hours, the close quarters and the smell of the chemicals got to be too much so I took a break out on deck. The wind had dropped, but the seas were still angry and the sky a grim overcast. Then out of the blue, a twin-engine, 12-passenger prop plane passed directly overhead. The plane was outfitted with special navigational antennae, clearly there for only one purpose: to determine our exact location. It crossed back and forth over us, first in one direction, then another. But whoever it was, he was out of luck, since we were recovering a transponder and a mile or more away from the *Titanic*. Probably Jack Grimm, I thought.

Moments later, Martin emerged from the photo lab to report that we had excellent color images – but I was too tired to feel much sense of triumph. My remaining energy was needed to take care of business. Immediately, I gave irreversible orders to recover the last transponder. As it rose swiftly back to the surface, our precise tracking net was destroyed for good. The *Titanic* was once again lost in the deep, but not that lost. During our short time on the scene, we had collected hundreds of satellite fixes. Returning to the *Titanic* and landing *Alvin* on her deck would be a piece of cake.

With the photo-processing finally complete, Martin Bowen catches a few well-deserved winks on the fantail. ANGUS is in the background.

With our operations over, there was still one more job for me to do – deal with the media. Woods Hole had asked me to talk to as many reporters as possible and it seemed like every print and television journalist in North America wanted a few words of wisdom from Dr. Ballard. I had expected people to be excited about our finding the *Titanic*, but never in my wildest dreams had I anticipated this level of excitement.

Punchy from lack of sleep, I stumbled up to the radio room and began conducting interviews. The questions asked ran the gamut. Most reporters wanted to know the condition of the ship and whether we'd seen any signs of human remains. I did my best to answer them all, but I was near the end of my tether. *Argo* and ANGUS had finished their work, the seas were finally subsiding, the *Knorr* was just about to head toward the shore, and I should have been in bed. But I managed to hang in there, until I talked to Tom Brokaw of the NBC *Nightly News*.

Just as I began to talk to Brokaw, I happened to glance out the porthole. Suddenly, I realized that *Knorr* had finished recovering our final transponder and was now underway toward home. We were leaving the *Titanic* behind before I'd made my peace with her. Just at that moment Tom asked how I felt. Well, right then I felt terrible and it was all I could do to hold back the choking that rose in my throat. My resistance was gone and my emotions were quickly overwhelming me. Abruptly, I signed off and bolted from the radio room.

I went out through the back of the lab so no one would see me and down onto the now-empty fantail. The sun was just breaking through the clouds as I looked at *Knorr*'s beautiful and peaceful wake streaming out toward the blue horizon. My emotions were mixed: there was a feeling of sadness and regret that we had come and gone so quickly and at the same time a warm satisfaction at having finally ended the *Titanic*'s long journey. I'm not a particularly religious person, but I suppose you could say this was a religious moment, similar perhaps to the impromptu memorial service held on the fantail the night of our discovery a mere four and a half days ago. It was as if those who had perished aboard the *Titanic* could finally rest. That's how I felt.

For the last four and a half days, I had not managed a wink of sleep. Sleep. What a wonderful, blissful thought. I headed aft, through the main lab and up two sets of ladders toward my quarters. Then as I hobbled down the final passageway, I collapsed. My feet simply went out from underneath me and I found myself on the deck. This was a new experience for me and it was an interesting sensation – disorienting, almost comic. Then I started to feel embarrassed. What if someone had observed the great Captain Nemo slump to the floor? Luckily the passageway was deserted. Carefully, I got back up and made it to my bunk still on my feet.

Now, finally, I slept. When I awoke, it was nighttime and the good ship *Knorr* steamed quietly and steadily toward the tumult on the shore.

A helicopter hovering over the Knorr *lowers a basket to pick up film and video of our discovery.*

What should have been a pleasant trip home, with time for reflection and decompression, turned into a sour and disheartening experience. The bond of cooperation I'd built up over many years of working with French oceanographers seemed about to break.

Naively, I now realize, we had not agreed in advance on a set policy for releasing the news of our discovery to the waiting world, or for the disposition of video footage and still images. We hadn't dreamed people would get so excited about our finding the ship, and we simply hadn't thought through all the ramifications of dealing with the news media while in the midst of a complex technical operation at sea in difficult conditions. It didn't help, either, that all of us were exhausted.

The trouble actually had begun on Sunday morning with the arrival of a helicopter from a Canadian television network which had provided funds to help cover the documentation budget of our expedition. The helicopter arrived with a news crew on board and asked if they could place the crew on board *Knorr* to report firsthand on this fast-breaking news event. I told them that was out of the question. We weren't giving exclusive access to anyone. But they could certainly have the "scoop" of filming us on site from the air. After all, they had earned it by being the only network to back us.

Jean-Louis, Jean Jarry, and I also saw the helicopter as an opportunity to regain some control over the news coverage of our own expedition, coverage which seemed to have gone bizarrely awry. The story in Sunday's London *Observer* had been followed by totally false news reports saying that we were actually salvaging the *Titanic* wreckage. Over the radio we'd even heard that protests against our supposed actions had been lodged in the United Nations. That had everyone on board upset. So we elected to use the Canadian helicopter as a courier to carry the first pictures of our discovery ashore. We chose the initial footage of the boiler and film of the jubilation in the van. These images would begin to tell the true story of the finding of the *Titanic*. As we watched the helicopter disappear into the gathering storm and returned to our *Argo* runs over the wreck, we were satisfied that our story would finally get told accurately.

The next thing I knew, Woods Hole was on the phone, not to congratulate us, but to complain about the apparent news exclusive we'd given out. The images of our discovery had gone on air, but not all the big U.S. networks had them yet. Those who didn't were furious and

(Left) The forecastle of the Titanic's *sister ship*, Olympic, *looking aft toward the bridge.*

(Below) The same area on the Titanic's *decks, seen from above. The huge anchor chains are clearly visible.*

(Right) The crow's nest on the fallen foremast.

(Far right) This picture of the fore-castle and the forward edge of the Well Deck of the Olympic *in New York after her 1911 maiden voyage closely parallels how the same area on the* Titanic *would have looked.*

threatened Woods Hole with lawsuits. Suddenly, a quiet scientific community in a remote corner of Cape Cod – with most people off enjoying the Labor Day Weekend – was being subjected to unheard of media pressure.

Immediately, I got on the phone to all concerned, explaining our position. News was news and the tapes we had sent ashore could be used by anyone. A scoop was one thing, but an exclusive was something entirely different. No one was to blame. Woods Hole was simply unprepared for the media onslaught, and this problem was aggravated by the fact it was a holiday long weekend.

Now, as we sailed toward Woods Hole, my French colleagues and I concocted a careful scheme to show off some of our ANGUS pictures. There was frequent contact with IFREMER in Paris and with Woods Hole management. These were high-quality images and we wanted to be sure that they were released simultaneously to all North American television networks and to the French media.

On September 6, as we steamed home, another helicopter flew out to the *Knorr*, this one chartered by all three American TV networks. When it returned to Newfoundland, Bernard Pillaud and Steve Gegg went with it, carrying multiple copies of the ANGUS and *Argo* footage we'd agreed to release. One Frenchman and one American would make sure that this time our plan was carried out to the letter.

When the helicopter landed at St. John's Airport, a throng of reporters lay in wait as a handsome young American and a dashing Frenchman emerged. They must have looked a little like astronauts returning from a trip to the moon. How could Woods Hole and IFREMER withhold such important images from a waiting world? The media pressure proved too great and Woods Hole relented, releasing the material. That night, while Bernard was still flying across the Atlantic, French television viewers saw our newly minted *Titanic* images on their screens before IFREMER could release them; they had been picked up from the American networks via satellite.

Quite understandably, IFREMER was furious at this apparent breach of our understanding, an anger compounded by the dawning realization of just how valuable these images were. I'd never had any plans to

Our discovery of the Titanic *was front page news around the world.*

The discoverers of the Titanic *pose on the* Knorr's *fantail.*

"sell" the news, but now Paris wanted to. Unfortunately, our earlier agreements did not make this point clear. So, as we headed toward a hero's welcome on the American shore, IFREMER and Woods Hole were locked in an unfortunate conflict over who owned the images from our *Titanic* expedition and how they would be used. Jean Jarry, who was IFREMER's head-office man on board, was caught in the middle – feeling the full pressure of his bosses back in Paris. My old friend Jean-Louis couldn't believe what was happening and spent most of his time in his cabin. I watched helplessly as all the good feelings of our voyage and 13 years of joint American and French cooperation seemed to slip away.

The low point of the trip home came when Emory Kristof decided he wanted a group picture of the victorious *Titanic* discoverers posed on the fantail with *Argo* and ANGUS in the background. By this stage none of us felt much like smiling, but at Kristof's insistence we reluctantly agreed. We made poor subjects, our forced smiles disguising the hurt underneath. Despite this setback, however, I wanted our homecoming to be a joint U.S./French celebration. And I spent two days polishing the brief remarks I would make to the waiting press.

What I would be able to say would be based on only partial knowledge of the state of the wreck. Careful analysis of the ANGUS footage over the next several months would reveal that a second large section of the hull rested roughly 2,000 feet to the south of the bow. This was the stern, but beyond that we knew little about its condition. We would also discover that all four funnels appeared to be gone. But the region of the tear on the bow section, and much of the larger debris field, remained a mystery, and we knew nothing about what lay between the bow and the stern. Only if we returned would we know the complete nature of the *Titanic*'s wreck.

(Top) A congratulatory banner hangs on the facade of the Bigelow Building, WHOI's original headquarters.

(Above) A big crowd greeted us when we docked at Woods Hole. Rear Admiral Brad Mooney, Chief of Naval Research and sponsor of the Argo/Jason *program, comes aboard.*

On the clear, warm morning of September 9, 1985, as we steamed down Nantucket Sound, *Knorr* was mobbed by helicopters, small planes, and pleasure craft running circles around us and blowing their horns. A boat had already delivered a small welcoming party – including Woods Hole Director John Steele and two of his staff; Hugh O'Neill, representing the Secretary of the Navy; and my wife Marjorie and our two sons Todd and Douglas. Having my family there was especially important to me. They had paid a tremendous price over the years during my long months away from home, but they'd never complained. Along with my parents, they have long been my most important rooting section.

As we turned the corner and entered the narrow channel leading to Woods Hole's marine facility, I couldn't believe my eyes. The dock was a mass of people filling every available inch of space. To the right, the networks had erected a wall of satellite antennae already sending their signals back to New York and around the world. In the middle of the dock was a makeshift platform bristling with television cameras and reporters – the media demanded and got the best view. Banners were flying, a band was playing, schoolchildren were hanging onto helium-filled balloons. As we neared our berth, a cannon boomed out a salute. It was as if the circus had come to town. In many ways it had.

I thought of the very different crowd that had met the *Carpathia* when she sailed into New York on the stormy evening of April 18, 1912, three and a half days after the tragedy. The offices of the White Star

Line had been besieged by anxious crowds – many of them relatives of the passengers. Reporters had waited like sharks to prey on any survivors willing to sell their story. I pushed such thoughts away.

Since this was a celebration, I decided to give the people a little bit of a show. Climbing up to the bridge, I asked Captain Bowen to stop *Knorr* less than 100 yards from the dock and to put his ship into a full 360-degree spin. (Few in the crowd knew of *Knorr*'s unique propulsion system.) Then the captain brought his ship gently against the dock.

With the gangplank in position, proud wives and children streamed aboard for a hug and a kiss and a firsthand look at *Argo* and its control center, where every monitor was alive with images of the *Titanic*. Inside the van champagne corks exploded into the air.

Now it was time to meet the press. As Jean-Louis and I crossed the gangway to a waiting car, the reporters and cameramen jamming the makeshift platform started shouting for me to make some gesture – something the cameras could make immortal. Without thinking, I gave them the thumbs-up sign and stuck out my tongue – from hero to buffoon in ten seconds. That silly victory picture instantly flashed around the world still haunts me.

A few minutes later we entered the side door of the Woods Hole Oceanographic Institution's Redfield Auditorium to be met by a wall of cameras and a podium full of microphones. In that moment they looked threatening, like a mass of spears poised to strike. As I made my way toward my place on the platform amid popping flashbulbs, I remembered one of George C. Scott's lines in the movie *Patton*. In it, Patton says that whenever a victorious Roman general returned to Rome at the head of his army, riding in a chariot surrounded by slaves, a young man always stood at his side reminding him that fame and glory were fleeting. Today, we were the main show in town. Tomorrow, the media circus would have moved on to another event.

Jean-Louis went first, speaking so softly that the press strained to make out his words. Both of us were still exhausted, and the emotion of the moment was taking over. As always, however, his words were gracious and eloquent. Despite any feuding between our countries, ours was a friendship and a partnership that went back a long way.

He began by briefly recapping the search and discovery. Then he went on to speak of our expedition's teamwork. "Our results were not obtained easily. They are the product of highly skilled teams on both ships who worked in a closely coordinated manner. The French-American cooperation took root because of the inspiration of Bob Ballard who made this discovery possible. Moreover, Dr. Ballard inspired among us all the idea that the success of the discovery must be assumed with the greatest respect and dignity befitting the *Titanic*. The endeavor between France and America has been technically and spritually difficult, yet the actual R.M.S. *Titanic* site was explored with her dignity in mind at all times. We hope that the work in the deep ocean between France and America will continue."

Now it was my turn to give credit where credit was due. I had given a thousand speeches in the past, but this one proved to be the most difficult to write or make, even though it would only take two minutes to say. I took a deep breath and began reading.

"This summer's joint expedition by the United States and France was a highly technical undertaking involving the finest technology of these

At the podium with Jean-Louis as we prepare to meet the press in Woods Hole's Redfield Auditorium.

two countries. In the field of deep submergence exploration, France and America are equal. But this summer's campaign was also the compassionate undertaking of two individuals who are human first and a Frenchman and an American second.'' I went on to talk of Jean-Louis' stature in his profession and the technical excellence of the SAR sonar system. I praised him as ''a quiet and gentle man'' with whom it had been a privilege to work.

"The *Titanic* lies in 13,000 feet of water on a gently sloping alpine-like countryside overlooking a small canyon below. Its bow faces north and the ship sits upright on the bottom. There is no light at this great depth and little life can be found. It is a quiet and peaceful and fitting place for the remains of this greatest of sea tragedies to rest. May it forever remain that way and may God bless these found souls.''

I had already escaped with my family through a side door and into a waiting Woods Hole car when I realized that I hadn't said goodbye to Jean-Louis. Then I spotted him in the very crowd of reporters and photographers I'd hope to escape. But I had no idea when I'd see him again. In a few hours, he'd be on a plane to France and, the next day, he'd be holding a press conference in Paris while I was doing the same thing at the *National Geographic*'s Washington, D.C. headquarters.

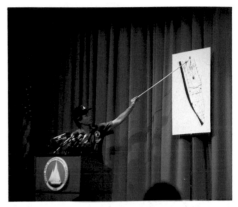

Two days later, I held a press conference at the National Geographic Society headquarters in Washington D.C. Here I indicate on a chart of the Titanic where our ANGUS pictures came from.

I jumped out of the car and into the sea of reporters, all of them wanting a few pithy words for the nightly news. But Jean-Louis and I ignored them. The media buzz became a background blurr and the only person I could see and hear was Jean-Louis. It was as if we were still out at sea, quietly talking on the fantail as we reconsidered the day's events or plotted some new twist in our search strategy. We swore to hang together, whatever happened, then shook hands and I fought my way back to the car. Soon I was racing away from this craziness.

I wondered then whether Jean-Louis and I would revisit the *Titanic* together. Whatever happened, nothing could take our accomplishment away from us.

(Left) In the front row at the press conference are: (left to right) John Steele, Director of WHOI; John Lehman, Secretary of the Navy; Guy Nichols, Chairman of WHOI; and Admiral Brad Mooney. My wife Marjorie is seated behind Secretary Lehman.

CHAPTER 8
Touring The *Titanic*

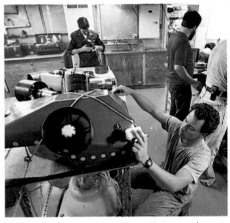

(Above) *Martin Bowen at work on* Jason Jr.

(Opposite) Alvin *is rolled out onto the fantail to be readied for the morning launch.*

W E RETURNED A YEAR LATER TO TAKE A CLOSER LOOK AT THE WRECK and this time, finding the *Titanic* was easy. Our satellite fixes from the previous year meant we could simply sail the 900 miles straight from Woods Hole to the site – and that's exactly what we did, arriving in the early evening of July 12, 1986. And the luck that had smiled on us during 1985 seemed to be with us still: the weather was fine – the sea calm and the night clear – and spirits were high on board our new ship the *Atlantis* II as we launched the first of three transponder beacons that would form our tracking "net" around the wreck. With only 12 days on site, I didn't want to waste a single moment.

As the saying goes, what a difference a year makes – in both good ways and bad. This expedition, primarily funded by the U.S. Navy like last year's, was being undertaken with Woods Hole's full blessing and official support. Our technical goal was to demonstrate the capabilities of *Jason Junior* – the prototype of our remotely controlled underwater robot. And, with "*JJ*'s" help, we intended to come back with beautiful pictures of the exterior and interior of the ship – a comprehensive visual record of a legendary wreck.

Sadly, this year's *Titanic* expedition was being conducted without the French. After the disagreements arising from the 1985 expedition, relations between Woods Hole and IFREMER had hit rock bottom. But olive branches had been extended by both sides and, for a time, it even looked as though a French ship and a French sub (*Nautile*) would be joining us at the site. When I learned that the French hadn't been able to raise the funds for a second *Titanic* expedition, I invited Jean-Louis Michel, my co-leader in 1985, and long-time friend Claude Riffaud, who was now heading IFREMER's *Titanic* project, to come as my guests. Unfortunately, neither was able to make it.

The absence of Jean-Louis and his French colleagues not only struck a note of melancholy amidst our generally high spirits, it introduced an additional element of risk. This year, we would explore the *Titanic* by manned submersible – my old friend *Alvin* – and without the French we would be diving without a back-up submarine in the event of trouble. As a result, we would be like astronauts landing on a distant planet millions of miles from home with no hope of rescue should anything go wrong.

Captain Reuben Baker brought *Atlantis II* about and began inching toward the spot beneath which the *Titanic* should lie, while I stood in the top lab just aft of the bridge and watched the sonar printout from the ship's echo sounder. Every second, a ping went out from the transducer attached to the ship's hull and, seconds later – like a shot fired into the Grand Canyon – a rapid succession of echoes came back from the bottom setting off a corresponding succession of burn marks on a rotating drum of paper – a sonar picture. Minute by minute, the flat sediment-covered ocean floor took shape on the moving record. Then, suddenly, a faint second echo began to appear. An object was rising up toward us, too large to be an outcrop or other natural feature. We were directly over the wreck, its coordinates locked into our computer. Visions of the *Titanic* danced in my head as I turned in for the night, and I'm sure I wasn't the only one on board that night who was dreaming about the ship.

Our first dive to the *Titanic* started out in picture-perfect fashion. It was another gorgeous summer day with the sun already high in the sky. At 7 a.m., *Alvin* was rolled out of its hangar on the stern of *Atlantis* II and positioned under the huge blue A-frame that loomed above the fantail. This frame would lift *Alvin* from the deck and retrieve it from the water. *Alvin*'s and *JJ*'s support crews immediately went to work. Like a space launch, a careful sequence had to be followed, involving a lengthy series of safety checks – a thick pile of check-off forms were signed and countersigned: battery check, life-support system check, acoustic telephone check, sonar check, back-up battery check, and so on.

Four heavy weights were rolled out in their trolleys and attached to the sub's sides. Unlike conventional submarines, *Alvin* can't use air ballast tanks to control its buoyancy in deep water – the pressure is too great – so instead, it has a complex flotation system. Then three tubs containing the freshly charged batteries were topped off with pressure-compensating oil, which takes up a lot less space than individual pressure chambers.

At 8:15 a.m., it was all systems go. Ralph Hollis, co-pilot Dudley Foster, and I, having removed our shoes, descended the ladder leading down through *Alvin*'s red fiberglass "turret," designed to keep waves from splashing water into the open hatch while the sub bobs on the surface. Then we climbed down into the seven-foot-diameter pressure sphere, careful not to brush against the well-greased hatch. (The grease is needed to insure a good seal and is next-to-impossible to get out of your clothes.) Once inside, expertise in yoga or contortionism would have helped as we now had to wad ourselves into balls and squeeze into the tiny cabin, hemmed in on three sides by panels of instruments and boxes of virgin video tape waiting to record some history. For the duration of the voyage, none of us would have room to stretch out or stand up – three sardines in a spherical can.

Ralph then closed the hatch from inside the sub as I turned on our oxygen tank – the sole source of air – slowly bleeding its life-supporting contents into the sphere. Already the sub was becoming stuffy, as Ralph turned on the lithium hydroxide blower which recycles the cabin's air to remove dangerous carbon dioxide.

Outside our tiny craft, the A-frame had begun to swing us out over the fantail, rocking us gently like a pendulum. The point when the sub is suspended half over the deck and half over the water is always one of the most dangerous moments of a dive. Should *Alvin* suddenly fall there could be severe damage to the sub and injury to the occupants.

As soon as the sub hit the water and the lift line was released, divers swarmed over *Alvin*'s hull, checking that everything was ready for descent. Inside, Ralph was rapidly rechecking all systems now that the sub was "wet." Each phase of the operation was carefully directed by

(Top) In stocking feet, and being careful not to rub against the greased hatch, I prepare to descend through the red turret-like "sail" into the sub.

(Above) The most dangerous point in the launch sequence is when Alvin *is suspended partway out over the water.*

the surface control team in the top lab on board *Atlantis II*, in radio contact both with the interior of the sub and the inflatable rubber dinghy waiting to pick up the divers.

At 8:35 a.m., the surface controller – always a pilot from the *Alvin* team – gave Ralph clearance to flood our air ballast tanks and begin our descent. The four weights attached to *Alvin* would now send us straight to the bottom. These worked on the same principle used by sponge divers: grab a rock, jump into the ocean, and let the rock get you down as fast as possible without having to expend valuable energy; when you arrive, drop the rock and go to work. With *Alvin*, when we wanted to head home, we dropped two more weights and started up. The idea was to minimize the use of the propellers – and battery power – both on the way down and on the way up.

I felt completely confident with Chief Pilot Ralph Hollis at the controls. I'd known him ever since he joined the Alvin Group in early 1975. And I'd known Dudley Foster even longer: we'd met during Project Famous, 12 years before. Between us, we had approximately 500 dives worth of experience.

In many ways the backbone of the 1986 expedition was the Alvin Group of deep-submersible pilots. Most of them had joined long after I'd begun diving in the sub in the early seventies, but collectively they had enormous experience in the deep ocean. I also knew that some of them, most notably Ralph Hollis, resented the way my Deep Submergence Laboratory was now capturing the headlines – and the fact that I had more than once predicted publicly that *Argo* and *Jason* would someday make *Alvin* obsolete.

Over the years, Ralph had come to embody the soul of *Alvin* and now took any comments against his sub personally. He and many others in the Alvin Group had never forgiven me for an interview I'd done a few years back for the local Woods Hole newspaper. The article had read: "Ballard says manned submersibles are doomed." Understandably, Ralph and his colleagues hadn't let me forget that one. In fact, their sub was in no immediate danger of being out of work; it simply represented technology that had had its day in the sun.

As the sub slipped silently below the surface, a translucent jellyfish drifted past my viewport, its stinging tentacles dangling down several feet. I glanced at the *Jason Jr.* control panel. Today *JJ* would stay in his specially constructed garage on the front of *Alvin*, but tomorrow Martin Bowen would be on board to pilot our cute little "swimming eyeball" over the wreck. Like the yet-to-be-built *Jason*, *Jason Jr.* was a remotely operated vehicle (ROV) – an underwater robot. And unlike *Jason*, *JJ* was light enough to be deployed from a manned submersible. Both would operate on a 250-foot tether and have a telemetry system, imaging cameras, and propulsion plant. But *JJ* didn't have the heavy arms and multiple color eyes we planned for *Jason*. If *JJ* worked as planned, we would be able to investigate many places on the wreck that *Alvin* couldn't safely reach.

(Top) With the final checks complete, divers detach the safety line readying Alvin *to take the plunge.*

(Above) With JJ *snugly in his garage,* Alvin *gets ready to descend.*

Today, we would find out if 12,500 feet of freezing salt water gave *JJ* cold feet. But the main purpose of this first dive was to see how dangerous the *Titanic* would be for *Alvin*'s cadre of seasoned pilots – and to get a good first look at the ship up close.

During our time on the bottom, I hoped to survey the bow section from high above the wreckage. We would do this using one of *Argo*'s highly sensitive black-and-white SIT cameras which we had mounted on *Alvin*'s undercarriage for this mission. On subsequent dives, we would be able to hover safely out of danger and pick out places to work before risking the sub up close. The fear of entanglement was ever present in our minds. We all knew that if anything terrible was going to happen, it would be because *Alvin* got trapped in wreckage and was unable to free itself.

Because we were diving without a back-up, I'd had to convince the Navy that we had worked out adequate safety precautions. First, I would only land on pre-surveyed sites, pumping ballast to become heavy and then deploying *JJ* from his garage in front of *Alvin*. Second, *JJ* would take all the really dangerous risks. In the event *JJ* became inextricably entangled, a cable cutter mounted on the garage could quickly cut his tether so that we could move away unharmed.

Alvin also had a last-ditch escape measure in an emergency, recommended only if all other measures failed. This meant jettisoning the entire after two-thirds of the sub and letting the pressure sphere rocket to the surface. We might get home, but most of *Alvin* would be lost. And since this escape plan had never been put into effect, we could only guess what would happen to the passengers on their rapid rise to the surface. The sphere might tumble uncontrollably, treating human beings and instruments like the contents of a washing machine. The sphere would certainly make it to the surface, but would we survive the trip?

JJ is controled by a console (left) held by an operator inside *Alvin*. Buttons in the handgrip (A) activate the robot's vertical thrusters and control the tether to *Alvin*. photo trigger (B) activates the still camera; a companion button (C) adjusts the video camera tilt. The video monit (D) displays *JJ*'s field of vision. Switches (E) work moto and lights. Other switches (F) operate the videotape. Joystick (G) controls horizontal maneuvers.

Light

Reflective Disks

Tether to *Alvin*

Foam Flotation Housing

Docking Rail

Video Camera

Thruster

35-mm Still Camera

Inboard Electronics

Depth Sensor

Compass

Strobe Light

Jason Jr. secured in garage by air bag

Alvin and *Jason Junior*

A diagram showing Jason Jr. *and* Alvin *as they were set up for our 1986 expedition.*

On a few occasions, *Alvin* had come close to this emergency bail-out point. The most serious of these was in 1974 during the exploration of the Mid-Atlantic Ridge. For over four hours, it was wedged inside a rocky crevice in 9,000 feet of water where overhanging lava outcrops would have prevented the released pressure sphere from rising straight up – which meant almost certain death. Fortunately, the crevice was in relatively fresh "glassy" lava flows that could be chipped and broken. Finally, the pilot was able to bang the sub back and forth until eventually the rock shattered and *Alvin* broke free.

None of us had been on that particular dive and I pushed such thoughts from my mind as we accelerated downward. Within a minute of leaving the surface, the pitching and rolling of the sub had stopped. We had sunk 100 feet and daylight rapidly faded into deeper and deeper blues as the sub reached its maximum descent speed of 100 feet per minute. At this rate it would take two-and-a-half hours to reach the bottom – a peaceful free-fall in utter darkness.

Inside our inner space capsule, it was still quite warm and stuffy, but the surrounding ice-cold water would soon cool the titanium-alloy hull and leaning against it would become quite unpleasant. Suddenly, a white-tipped shark materialized outside my window, silently scouting *Alvin* for a moment before swimming away. Attracted by the unusual noise and behavior of deep submersibles, sharks often appear soon after *Alvin* enters the water. It was comforting to know that several inches of metal protected us.

(1) Still camera with strobe. (2) Manipulator arm with lights and still and video cameras. (3) Cable winch and reel. (4) Scanning sonar. (5) Hatch. (6) Titanium sphere. (7) Three viewing ports. (8) Jettisonable iron ballast. (9) Acoustic telephone. (10) Hoisting bitt. (11) Tanks for air and variable seawater ballast. (12) Batteries. (13) Pressure housing for electric controls. (14) Thrusters. (15) Emergency tether cutter. (16) Down-looking low-light-level black-and-white TV camera, or SIT camera. (17) Forward-looking SIT camera.

I wondered what Ralph was thinking. He seldom let anyone know; his grizzled appearance and gruff demeanor kept most people at a distance. We'd been friends – in the way that people who work together are often friends – but that was before I'd left the Alvin Group and had started up the competition. He was the one who'd given *JJ* the derogatory nickname, "dope on a rope," originally applied to ANGUS.

While Dudley ran a few tests on *Jason Jr.*, I loaded our video recorders with fresh cassettes as Vivaldi's "Four Seasons" played softly in the background. (The music would be switched off once we reached the bottom and went to work.) Normally, *Alvin* had only one video camera, a low-light-level camera mounted on the forward bow that helped the pilot see where he was going. Its recorder, mounted in the science rack behind us, also recorded the conversations going on inside the sphere.

For this mission we had three additional video tape decks inside the already cramped space – and all of them would require constant reloading. One was connected to the color camera mounted on *Alvin*'s arm, which would capture our best video images. Since the arm could move within a range of several degrees, it would provide close-up images as *Alvin* crossed the *Titanic*'s deck and would also give us a tracking shot of *JJ* when he was prowling outside his garage. The arm was also loaded with a still camera, strobe lights, and television lights, giving the entire rig the appearance of *Sesame Street*'s most famous puppet character, Big Bird, which became the camera system's nickname.

A second tape deck was hooked up to the color video camera in *JJ* and the third was connected to the down-looking black-and-white SIT camera that we would use for our high-altitude surveys of the wreck and to spot suitable landing sites.

Ralph, as pilot, sat on a small stool in the center of the sphere looking out the forward viewport. Dudley and I half sat, half lay on *Alvin*'s small deck staring out through the port and starboard viewports respectively. In the first few minutes of the descent, we had all been making our nests in the sphere, arranging blankets and clothes as comfortably as possible. Given the close quarters, Ralph would often crunch my ankle with his foot as he concentrated on driving the sub. At other times, the overhead panel would snag my hair and, if I shifted to try and get more comfortable, the cassette machines would poke me in the back. Then, if inadvertently I let my socked foot hit the hull, it would come away cold and wet. During the long hours in these uncomfortable conditions, my legs frequently fell asleep and occasionally I'd get a bad cramp in my hip. At times like that the pressure sphere took on more the character of a torture chamber than a space capsule.

But the long fall to the bottom is usually a kind of lulling experience. The interior gets darker and darker and begins to cool until, after less than 15 minutes, we have reached a depth of 1,200 feet and total darkness. To conserve power, the outside lights are left off and the only illumination comes from three small red-and-white lights inside the sphere. After being attacked once by a swordfish – which actually got its sword stuck in *Alvin*'s hull near a glowing window – I'd learned even these interior lights should be turned off at times.

However, there wasn't time for quiet contemplation today. Almost immediately, we had technical problems to worry about. July 13 was proving unlucky. First, we discovered that *Alvin*'s sector-scanning sonar (originally developed for hunting mines) had stopped working. Either

Checking out the hand-held video camera used to take footage inside the sub.

the cold seawater or the rapidly increasing water pressure had somehow gotten to it. Without this sonar, we were blind beyond the few yards we could see and now would have to rely on our surface navigator to guide us to the *Titanic*'s side.

A few minutes later, at about 2,000 feet, we passed through what is known as a deep scattering layer, so named because it shows up as a cloud-like blur on a sonar. In fact, it is composed of thousands and thousands of small creatures that live in this depth range during the day and migrate to feed near the surface at night. Many of them are bioluminescent, their small bodies exploding like fireworks as our pressure wake warns them of an intrusive presence. Chains of individual animals commonly form strings of lights about six to eight inches long. Apparently when they are frightened, each bead suddenly brightens; the flashes begin at one end and travel down the string in a fraction of a second. When I first saw this, I thought it looked like a tiny passenger train passing by at night with only the lighted windows visible.

By the time we passed 5,000 feet, almost one hour into our descent, the sub was cold and we were putting on our first layers of extra clothing. The moisture in the air from our breathing had begun to condense on the now-freezing hull, forming drops of water that dripped from the hatch and ran down the inside wall to collect in the bilge. Seventeen years before, on my first dive in *Alvin*, I'd seen these droplets and become convinced the sub was leaking. The pilot had only smiled and explained to the nervous neophyte what was happening. All I had to do was put a drop on my tongue to discover the water was sweet not salty.

Over the years, I'd learned how to stay healthy while spending so much time underwater. Today, I was wearing a toque from my sons' hockey team to keep my head warm and I had extra clothes if I needed them. I'd also become adept at staying away from the cold hull. Head and lung ailments are common among those who dive frequently in deep submersibles. I always take an antihistamine before a dive to keep my lungs and sinuses clear.

Chief Alvin *pilot Ralph Hollis talking to the* Atlantis II *on the underwater telephone.*

Ten minutes later, as we hit 6,000 feet, Ralph noticed a salt-water leak into the battery pack that powers the sub and its array of instruments. At first, it showed up on our instrument panel as a small leak, but as the level of seawater in the battery tub rose, the leak turned into a hard electrical ground: this meant the protective oil in which the batteries were bathed was being replaced by short-circuiting seawater. Thankfully, we have a back-up battery inside the sphere for emergency use, so this situation only threatened our mission, not our lives. But if we let the batteries deteriorate beyond a certain point, they would consume themselves and our 1986 *Titanic* expedition would be over. Our bottom time would be awfully short today.

The next hour and a half passed uneventfully. Vivaldi gave way to Beethoven on the sub's stereo and there was little talking as we fell silently, swiftly downward. The interior was getting very cold – in the low 50s – and I'd now put on a sweatshirt over my turtleneck sweater.

As we neared the bottom, the *Alvin* navigator aboard *Atlantis* II began driving us in squares. Apparently his transponders were sending him confusing data – maybe one of them was malfunctioning. Ordinarily, he should have been able to steer us straight to the wreck. But his directions, echoed down to us on the underwater acoustic telephone, indicated that he too was lost. He was sending us first in one direction, then another.

Our down-looking echo sounder, which was still functioning, indicated the bottom was 600 feet below and we were closing fast. We could have dropped weights then, attained neutral buoyancy, and powered ourselves the remaining distance to the bottom. But Ralph, being a pro, waited until the last minute, conserving power, and only dropped our descent weights 60 to 100 feet above the bottom.

We'd arrived. The only trouble was we had no idea where we were.

As we gently descended the remaining distance with our outside lights now piercing the blackness, the featureless bottom slowly emerged from the dark green gloom. The first thing that indicated its presence was our own shadow, cast by *Alvin*'s light and growing sharper as we dropped lower. We stared out of our viewports, straining to see some sign of the wreck. No *Titanic*, no debris, just a gently rolling countryside of mud, much like an alpine meadow after a blanket of snow has all but erased its features: a bump here, what appeared to be a covered valley over there. Outside the windows, a gentle "snow" was falling, underwater particles blown by the current. If the sonar had been working, the *Titanic* would show up as a giant blip on the screen and finding her would be a simple matter.

So close and yet so far away. The ship lay somewhere near us, probably no more than 400 feet, the distance from home plate to the center field wall in Fenway Park. At the surface, such a distance would mean nothing, but here, more than two miles down below in this Stygian murk, a few hundred feet might as well be a thousand miles.

Then the damn alarm buzzer started, indicating that the short in our batteries had reached a critical point. Ralph was already thinking about returning to the surface. Here I was trapped inside a metal sphere, down on my hands and knees on *Alvin*'s tiny deck, peering at nothing but mud out the side viewport as we hovered three feet off the bottom. It had taken 13 long years to get to this point. Now *Alvin*, the most reliable of my tools, was having a bad day.

None of us wanted to give up and go home empty-handed – least of all Ralph, whose pride in *Alvin* was on the line. There was nothing left

(Right) Bundled up in the darkened sub, I hold up the Explorers' Club flag for the camera.

(Opposite, top) This photograph of the Olympic *in graving dock in Belfast, resembles the towering wall of steel that confronted us on the ocean floor.*

(Opposite, bottom) We shine a light on the Titanic's *hull plates.*

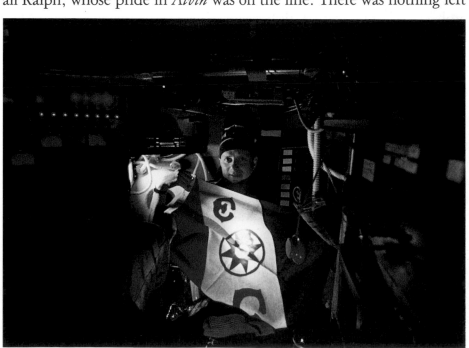

to do but guess where the *Titanic* was and blindly go there. The snow-storm of particles was blowing from the south-southeast at between a half and three-quarters of a knot; I figured this must have pushed us to the north of our desired location. After a brief discussion, we began driving south. *Alvin*, now gently touching the bottom with its single runner, was like a one-legged skier gliding over virgin snow, leaving a lonely track behind us. This ski keeps the bottom of the sub from plowing into the muck and kicking up a big cloud of sediment.

Now the alarm grew louder and more shrill as the tension in the sub mounted. Ralph was about to pull the plug, when finally our navigator chimed in from the surface: "*Alvin*, this is *A-II*. Tracking is now working. *Titanic* should bear 50 yards to the west of your present location." We had guessed right and had only just missed the ship. We were running parallel along its side.

Ralph turned *Alvin* to the west as we strained our eyes to see. Suddenly, the bottom began to look strange: though devoid of debris, it began to slope sharply upward – too steeply to be a natural underwater feature. It was as though this mound of mud and small boulders had been bulldozed into place. My heartbeat quickened.

"Ralph," I said, "come right. I think I see a wall of black just on the other side of that mud mound." Ralph did as I asked and inched *Alvin* forward until he was stopped by a sight unlike any he'd encountered in hundreds of deep-ocean dives: directly in front of us was an apparently endless slab of black steel rising out of the bottom – the massive hull of the *Titanic*. I thought of Edmund Hillary standing at the summit of Mount Everest, of some future space traveler peering over the edge of the known universe. Slowly, I let out my breath; I didn't realize I'd been holding it.

But no sooner had I persuaded Ralph to let me have a look through his forward viewport, than he dropped *Alvin*'s weights and we began hurtling toward the surface – soon reaching our maximum ascent rate of 100 feet a minute. I had seen the *Titanic*, but not even long enough to know exactly where on the bow we had come in. If we wanted to dive tomorrow, we had to get back on board and fix our growing list of problems. Thank God Ralph had turned that head-splitting alarm buzzer off.

As we rose swiftly back toward warmth and daylight, I reflected among other things on the past 13 years during which I had spent an average of four months out of every twelve at sea. I had passed countless hours on my hands and knees, working in the dark of the deep ocean. I'd participated in exciting discoveries thanks to the work of *Alvin* and the world's other champion manned deep diver, the French *Cyana*. But diving was often so frustrating and so fleeting. For less than two minutes, we had glimpsed the *Titanic*'s towering hull. That was all we had to show for six hour's work. I couldn't help wondering how long the repairs would take – or whether they could be made at all. And what if the weather deteriorated? Would this be my one and only glimpse of the *Titanic*? Had I come all this way for nothing? I fought back my black mood, but such depressing thoughts continued to mount.

The ascent is usually a time when rock music is playing on the stereo and the people in the sub joke and unwind after a job well done. Not today. For the next two hours we sat in virtual silence, meditating on our failure.

I was still in a grim mood when I emerged from the sub into the waiting crowd on the fantail of *Atlantis II*. My only comment when asked about the situation was, ''I saw the ship for about ten seconds. They're going to be up all night. They've got a sick puppy and they've got to fix it.'' It was at times like this that I wished Jean-Louis were with me – we had shared disappointment as well as triumph and could commiserate quietly together.

This year, I was in command of a ship and crew of 50 men and women ideally suited to the very specific task at hand. The *Atlantis II* is a slightly smaller ship than *Knorr* and lacks *Knorr*'s sophisticated cycloidal propulsion system. She's a work horse, not a fancy Kentucky trotter, and in 1986 that's exactly what I needed.

The team on board, which included a few familiar faces from our 1985 expedition, was drawn primarily from the Deep Submergence Laboratory. Added to these members of my immediate ''family'' were a few experts from private industry who were working with us in the development of the *Argo/Jason* system.

The core of the 1986 team was Chris von Alt, the Deep Submergence Laboratory's latest whiz kid, and the mastermind behind *Jason Jr.* Chris was equally at home at sea or in the lab, a no-nonsense, can-do type of engineer who wouldn't run from a high-pressure challenge. The precise person for the job.

Chris worked with a small team drawn primarily from the *Argo* group, including Martin Bowen, our resident expert on flying remotely operated vehicles, and Emile Bergeron, techie par excellence. When we arrived on site, we had never tested our new robot at ocean depths and we didn't know whether it would stand up to the pressure, exceeding 6,000 pounds per square inch, found there. But in principle we were sure *JJ* could do the job.

The ANGUS team was also on board, though somewhat out of the limelight. Each night, while most of the crew was asleep, Earl Young, Tom Crook, and Tom Dettweiler would methodically tow ANGUS back and forth across the *Titanic*'s debris field and stern section, which had all but eluded us last year. While *Alvin* dove on the wreck's bow, ANGUS paved the way for our final dives to the stern.

Honorary members of the ANGUS team in 1986 were Bill Lange and Dr. Elazar ''Al'' Uchupi. Lange, of course, had been in the control van for the 1985 discovery – one of the first people to see the *Titanic*'s boiler. In preparation for this year's cruise, he had worked with Al reviewing every image taken by ANGUS and *Argo* in 1985. By the time summer rolled around, Al and Bill had become *Titanic* experts and I wanted them both on the 1986 cruise to analyze the pictures we brought up from the bottom.

Al Uchupi's 20 years of field work made him, in my estimation, the most accomplished marine geomorphologist in the world – intimately acquainted with every variant of underwater landscape from ripple marks to landslides. On top of that, he has a photographic memory – which came in handy when poring over literally tens of thousands of still pictures and thousands of feet of video. With Jean-Louis absent, Al was my alter ego, the one man I felt I could completely rely on to be in charge. While I slept, I knew that he would be getting the job done.

The *Alvin* crew worked all through the night to cure their sick submarine, an operation rarely attempted at sea. Replacing one of *Alvin*'s

(Top) Emerging from the cold sub after the foreshortened first dive.

(Above) JJ's team at work. Left to right: *Emile Bergeron, Chris von Alt, Martin Bowen, and Brent Miller.*

heavy battery banks was dangerous and difficult in the best of conditions. Fortunately the weather remained clear, the seas flat calm, and I was confident I wouldn't return home empty-handed. Besides, Ralph didn't want egg on his face in the contest with *Argo/Jason*.

Overnight, *Jason Jr.*'s crew also made sure their boy had survived his first deep dive in good shape. They made a number of last-minute checks before giving the thumbs up. This morning, it appeared that all systems were go.

It was still relatively calm in the North Atlantic, but the sky was overcast and gray.

Ralph Hollis was again our pilot on today's dive, but this time Martin Bowen was along to maneuver *JJ*'s first deep-sea deployment. Martin hadn't forgotten his role in the near-loss of *Argo* the previous year. I knew he was determined to turn *JJ* into the star of our 1986 expedition.

Our dive plan was essentially the same as yesterday's: acquire the *Titanic* on sonar upon reaching the bottom, close to visual range, rise up the hull making sure we avoided any overhanging wreckage, and conduct a detailed survey of the ship using our down-looking *Argo* camera. Then, if all went well, we'd pick a site, land, and then try to launch *JJ*.

As part of my preparation for the 1986 expedition, I had carefully reviewed the 1985 ANGUS photographs, constructing a number of mosaics of possible landing sites on the wreck. Of these, the one I was most interested in was a site near the entrance to the forward Grand Staircase. (A similar glass-domed staircase, though slightly less grand, had existed between the third and fourth funnels. But as far as we knew at this point, that part of the ship was now a hopeless wreck.) I had long been attracted to the forward staircase – not only because it seemed to symbolize the ship's luxury, but because it promised to take me deep inside the first-class compartments of the ship. Luckily, it appeared to be the safest of all potential landing locations, a large flat deck surface stretching between the number 1 funnel opening and the staircase opening. The roof was still intact over the aft part of the officers' quarters and it was one of the highest decks on the ship. The smokestack was gone and with it the guy wires that might have fouled our craft, as well as a ventilation duct that had once run across the deck. The elegant glass dome that had once covered the staircase had not survived the descent to the bottom, leaving an easy entrance for *JJ*. There were sections of railings left at the port and starboard edges of this deck, but these would be easy to avoid. Overall, it was as if someone had gone down there with a bulldozer and cleared a landing pad for our submersible helicopter.

There was another potential landing point on the Boat Deck forward and to the side of the bridge, next to where the wheelhouse once stood. But here, the ANGUS pictures were confusing and didn't appear to agree with our historical drawings and photos. Both port and starboard bulkheads just aft of the bridge, including those in the area of the captain's cabin, had collapsed outward and the roof was caved in as if a giant had brought his fist down on it. True, the forward mast with the crow's nest – its base crimped but still fitted to the Forecastle Deck – had fallen aft and landed on the port wing of the bridge, but that surely had not been a blow sufficient to account for the devastation. Curiously, a strange, anomalous object on top of what seemed to be the wheelhouse resembled a modern radio direction-finder – but that sort of antenna didn't exist in 1912.

(Top) Al Uchupi and Dudley Foster chat in the top lab from where Alvin'*s surface controller directs the sub to its target – we hope.*

(Above) The Alvin *crew works on the sub's faulty battery tubs to get them ready for the next day's dive.*

113

Another likely landing for us was the *Titanic*'s expansive Forecastle Deck near the opening to hatch number 1. According to our 1985 pictures, all three hatches forward of the bridge were open and in theory suitable for *JJ* penetration – if we could land our sub close enough to them. But two of these were down on the Well Deck – the deck that dips down between the forecastle and the bridge – and it looked scary. Not only did the forward mast traverse it, but a formidable array of nasty-looking cables still connected the fallen mast to the ship. Last year, in our hair-raising attempt to get close enough for clear pictures, we had almost flown ANGUS underneath the mast by accident and had actually grazed the crow's nest. If *Alvin* got caught in those cables it could well be "game over."

Although the surface weather was now beginning to worsen with a storm front approaching and the seas building, the launch went without a hitch. But again problems arose shortly after we left the surface. This time it was *JJ*'s turn: his motors had somehow become flooded, rendering them useless. I could see that Martin, geared up for his first dive, shared my frustration. I could abort the trip now, return to the ship, get the motors fixed, and jump back into the water. But that would reduce valuable time at the wreck. Ralph was adamant that we stick strictly to *Alvin* regulations and leave the bottom no later than 3 p.m. each day, no matter what, so the crew could be back on board in time for dinner. I understood the logic behind the rules – the importance of maintaining a regular work routine (*Alvin* makes an average of 150 to 160 dives a year) – but I would have appreciated some flexibility given the historic nature of our mission. The situation infuriated me, but I kept quiet. More than once, I would privately curse the inflexiblity that prevented us from lingering longer when we were in the middle of something interesting.

I decided to continue the dive and hope that no other problems got in our way; even without *JJ* a lot could be done. Poor Martin would just have to sit it out. Soon we were falling through pitch darkness toward the seabed far below. By the time we reached the bottom, it was beginning to seem like our first dive all over again. *Alvin*'s mine-hunting sonar was again on the blink and we had another ground on the electrical system. This time, however, there were two big differences: despite the ground, we had no leak indications; and the tracking from *Atlantis II* seemed to be working fine. A message came from the surface: "Target bears 180°."

Our second view of the *Titanic* was breathtaking. As we glided soundlessly across the bottom on our single ski, out of the darkness loomed the razor's edge of the bow – the great ship towered above us and suddenly it seemed to be coming right at us, about to run *Alvin* over. My first impulse was that we had to get out of the way – but the *Titanic* wasn't going anywhere. Gently, Ralph brought the sub closer until we could see the bow more clearly. It was buried more than 60 feet in bottom mud. Both anchors still hung in place, the port one about six feet above the bottom, the starboard one resting just at mud level. I felt myself smiling. The would-be salvagers were out of luck; the *Titanic* was far too deeply buried for anyone to pull her out of the ooze.

As we moved closer, it seemed as though the metal hull was slowly melting away. Rivers of rust covered the side of the ship, some of it running the full length of the exposed vertical hull plating and pouring

The port anchor.

JJ's headlights look back at us as Alvin *illuminates the knife edge of the bow that plowed into the mud.*

out over the bottom sediment where it formed great ponds as much as 30 to 40 feet across covered by a reddish-yellow crust. The blood of the great ship lay in pools on the ocean floor.

Then, as we rose in slow motion up the ghostly wall of the port bow, our running lights reflected off the still-unbroken glass of portholes in a way that made me think of cats' eyes gleaming in the dark. In places, the rust about them formed eyelashes; sometimes tears: as though the *Titanic* were weeping over her fate. Near the upper railing – still largely intact – reddish-brown stalactites of rust hung down as much as several feet, looking like long needle-like icicles. This phenomenon, the result of iron-eating bacteria, was well known, but never had they been seen on such a massive scale. I subsequently dubbed them ''rusticles,'' a name which seems to have stuck.

These rust features turned out to be very fragile. If touched by *Alvin* or dislodged by the thrust from one of our propellers, they disappeared in a cloud of smoke. Once the foamy crust had been knocked away, the steel beneath appeared almost perfectly preserved, only slightly pitted. I mused for a moment on what it would be like taking a steel brush to the hull and cleaning the ship to its former smoothness. But I had made a promise to myself to leave the ship undisturbed.

Carefully, I counted the portholes aft from the anchor to locate the position where the ship's name should be, but I could see nothing. If I'd been able to remove the rust, the letters ought to have been visible since they were cut slightly into the hull as well as painted. In fact, looking later at some of our videotape, we could just barely make out what looks like the faint outline of a ''C'' on the port bow. But this image did not show up in our still pictures.

Alvin rose further, cleared the railing forward of the number 1 hatch, and Ralph maneuvered out over the *Titanic*'s mighty forward deck. All at once, I was forcibly struck by the sheer size of everything: giant bitts (usually called bollards in 1912), the huge links of the anchor chains, and even bigger shiny bronze-topped capstans. When you were there, on the spot, it really was titanic. Until now, the ship for me had been somehow ghostly, distant, and incorporeal. Now it was very close, very material, very real.

As always when we were working, the three people in the sub exchanged few words that didn't have to do with the job at hand. Martin, stymied by *JJ*'s fickleness, looked through the port window quietly and in awe. There was nothing for him to do except gape and think about tomorrow. I was busy snapping pictures through the starboard viewport and instructing Ralph on where to go.

I strained to get a look at the deck's wood planking just four feet below us. Then my heart dropped to my stomach and I muttered, ''It's gone!'' Except for a few tidbits here and there, the wood had been replaced by thousands upon thousands of small, white hollow calcareous tubes one to two inches in length – the protective homes of now-dead wood-boring molluscs. Gone was our hope of finding much *Titanic* woodwork intact, her beauty unblemished by the years. Myriads of little worms had done more damage than the iceberg, wreaked more havoc than the corroding seawater.

Now I could see beyond the illusion of last year's footage. The appearance of decking in our ANGUS photos had been created by the thin lines of resin and caulking that had originally been between the

(Top) The rusticle on the porthole for first-class stateroom C-46 gives the impression of a weeping eye.

(Above) JJ explores the starboard Forecastle Deck, his lights illuminating a bollard, also known as a bitt.

(Opposite) One of the Titanic*'s huge bronze-topped capstans.*

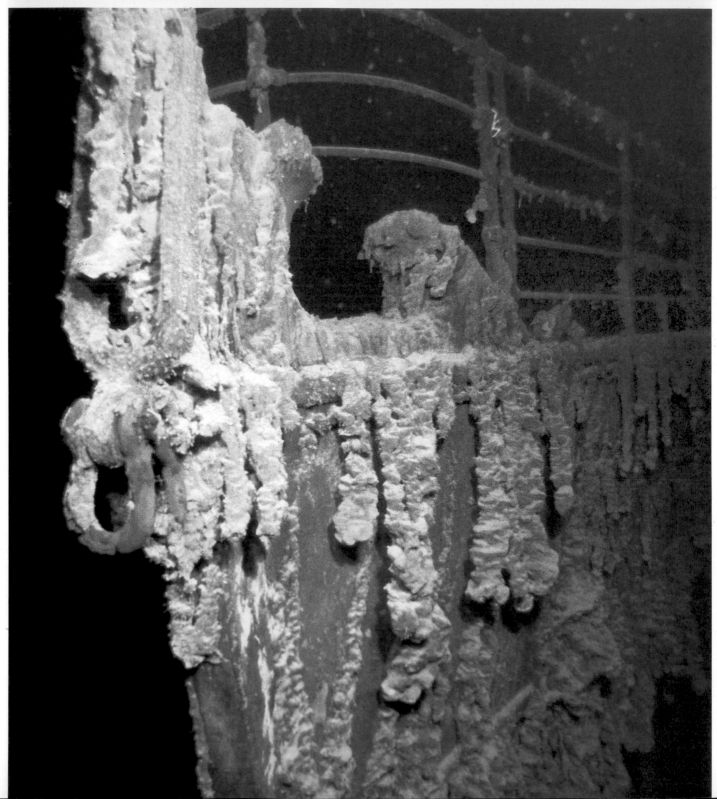

planks. That had remained, producing a laminated pattern, but the wood was virtually all gone. Immediately, I began to wonder whether the metal sub-deck would support us when *Alvin* made its first landing.

Alvin crossed just above one of the great bronze-topped capstans, and landed on the deck just forward and to the starboard of the *Titanic*'s mast. We were on tenterhooks, afraid the deck might not support *Alvin*'s weight once we'd pumped enough ballast to rest comfortably. As the sub settled, it made a kind of muffled crunching noise. If the steel plating gave way, we could crash downward belowdecks before Ralph had time to drop our weights. At best, the day's dive would be over; at worst, we'd be trapped in collapsing wreckage. But we settled firmly. That meant there was a good chance the *Titanic* would be able to support our weight at future landing sites.

The deck strength tested, we carefully lifted off and headed aft into the "wind," heading along the starboard side between the center line and the railing. The starboard forecastle railing was remarkably intact, almost unmarred by rusticles. The bottom current blowing across the deck was as strong as the day before – between a half and three-quarters of a knot. Particles suspended in the water blew in our faces so I switched to our down-looking *Argo* camera in time to catch a panorama of the Well Deck as it passed several yards below us. I could see a clutter of cables and the forward cargo cranes, their booms knocked aft off their supports. This was not the place to risk landing *Alvin*.

Ralph was worried: "This current is strong and I can't see in the haze."

"We're fine," I reassured him, my eyes still on the video monitor. "The bridge should be dead ahead. Come right."

As we passed over the big cranes in the after portion of the Well Deck, I could see that they were surprisingly intact, unlike those in the ANGUS pictures of the debris field. Then the dim outline of the superstructure of the ship came into view, rising in three grand steps to the bridge: first B Deck, then A, and then the forward Boat Deck, location of the bridge, and the officers' quarters. As the vague outline of the bridge area appeared, I realized why last year's ANGUS footage of this portion of the ship was so confusing. The wooden wheelhouse was completely gone, probably knocked away in the sinking. Apart from strips of teak wood fitted to the Boat Deck outlining where the wheelhouse had stood, there was no trace of the structure. The object I had thought was a strange-looking radio antenna was in fact the ship's bronze telemotor control, where the wheel was once attached. The wooden wheel itself was gone but, remarkably, the huge bronze base was standing intact and kept polished to a shine over the years by the current. Various conduits and the rudder order indicator arrow were still there.

We landed briefly to test the solidity of this second site. Then Ralph reported to the surface that there was a new leak indication in one of our battery tanks. He'd noted the first one moments before. Talking on the acoustic telephone is rather like having a conversation in a well. There's an echoey quality to the sound and the end of your last message to the surface bounces back to you about the same time as the response. As I listened to his conversation with someone two and a half miles up, I wondered how much time we had left today. There was so much more I wanted to see. Surface control gave us clearance to continue for another 15 or 20 minutes. *(Continued on page 128)*

*(Opposite, top, left) The point of the bow from the port side. **(Opposite, top, right)** JJ illuminates a windlass on the starboard bow. **(Opposite, bottom)** The prow adorned with rusticles.*

*(Top) This 1985 ANGUS picture shows why we believed the deck planking to be intact. **(Above)** A 1986 deck shot shows that the caulking is nearly all that remains.*

119

The diagram (below) shows the forward section of the ship from the bow to the break, and is keyed to the mosaic (above).

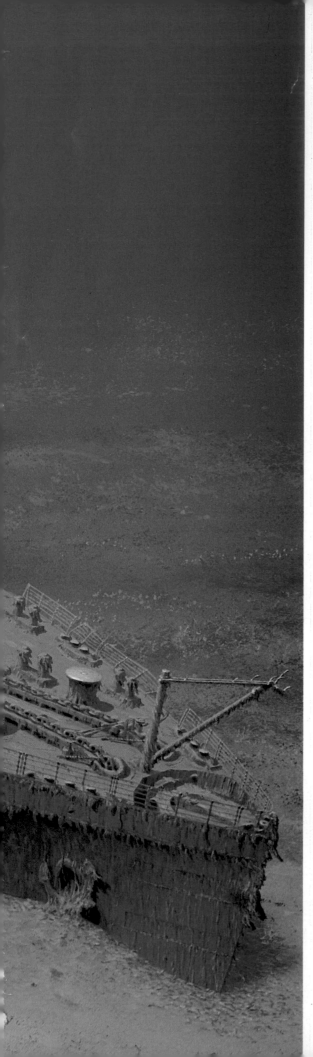

The Bow Section

A front view seen from the starboard side

This painting shows how the *Titanic*'s bow plowed into the bottom upon impact, burying itself up to the base of the starboard anchor. On the forecastle, the anchor chains remain in place between gleaming capstans, and the fallen foremast still supports the crow's nest from which a lookout gave the fatal message, "Iceberg, right ahead!"

(1) *Main first-class gangway doors, D Deck.*

(2) *After davit for lifeboat No. 7, its arm broken off.*

(3) *First-class dining saloon.*

(4) *Arched gymnasium windows.*

(5) *First-class entrance to Grand Staircase and gymnasium.*

(6) *Gaping expansion joint.*

(7) *Stokehold (boiler room) vents.*

(8) *Fallen starboard bridge cab.*

(9) *Bulwark rail of bridge wing, fallen forward.*

(10) *Bronze telemotor control.*

(11) *Forward port davit for lifeboat No. 2 which launched collapsible D, the last boat to leave the ship.*

(12) *Forward B-Deck first-class staterooms.*

(13) *Still-closed gate between Well Deck (third class) and B Deck (first class).*

(14) *Possible ice damage: creased plates with horizontally opened seams.*

(15) *Cargo crane.*

(16) *Bitts (bollards).*

(17) *Steam winch.*

(18) *Number 1 hatch.*

(19) *Windlasses.*

(20) *Center anchor stowed in its well.*

(21) *Anchor crane.*

A *Titanic* Bow Section Mosaic

Our deep-towed sled ANGUS made dozens of passes over the *Titanic* wreck and the debris field, taking more than 53,000 photographs from a height of approximately 25 feet. After the expedition, we began the painstaking task of trying to create a photographic "mosaic" of the approximately 470 feet of the *Titanic*'s intact forward section. Woods Hole technician John Porteous spent months assembling a jigsaw puzzle of adjoining images – an extremely complex task given the range of distances, camera angles and lighting conditions. The more than 100 images selected were then adjusted and re-assembled in collaboration with the *National Geographic* Society to create the mosaic shown above.

1. Anchor crane.
2. Anchor chains.
3. Bitts (bollards).
4. Windlasses.
5. Capstan
6. Number 1 hatch.
7. Breakwater.
8. Crew galley skylight.
9. Base of foremast fallen on steam winches.
10. Number 2 hatch.
11. Crow's nest.
12. Number 3 hatch.
13. Well-Deck cranes.
14. Top of remaining foremast on bridge.
15. Steering telemotor where wheelhouse was.

16. Forward davit for lifeboat No. 1.
17. Forward davit for lifeboat No. 2.
18. Peeled-out wall of officers' quarters.
19. Stokehold vents (4).
20. Number 1 funnel opening.
21. Officers' bathroom skylight.
22. Forward expansion joint.
23. Marconi office skylight.
24. First-class forward staircase.
25. Collapsed roof of gymnasium.
26. Number 2 funnel opening.
27. Accommodation vent fan and motor housing (see page 163).
28. Raised roof over reading and writing room.
29. Area where decks slant downward.
30. Compass platform amidships (missing).

The Bridge

The telemotor that held the ship's wheel stands alone on the devastated bridge.

(Below) The bronze steering telemotor from the wheel-house. (Right) How it looked with the wheel in place.

(Below) The only picture that exists of Captain Smith standing on the Titanic's bridge. Through the window, one of the bridge telegraphs can be seen.

(Above) A painting of the bridge area showing Alvin illuminating the telemotor while JJ takes a closer look at the crow's nest.

(Left) The base of the wheelhouse is all that remains of the structure.

(Right) The Titanic's bridge with the shadow of the foremast visible. (Far right) The base of the foremast rests on the steam winches seen in the lower right of the bridge photograph.

"Ralph, I want you to lift up from this site and head directly to the Grand Staircase opening."

I directed him up and aft. A blast from *Alvin*'s prop kicked up the sediment on the wheelhouse floor, temporarily engulfing us in a cloud of dust. Soon we entered clearer water as the current blew the cloud downwind toward the bow. Again I switched to the down-looking video camera, which gave me a good black-and-white picture of the ship beneath us as *Alvin* cleared the gaping hole where the number 1 smokestack once stood. All that remained of the massive funnel were a few jagged sections of metal rising eight feet or so above the deck. In one way I wished the stacks were still there; they would have made the hull look so much more dignified. But their absence, along with their numerous stabilizing guy lines, made working above the ship much safer. Martin and I could barely control our excitement as the ship unfolded beneath us.

We quickly crossed the deck aft of the smokestack hole and arrived over the Grand Staircase opening.

"It's gigantic," commented Ralph. "We don't need *JJ*. I can take *Alvin* down that opening."

He was half joking, half serious, but I didn't rise to the bait. "That's all right, Ralph. I think we'll stick to the original plan and land *Alvin* on the deck and let *JJ* go down that hole, not us." But that mission was for a later dive and a healthy robot. Today I wanted to continue the tour.

Heading west, *Alvin* cleared the port side of the ship and the Boat Deck fell behind us into darkness. At my request, Ralph now pivoted our sub back around, dropped down, and came in along the A-Deck windows, the enclosed first-class promenade. As we did this, the hull of the ship began to act as a "wind break," protecting us from the current. Clearly, the port side of the ship was the best place to work when the current was strong.

Huge rusticles hung from the overhang made by A Deck. These partially obscured the smaller windows looking into B-Deck staterooms just below. As I peered entranced through my viewport, I could easily imagine people walking down the promenade, looking out of the windows I was now looking into. Either the outer glass was missing or the windows had been cranked down out of sight because I could see

The port side of the A-Deck promenade.

through them to the interior windows on the inboard side of the enclosed promenade off of which *Alvin*'s headlights reflected. The effect was eerie, as if a party were going on in the first-class section of the ship and lights were shining out through the closed windows.

Here I was on the bottom of the ocean peering at recognizable, man-made artifacts designed and built for another world. I was looking through windows out of which people had once looked, decks along which they had walked, rooms where they had slept, joked, made love. It was like landing on the surface of Mars only to find the remains of an ancient civilization similar to our own – a live episode from *The Twilight Zone*.

Ralph now began to bring *Alvin* up toward the Boat Deck. Suddenly the sub shuddered, made a clanging noise, and a waterfall of rust covered our viewports.

"Ralph, we've hit something!" I exclaimed. "What is it?"

"I don't know," replied the pilot. "We should be clear of any overhang. I'm backing off."

Unseen overhangs are the nightmare of the deep-submersible pilot. Gingerly backing out from the hull, Ralph brought us slowly upward. Directly in front of our forward viewport, a big davit block slid by – only inches away. This was what we'd hit. It was attached to one of the *Titanic*'s long, curved lifeboat davits which had fallen onto the deck and hung several feet out over the side. This was the after davit for lifeboat No. 8 – a sight to chill the heart of the hardiest explorer. No. 8 was the boat Mrs. Ida Straus had refused to enter, the boat steered through much of the night by the doughty Countess of Rothes. Suddenly it seemed as if the Boat Deck was crowded with passengers echoing with the cry, "Women and children first!"

Isidor and Ida Straus.

We continued rising and headed aft once more, in search of the severed end of the bow section. Just beyond the number 2 funnel opening, the deck plunged at a precipitous angle and Ralph tried to chase it down, crossing diagonally toward the starboard side of the ship. But our sub was now being buffeted by the full force of the current and Ralph was having trouble holding *Alvin*'s head to wind. As we turned south into the current, what I saw out the starboard viewport I didn't like. The graceful lines of the ship had disappeared in a maelstrom of twisted and torn steel plating, upturned portholes, and jumbled wreckage protruding in our direction, too close for comfort, ready to poke out *Alvin*'s right eye.

"Swing back to the left! I have wreckage just out of my viewport and it's getting close. Swing left!" It was moments like these that all deep-submariners lived in fear of.

"It won't come around into the current!" Ralph returned.

"Then come up. Let's get out of here! It's too dangerous. Continue driving forward until we clear the tear. Let's go along the starboard side of the ship to the bow."

It was probably worse for Martin, stuck at the left-side viewport and unable to see the danger. He said nothing, but the tension must have been getting to him – all this time just watching and waiting.

Once again *Alvin* was acting up and Ralph informed me that I'd better start thinking about going home. We had been on the bottom less than two-and-a-half hours. Surface control informed us that the weather topside was getting worse. Every minute we now delayed would make *Alvin*'s surface recovery more dangerous. But I couldn't bear to leave the ship until the last possible minute – not now that I'd finally found her.

Ralph reluctantly agreed to make a few high altitude runs back and forth between the midships tear and the bow so I could determine other places to land tomorrow when I planned to make our first penetrations with *JJ*. Few words were spoken as we passed back and forth along the length of the lifeless hull.

Suddenly that infernal alarm went off again, indicating that the battery grounds were steadily getting worse. Surface control chimed in to inform us that the weather upstairs was deteriorating. Our time had run out. Ralph drove *Alvin* away from the wreck, dropped his weights, and we began our ascent.

I popped a cassette in the stereo – the soundtrack from *Flashdance* was my favored music for the way up – as we began to unwind. It's funny, but we always played classical music on the way down and rock on the way up. The upbeat music fits in well with the feeling of accomplishment after a good dive and spurs the joking and small talk that seem to flow at such times.

Mike Mahre works on JJ's after thrusters.

Two and a half hours later, as we approached the shallow, day-lit layers, *Alvin* began to heave as the seas at the surface made themselves felt. When we broke through the surface, the sub suddenly pitched forward throwing an array of bottles, tissue boxes, and video cassettes crashing down on my head.

Suddenly Ralph yelled, "*JJ* is out of his garage!"

We were helpless inside the wildly pitching sub as *JJ* fell downward. *Alvin*'s heaving action was causing his tether to snap like a whip, and the cable was chafing against the cable cutter and in danger of severing. If that happened, *JJ* would be lost forever, before even having one chance to perform. Ralph grabbed *Alvin*'s radio mike to contact the surface controller as divers swarmed out of their dinghy onto the sub, oblivious to the crisis.

"*A-II*, this is *Alvin*. Get the divers in the water immediately and put a safety line on *JJ*!"

But his directive was lost in the confusion. Bridge, surface control, launch coordinator, and the rubber boat carrying the support divers all had radios and everybody seemed be talking at once as preparations were made to recover the sub. Vainly I tried to signal them through the viewport. No luck. The divers were too busy getting ready to attach safety lines to the front of the sub. At last, we got in touch with the support boat and Ralph practically shouted, "Get a safety line on *JJ* now!" The divers rushed to rescue *JJ* and soon he was safely on the support boat. Since the water was too rough for the divers to manhandle *JJ* back into his garage, the only alternative was to cut his tether. With frightful ease, the cable cutter did its work, the crisis was over, and we were soon all back safely on board *Atlantis II*.

We had spent a total of two hours and fifty minutes examining the *Titanic*'s entire forward section from the bow to the forward base of where the number 3 funnel once stood, marking the aftermost part of the broken-off bow section. Soon our video studio was jammed with people eager for their first glimpse of the *Titanic* close up. We didn't disappoint them.

Meanwhile, Chris von Alt and his team had *JJ* on the table preparing for an all-night operation. Not only did they have to replace the cut tether cable, they wanted to get to the root of *JJ*'s poor performance on his debut voyage and to eliminate a "noise" we'd noted was interfering with the video signal. As well, they wanted to prevent him from again coming loose from his garage when we hit the surface.

As I collapsed in my bunk, I vowed that if *JJ* was working properly we'd go down the Grand Staircase tomorrow. Each dive could be our last and, given *Alvin*'s recurring battery problems, there wasn't time to warm up to the challenge. Tomorrow we would go for broke.

While I slept, the *Jason Jr.* team did its work. Chris even rigged up an ingenious way of keeping *JJ* in place during rough launches and recoveries: an inflated air bladder made of black rubber – similar to an inner tube – placed in the front of the garage. At the surface, it would keep our boy snugly stowed. On the bottom, the water pressure would compress the air inside the bladder, collapsing it flat and freeing *JJ* to move in and out of his garage on command.

The main storm missed us and by morning the weather had abated, but again my hopes for a perfect day quickly vanished. As we readied for launching, Chris checked out *JJ*'s system from inside the sphere only to discover that one of his four motors was jammed. It had been running fine when tested out of its housing; now it was hitting the protective shroud.

Dudley Foster at the Alvin *controls.*

Although Dudley Foster would be piloting today, his boss Ralph Hollis was quick to remind me that any delay meant time lost on the bottom – we would still have to be back on the surface in time for dinner. . . .

For the next three hours I stood around in mounting disbelief as one glitch appeared after another. Once *JJ*'s port motor was fixed, the starboard one failed to function. While Martin replaced a capacitor in *Alvin*'s arm camera, Chris changed a blown-out bulb in *JJ*'s strobe. Precious time was slipping away.

Finally, at 11:18 a.m., *Alvin* was falling toward the bottom with *JJ* nestled snugly in his garage. Martin Bowen would finally get to operate our eye-on-a-string – if it was still working when we got to the bottom.

It was nearly two o'clock when we neared the sea floor and I put my favorite arrival tape on the sub stereo – the Boston Pops playing the themes from *E.T.*, *Chariots of Fire*, and *Raiders of the Lost Ark*. This was the perfect music to psyche everyone up for the dive (we used to joke that *E.T.* was *JJ*'s song and that *Raiders of the Lost Ark* was the theme song for our expedition). With the orchestra going full blast, Dudley dropped the descent weights and leveled off just below 328 feet altitude off the *Titanic*'s port side. It was a beautiful underwater day for diving, with only a gentle current blowing. We moved quickly through a field of light debris full of white third-class china coffee cups bearing the insignia of the White Star Line. Within moments, the *Titanic*'s massive hull emerged from the darkness. We were coming in on the port side, this time near the aftermost part of the bow section.

With so little time, Dudley piloted us quickly up the ship's side and across the port Boat Deck toward the staircase opening. Barely clearing the rail on the deck above, we jumped up to the area where I wanted to make our landing.

I pointed out the big opening above the Grand Staircase.

"Got it," was Dudley's reply.

"Now, spin the sub slightly to the right and land next to that small vertical pipe." The pipe, centered amidships, had been a vent for the large elevator shaft below it and us.

I directed the pilot to move forward to the very edge of the opening and set down *Alvin*, facing aft, with *JJ*'s garage next to the elevator vent. We landed gently on the deck and Dudley turned on the ballast pumps, their squealing noise echoing through our tiny sphere. Slowly, our rocking motion disappeared. We didn't want to be too heavy, just enough to stay firmly in place.

Alvin now rested quietly on the topmost deck of the R.M.S. *Titanic* directly above the shaft where three elevators had carried first-class passengers from belowdecks should they not wish to climb the elegant Grand Staircase. We, however, would take the stairs.

Martin was extremely nervous, not so much because he felt a lack of experience but because this was the first real test for *JJ*. Almost all his attention would be focused on a video monitor inside our sub while he projected his mind away from his body and inside a single remotely controlled swimming eyeball.

The *JJ* control box sat on Martin's lap. With his right hand he operated the joystick, a lever that looked like it belonged to a Pac-Man game. When Martin pushed the lever in any of 360 directions, *JJ* would go the way he pushed. If he twisted it clockwise, *JJ* would spin clockwise on his axis, and so on. His left hand clutched a pistol-grip control. When he pushed away on the button near his thumb, *JJ* would go down; pull it toward him and *JJ* would go up. When he pulled his trigger finger once, the cable would start to unwind from its reel; pull it again and the cable started pulling *JJ* back into his garage. If he rolled a knob with his middle finger, *JJ*'s eye rolled up and down within a range of 170°. If he pushed another knob with the same finger, *JJ*'s strobe light flashed on and a color picture was taken by a still camera mounted next to *JJ*'s video eye. Martin had spent many hours practicing these maneuvers with *JJ* in a pool back at Woods Hole. Now that training would be put to the test.

Cautiously, *JJ* left his garage. Then Martin turned him around to look back at *Alvin* resting on the deck. It was the first time we'd actually seen ourselves on the video monitor, through *JJ*'s eye. There we were inside a tiny submersible surrounded by darkness and incredible pressure, our running lights looking like the eyes of a deep-sea monster.

JJ turned away and slowly floated out over the staircase. For an instant he swerved drunkenly until Martin got him under control. As I watched *JJ* on Big Bird's video screen, I thought for a second that he was going to fall over the edge. Instead, four small motors turned *JJ* into an underwater hovercraft as he inched out over the yawning blackness.

I glanced at the red safety cover protecting *JJ*'s emergency decoupling switch. We'd already had to lift that cover once and cut *JJ*'s tether. That switch might save our lives, but if we had to use it down here, it would mean *JJ* was gone for good and half a million dollars down the drain. I fervently hoped we wouldn't need it again.

Our best route down appeared to be along the near or forward wall of the staircase opening, where an elaborate ornamental clock, decorated with the figures of Honor and Glory crowning Time, had once hung. It

Martin Bowen's face displays intense concentration as he works JJ's *controls.*

(Above) *The area of the Grand Staircase and Alvin's landing site. JJ has descended against the wall on which the clock once hung and is now exploring the remains of the staircase foyer.*

(Right) *JJ managed to penetrate as fa as B Deck and shine his lights down into C Deck.*

(Far right) *Only a scar remains on the wall where this clock depicting Honor and Glory crowning Time once hung.*

had graced the landing between the Boat Deck and A Deck. This route promised the least potential for obstruction and Martin hugged it closely as he paid out more cable and *JJ* dropped down. At first, *JJ* could see nothing but the rusty orange crust of the vertical bulkhead with rivets still visible. Hardly a trace remained of all that oak woodwork and paneling. Dudley inched *Alvin* forward so that Big Bird's camera could track our little explorer as he dropped deeper and deeper. But soon *JJ* was lost from view and Martin was completely on his own. I turned now to concentrate on the images appearing on *JJ*'s video screen in the back of the sub. Dudley stared too. This was the tensest moment of our dives so far.

A room appeared off of the port side foyer on A Deck, defined by the dim shapes of pillars. Martin swung *JJ* around for a closer look and suddenly he saw something off in the distance. "Look at that," he said softly. "Look at that chandelier."

Now I could see something, too. "No it *can't* be a chandelier," I said, more to myself than to Martin. "It couldn't possibly have survived." It was difficult to believe my eyes. The ship had fallen two-and-a-half miles, impacting the bottom with the force of a train running into a mountainside, and here was an almost perfectly preserved light fixture! Soon we could see more of them in the distance. "My God, it *is* a chandelier," I crowed. Indeed, that was what it looked like.

I told Martin to try to enter the room for a closer view. This would be a true test of *JJ*'s maneuverability: how close could we get without disturbing our object of study? Our robot left the stairwell, entered the room, and headed toward the fixture, in the process brushing up against rusticles hanging from the ceiling. The rust dissolved upon impact and suddenly *JJ* was engulfed in an orange murk, visibility zero. But by pitching *JJ*'s eye up we could again see our "chandelier." Martin moved closer until he was less than a foot away. A feathery sea pen sprouted from the light fixture, turning it into a crystal crown with a feather on top. We could plainly see the delicate designs in the brasswork surrounding and above the fixture, still bright and shiny. And there was the actual socket where a bulb had been fitted!

"Take a still picture, this is fantastic," I exulted.

"Bob, we are running short of bottom time. We have to return to the surface."

Dudley's words cut through my excitement like a knife. We were deep inside the *Titanic*, down the Grand Staircase, the fulfillment of a dream, and Dudley wanted to go home for dinner! I knew Dudley was just following orders, but I wanted to shout in protest. We had been at the bottom less than one hour – lots of battery time left. I could see Martin shared my frustration as he gently maneuvered *JJ* out of the room and back up the vertical wall.

Emerging from the black hole, our proud little robot soldier, an R2D2 of the deep, shone his lights toward our sub as we watched him approach on Big Bird's video. For a moment, I felt as though we were being visited by aliens. Instead of us looking out into an uninhabited world, something was looking back at us. Then *JJ* maneuvered in front of *Alvin*, his lights sweeping across our three viewports and bathing the interior in an unearthly glow. It reminded me of the scene in *Close Encounters of the Third Kind*, when the alien spaceship hovers over a truck, shining lights into its windows. Flying saucers aside, *JJ* had just walked on the surface of the moon and returned safely.

(Top) The A-Deck foyer of the first-class
Grand Staircase. (Left) A feathery sea
pen juts from a dangling light fixture
similar to those shown at the top of the
picture above. (Above) The base of this
pillar still bears some traces of its
original oak woodwork.

135

CHAPTER 9

Last Resting Place

TWO-AND-A-HALF HOURS AFTER LIFTING OFF FROM THE GRAND STAIRCASE, three aquanauts emerged from their underwater space capsule onto the fantail of *Atlantis II*, where a crowd of colleagues had gathered. Word of our successful dive had already spread and people were eager to hear firsthand about what we had seen below. If the expedition had ended now, I'd have had few regrets. We'd proven what we came here to prove. *JJ* had strolled in the first-class compartments of the *Titanic*!

Martin and I were ebullient, still hyped up from our trip down the staircase, as we attempted to recreate for those on the surface the experience of entering the *Titanic* for the first time. At one point, Martin quipped with forgivable exaggeration, "We went dancing in the ballroom!" I echoed his words. It didn't matter that there was no ballroom on the *Titanic*, or that our "chandelier" was a fairly ordinary light fixture, only one of nearly a hundred like it on the ship; the phrase simply captured our mood. I gave Martin a bear hug as the onlookers applauded.

The crowd on deck followed us into the video studio for our première presentation of "*Jason Junior* Descends the Staircase." Martin and I watched it with them, none of us tiring of the repeated showings. There before us on the video monitors, as *JJ* wheeled around the staircase well, we could now plainly make out the shape of the balconies and various deck levels. While the light fixture we had most closely studied was on the port side, others appeared on the starboard – then more and more of them, visible back into the darkness. Like the first one we'd seen, each had dropped from its original position in the ceiling and was hanging by its electrical wire. Some were intact with the cut-glass exteriors still fitted in their holdings. Others retained only the brass mounts.

More of the oak woodwork remained than I had first thought, giving rise to speculation that woodborers might not have completely decimated the interior wood deep in the ship. Some of the support columns still retained the decorative wood sheathing at their bases, their design just discernible. And horizontal wood trim was still visible on the edge of each deck level facing the stairwell. Unfortunately, we could see no trace of those beautiful wrought-iron balustrades I had admired in the old photographs. Maybe they were lying nearby covered with fallen rusticles; more likely they had fallen down the stairwell beyond the point we had dared venture with *JJ*. Or perhaps they had simply rusted completely away.

That evening, after supper and sunset, with *Alvin* and *JJ* being prepared for the next day's dive, I sent my daily report, describing our underwater exploits, ashore via satellite phone link. Then I dealt with the media, one network and wire service after another. Like last year,

(Above) The jubilation we all felt after our trip down the Grand Staircase, shows on my face.

(Opposite) Alvin *holds a broom indicating a "clean sweep" as one of us peers through the forward viewport.*

they were clamoring for news and I was amazed yet again by the intensity of the public's continuing fascination with the ship. Question after question was thrown at me. "Have you seen any bodies?" "How big is the gash?" "How dangerous is it down there?" "What is the most exciting thing you've seen so far?" "Have you found any valuables? Did you bring anything up?"

The question about salvage was asked again and again, but prior to the cruise I had ruled out bringing back anything from the bottom. There had been long discussions with everyone from Woods Hole's director of research, Dr. Derek Spencer, to the Smithsonian Institution. Naturally, the temptation was great. Maritime collectors around the world would have paid thousands of dollars for a piece of the ship. And artifacts could be easily recovered with *Alvin*'s powerful robot arm designed to collect biological and geological samples in the deep sea. How I would have loved a bottle of *Titanic* champagne for my own wine cellar. But from all our discussions it became clear the *Titanic* has no true archeological value. Although it is tempting to make the comparison, the *Titanic* is not a pyramid of the deep. We knew exactly how the ship was built and what was on board. Recovering a chamber pot or a wine bottle or a copper cooking pan would really just be pure treasure-hunting. My major funder, the Navy, wasn't interested in using taxpayers' money for this purpose. Nor was I.

Dive number four began in fog.

There are many true unopened "pyramids" in the deep sea. For example, thousands and thousands of ships were lost in the deep basins of the Mediterranean and wait to be discovered, ships of real archeological worth. Their cargoes merit careful documentation, recovery, and preservation. The *Titanic*'s didn't.

Post-dive checks on *Jason Jr.* had given him a clean bill of health, *Alvin*'s battery troubles appeared to have been solved, and this morning's launch began to look routine. Even the weather, which had been mostly good to us so far, continued to cooperate – grudgingly. Again the sea was calm, but a dense fog had rolled in. Nonetheless, dive number four, July 16, started with a spurt and sputter. *Alvin* had hardly lifted from its deck cradle when Will Sellars, our pilot for today, noticed a problem with one of *Alvin*'s cameras and decided to land back on deck to get it fixed. Fortunately, only ten minutes later we were over the side again and free of the ship.

The fog, however, added an element of danger. *Alvin*'s turret-like fiberglass "sail" is transparent to probing radar and a ship bearing down on us in this pea soup would never see us. So, while Will swiftly completed his final surface checks, *Atlantis* II stood guard, its radar scanning for intruders. Only one large blip appeared on the screen, the Navy's rescue ship USS *Ortolan* out of Charleston, South Carolina. *Ortolan* was keeping us friendly company.

Safety checks completed, Will flooded the tanks and *Alvin* sank into safer and quieter waters. It was odd to think that it was less dangerous sinking 12,500 feet down than hanging around on the surface – but given the thick fog, it was. For Martin and me the trip to the *Titanic* was becoming old hat, but this was Will Sellar's first time. Will hadn't been around as long as Ralph Hollis or Dudley Foster, but quite long enough to become an experienced pilot. I also knew that like his colleagues he'd follow the book: he had no choice. When it was time to leave, he'd leave, whether we were in the middle of some momentous discovery or not.

When the *Titanic* once again came into view, we headed for the wheel-house area. Conning *Alvin* into position, I asked Will to land near the brass remains of the steering mechanism, which glinted in our bright lights. Since the current was stronger than yesterday, Will had to control his excitement at seeing the *Titanic* for the first time in order to make a precise landing without damaging the wheel pedestal – or our sub.

At my request, he spun the sub around to face the wheel and the port side of the ship, setting down just outside the rectangular wooden frame on the deck where the wheelhouse had been. The upper part of the *Titanic*'s foremast was just beyond our forward lights and ahead to our right; where the ship's outer bridge had once stood with its many gleaming instruments, the deck just stopped, ending in a jagged, bent-down edge. It had been wrenched away, perhaps when the forward funnel fell during the sinking.

"All right, Bob. It's all yours," said Will with an audible sigh of relief.

Actually it was all Martin's, who now coached *JJ* out of his garage and toward what was left of the ship's wheel. Then he headed to the mast. Through *JJ*'s eyes we could see a brass running light still attached to the mast, and the fine metal wires inside the intact glass lamp.

Now I directed Martin to drive *JJ* along the sloping mast toward the crow's nest, warning him to watch out for the cables. If he stayed slightly above the mast he should be okay. *JJ* promptly disappeared from our viewports as his yellow cable paid out into the darkness and I watched the video monitor spellbound as our little friend did his tight-rope walk.

Martin's skill with *JJ* was almost as fascinating as what we were seeing. He played the control console like a concert musician, his fingers moving with quick precision across its array of knobs, levers, and switches. Suddenly, the crow's nest loomed into *JJ*'s view. He was now at the very spot where Frederick Fleet and Reginald Lee had been standing when they saw the iceberg appear without warning in the *Titanic*'s path. And *Alvin* was resting at almost the exact place where Sixth Officer James Moody had received the lookout's alarm call, and had relayed it to the

Two views of the ship's bronze telemotor control – one from 1986 and one from 1912.

This well-preserved running light on the fallen foremast is approximately eight inches wide.

139

watch commander, First Officer Murdoch. I recalled the fragment of dialogue between Fleet and Moody that seemed so incredibly calm and formally detached given the situation. Fleet: "Are you there?" Moody: "Yes. What did you see?" "Iceberg right ahead," replied Fleet. "Thank you," Moody politely responded. Thirty-seven seconds later came the impact. Looking out of *Alvin*'s window, I could imagine the helmsman turning the wheel hard-a-starboard in a vain attempt to avoid the collision.

The wonderful clarity of *JJ*'s video vision now revealed that the hole in the mast just above the twisted crow's nest, which we had previously assumed was the lookout's telephone hook-up, was actually much larger than we'd thought. It was in fact the hatch through which the lookouts climbed to enter and exit the crow's nest.

Now *JJ* dropped down beneath the crow's nest into the no-man's land of the Well Deck. In front lay the two large cranes used to load luggage into holds number 2 and 3. The scene was beautiful – the lines of windows looking out onto the Well Deck, the cables draped gracefully across, the detail of the cranes themselves – but dangerous. *JJ* was hemmed in by superstructure, cables, booms, and wreckage. And just as we'd feared, we encountered our first serious problem.

Martin drove *JJ* up to the forward bulkhead of C Deck, just abaft the port crane in the Well Deck, to take a look at a gate in the bulwark railing that kept third-class passengers from entering first class. The gate was still closed. Then he flew *JJ* along the row of B-Deck windows facing the bow looking for a broken one to peer into. The window to first-class cabin B-3 was gone and *JJ* glimpsed inside . . . . But no furniture or fixtures were visible, just the metal channels defining the ceiling and walls. As *JJ* passed from window to window along this forward end of B Deck, he could see the large steel doors that gave onto the deck. They were closed tight, their hinges and portholes intact.

But *JJ* had gone too far. Suddenly Martin noticed that his cable had become hung up on one of the jagged pieces of metal protruding from the bridge. Martin tried taking in the tether, but it began chafing against a piece of torn steel plate. "That's no good," he whispered, and tried driving *JJ* up and away in an effort to take the loops out, drawing it straight. *JJ* was turned toward us so he could watch the effect of this maneuver. As the distance widened between us and our robot, the tether finally came free.

"Bring him home," I said. This place was simply too risky. "Let's try another site."

With *JJ* safely in his garage, *Alvin* rose up from the wheelhouse, pivoted left, and crossed over what once was Captain Smith's cabin on the starboard side, its exterior bulkhead collapsed outward and lying on the deck. The interior side of a window passed within inches of my viewport and I could see a shiny brass worm gear used to open and close the upper portion of the window. Was this, I wondered, a window that Captain Smith had cranked open to let a little fresh air into his bedroom before turning in for the night?

"Watch it," I warned. "We are too close to a piece of railing. It's coming right for my viewport."

Will kicked *Alvin*'s stern around, rotating us free of the obstacle, and began to drop onto the starboard Boat Deck. *Alvin* was now facing aft toward the midships tear. The current, for some reason, had gone slack.

(Top) Purser Herbert McElroy and Captain Smith in front of the officers' quarters. (Above) This window matches the one behind McElroy and Smith above.

(Opposite, top) Big Bird's light illuminates first-class stateroom U on the starboard side of the Boat Deck. (Opposite, bottom, left) A window from Captain Smith's quarters on the peeled-out wall of the starboard side of the officers' quarters. (Opposite, bottom, right) JJ *looks into stateroom U.*

I swung *Alvin*'s mechanical arm to the right and trained Big Bird's cameras on the windows lining the Boat Deck. As we glided along, I felt as though I were visiting a ghost town in the wild west where suddenly one day everyone had closed up shop and left. Some windows were open, others closed.

A lifeless boat davit stood high on the starboard side, not cranked out after its last launch, but standing almost erect. This davit had seen more use than any other that night, having lowered both lifeboat No. 1 and collapsible C. Then it was cranked back in for yet another launch – collapsible A. But the *Titanic* had given a lurch and suddenly A was floating on its own. Steward Edward Brown jumped in, severed the lines just before a wave washed the boat clear of the ship, partially swamping it. A number of swimmers later gained its safety. Now we could see the davit still standing tall, waiting in vain for another boat launch. Ahead, an electrical winch sat slowly rusting on the deck and, along the deck's outer edge, I could see the row of chocks on which the *Titanic*'s lifeboats had rested.

It was on this very deck that the full spectrum of human behavior was played out in the three short hours between 11:40 p.m., when the ship hit the iceberg, and 2:20 a.m., when she disappeared beneath the waves. Alfred Rush, who had turned 18 during the voyage, refused to climb aboard a lifeboat with the women and children because he was now a man – and went down with the ship. Bruce Ismay, the wealthy president and managing director of International Mercantile Marine, which owned the White Star Line, had hopped into the partly filled collapsible C as it was about to be lowered away, and lived to regret his instinct for survival. After his public vilification as J. ''Brute'' Ismay, he became a recluse and eventually died a broken man. And from here you

(Above) The Olympic's starboard Boat Deck showing a winch used to raise lifeboats after test launchings. *(Below)* The same winch on the Titanic.

could have heard the *Titanic*'s brave band playing cheerful ragtime music to boost the crowd's spirits as the slope of the deck grew ever more alarming.

We had landed *Alvin* just aft of where Ismay had entered that boat, near where lifeboat No. 5 had once sat. Now we sent *JJ* over the side, following the same precarious route the lifeboats themselves had taken down to the water. One of them almost dumped its passengers before being righted. A pretty young Frenchwoman almost didn't make it into boat No. 9 and another woman completely missed boat No. 10, falling between the dangling lifeboat and the side of the ship. But some quick thinker had grabbed her ankle and, as she hung indelicately over the side, people on the deck below hauled her into the promenade.

Passenger Lawrence Beesley described what it was like to leave the towering ship in a tiny lifeboat: "It was exciting to feel the boat sink by jerks, foot by foot, as the ropes were paid out from above and shrieked as they passed through the pulley blocks, the new ropes and gear creaking under the strain of a boat laden with people, and the crew calling to the sailors above as the boat tilted slightly, now at one end, now at the other, 'Lower aft!' 'Lower stern!' and 'Lower together!' as she came level again. . . . It certainly was thrilling to see the black hull of the ship on one side and the sea, seventy feet below, on the other, or to pass down by cabins and saloons brilliantly lighted . . . .''

Looking through *JJ*'s eye into the A-Deck promenade, I could imagine the first-class passengers waiting patiently below, herded there by Lightoller who had had the good idea of speeding things up by loading some of the boats from the promenade. But the windows had been closed and many passengers had shuffled back up onto the Boat Deck. Eventually, however, the windows were opened and lifeboat No. 4 was

(Above) This 1912 photograph of the Titanic *shows the open forward A-Deck promenade which can also be seen (below) on the* Titanic *wreck.*

loaded and lowered from A Deck.

JJ kept descending, moving below the first-class stateroom windows of B Deck. As he passed, he peered in and caught a brief glimpse of the interior of cabin B-49. The aft wall and overhead were clearly visible, the steel channels bare where the decorative ceiling used to be. The walls appeared to be painted white and seemed fairly clean, but there was no sign of any wood paneling or furniture. As *JJ* continued down, the windows gave way to a steel wall punctuated by an endless row of viewports – C Deck. A few were open, some undoubtedly unlatched by first-class passengers after they had felt the ship's engine stopped, and who had peered out of them to see what, if anything, had happened. Some people in lifeboats recalled watching the seawater swirl in through these same open ports. By the time this part of the ship was underwater, these rooms had long been evacuated.

Martin brought *JJ* back to home base and then we sent him for a stroll aft along the Boat Deck. As he wended his way along, he looked in the windows of several first-class cabins and down now-exposed passageways until he came to the twin entrances to the Grand Staircase and the gymnasium. As *JJ* moved aft toward these entrances, he looked into windows of the foyer of the Grand Staircase. Although the roof had crashed in beyond a few feet, making his view only a short one, pillars could plainly be seen. Mounted high on the protective weather housing

JJ looks in the gym windows, while Alvin *rests in the distance on the Boat Deck.*

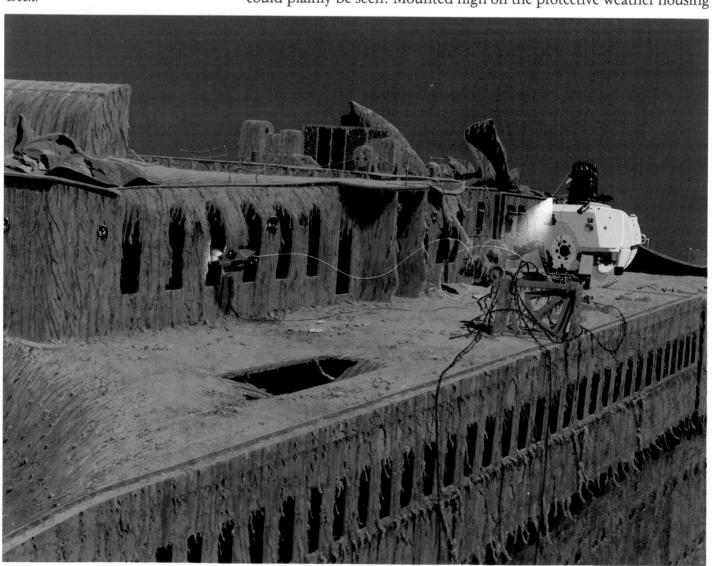

around the doorways, we could see the fitting that had held an electric sign bearing the words "First Class Entrance." *JJ* peeked into the doorway of the entrance to the Grand Staircase, spotting the door between its vestibule and the gym, before kicking up a dust storm and retreating.

As *JJ* slowly passed by the gymnasium windows, remnants of the equipment could be seen among the rubble, including a piece of metal grillwork that had protected the works of such contraptions as the electric camel, a turn-of-the-century exercise machine. Also visible were various wheel shapes and a handle. The ceiling was festooned with rusticles and collapsed downward on the inboard side. It was in this deserted gym that Colonel John Jacob Astor had calmed his pregnant young bride by explaining to her how a lifevest was packed with cork as he cut one open with a small pocket knife.

As I looked out of *Alvin*'s forward viewport, I could see *JJ* far off down the deck, turning this way and that to get a better view inside the doorways and various windows. It was almost as if our little robot had a mind of his own, seeming so deliberate and inquisitive. Martin was now controlling *JJ* with such skill that this floating eyeball had almost become an extension of his own body.

As Martin brought *JJ* home, I was thinking about going back down the Grand Staircase. Martin had done such a great job of getting us to within inches of that "chandelier" on our last dive, but we'd later discovered to our dismay that the still camera had jammed. We had good videotape, but no stills at all.

"I thought I was off the hook," joked Martin when I told him we were going back to the scene of yesterday's triumph.

Again we landed next to the remains of the elevator-shaft vent – this time on its port side – and again facing aft. *JJ* headed back down the stairwell. As *JJ* retraced his steps, I asked Martin to check several of the rooms on the starboard side of the ship. But we could see all sorts of wires drooping along under the ceiling and decided not to risk an entry. Finally, we relocated the light fixture we'd first seen, with its feather-like sea pen jauntily protruding, and Martin nosed *JJ* in close as I snapped off one still picture after another. Then Martin ventured even further into its depths. Very little was recognizable – except the columns, light fixtures, and wires – in the jumble of fallen rusticles scattered several inches deep on the floor. There was certainly no sign of the luxurious furniture that once graced the room.

We were now dangerously deep in the interior of the ship, and there was no sense taking any more chances with *JJ* than we already had. This fourth dive was turning into a banner day for *JJ*. We were doing exactly what we'd set out to accomplish – landing on one site after another and letting Martin and *JJ* do their thing. Our next stop was the bow.

Alvin landed gently on the bottom sediment a few feet from the knife-edge of the bow that towered overhead. Again I was awestruck by the size and majesty of the ship, its mighty prow plowing through the mud. From our vantage point there was no evidence this behemoth had been bothered by a mere iceberg. In a few moments, *JJ* was out of his cage and off to explore, a tiny figure against the great black hull. *JJ* flew up to the port anchor, resting at an angle in its hawsepipe, rust flowing off it in a frozen cascade, then rose further to look once more in vain for the *Titanic*'s name. Next he went higher and passed over the Forecastle Deck railing, across the auxiliary anchor crane to one of the large bronze

(Top) Rivers of rust flow off the port-side anchor.

(Above) The anchor as it looked when the ship was launched.

capstans nearby. Maneuvering to within an inch, Martin pitched *JJ*'s optical eye down and easily read the manufacturer's plate: "Napier Bros. Ltd., Engineers, Glasgow."

Reluctantly, Martin brought *JJ* home. It was time to head for the surface. We had landed at four separate sites, successfully deploying our robot on each occasion. The three of us were exhausted but elated as we headed for the surface to the sound of rock music. The floor of our cabin was a sea of video cassette tapes – our priceless *Titanic* salvage – as we joked and kibitzed, reliving the highlights of a fantastic day.

There are easy dives and hard dives and our fifth visit to the *Titanic*, on July 17, turned out to be a frustrating three hours and fifty-three minutes. Martin got the day off so that Chris von Alt, *JJ*'s architect, could try out his baby. Paul Tibbits, a recent addition to the *Alvin* team, was our pilot.

The current on the bottom was the strongest so far and the water was clouded with sediment. When we attempted to land on the bow, the sub smacked against the opening to number 1 hatch and a nearby capstan before we settled down. The thought of wreckage punching a hole in a viewport was a constant fear in our minds as the viewports are the only weak spots on the sub. Then we watched as *JJ* was blown like a kite in the submarine wind, his tether in danger of getting hopelessly wrapped around railings or wreckage. Having decided to keep *JJ* in his garage, we fared little better ourselves as we tried to investigate the region of the tear, the place where the bow had broken off, just forward of the number 3 smokestack. Yawing perilously close to the ugly wreckage, the current threw us dangerously out of control. But we saw enough to know that the decks of the ship had collapsed in on one another like a giant accordion. It was time to get out of here before the current swept us onto this treacherous shoal.

Paul was exhausted when we finally started for the surface, and all three of us were relieved to be floating peacefully upward after being tossed around by the storm below. Back on board *Atlantis II* we were tired and disappointed – especially Chris, who'd been denied his one and only chance to drive *JJ* in the deep. The *Titanic* was an elusive quarry: just when we thought we had her in our grasp again, she had slipped away.

That evening, I sat down with Al Uchupi to review the still-camera footage he and the ANGUS team had been gathering each night after *Alvin* and *JJ* returned from the bow section. Our next dive would be our first to the debris field and I wanted to make maximum use of the limited time that remained – only seven days. I had therefore asked Al to work up a map identifying the more interesting targets. I would carry this chart with me on the sub. That way we could save some time as the surface navigator led us from target to target.

ANGUS had so far mapped only a scattering of debris along the 1,970 feet separating the bow and the large stern piece we'd located last year. Most of the heavy debris seemed to be concentrated around this stern section and to the east of it, including all of the ship's smaller single-ended boilers. Al and I believed these had fallen out of the mid-portion of the ship when it broke in half at or near the surface. We surmised that these heavy round objects had fallen like giant bowling balls straight

In this video still shot by JJ, the manufacturer's plate is clearly legible on one of the bronze-topped capstans.

down to the bottom. In the vicinity of the stern section, there were additional pieces of large wreckage scattered in a larger field of lighter debris. As well as the boilers, ANGUS had spotted three ship's telegraphs.

This lighter material included some of the coal carried by the *Titanic* and many small fragments of wreckage including cups and plates, silver platters, and countless floor tiles apparently carried east of the stern section by the strong surface current running that night. I wondered what we would find when we went in for a close-up look.

My work with Al that evening was interrupted by a call from the radio room. ABC was on the line. Peter Jennings wanted to interview me for ABC's *Nightly News*. Like so many before him, he asked the inevitable question about the chances of finding human remains. "Well, Peter," I replied. "If we are ever going to find any bodies, it will come on tomorrow's dive to the debris field." In fact bodies were highly unlikely, but I thought there was a faint possibility of human skeletons. Certainly any sign of human remains was a chilling thought.

The morning of July 18 was another lovely sunny summer day. But as I reclined quietly by the starboard viewport inside our little sub – my home away from home – pondering Al's map, I couldn't help feeling edgy about the day's mission. I was anxious about what we would find down there. At least the risks in the debris field would be minimal for Jim Hardiman and his trainee co-pilot, John Salzig.

This was to be an *Alvin* training dive and *JJ* had been left behind since we wouldn't be needing him. The Alvin Group is constantly looking for pilots. Some, like Ralph and Dudley, stay with the program for years. Others leave after making a hundred dives or less. Given *Alvin*'s back-breaking schedule, that number of dives can be reached in less than five years. To insure a steady flow of well-trained new drivers, there is a rule that every seven dives we have to give up one seat to a pilot-in-training.

Today, our sixth descent to the bottom proved uneventful – no battery grounds, no malfunctioning sonar, no ominous alarm buzzers – and we found our target easily. Landing to the west, we approached the debris field along the ocean floor. As the first fragments of wreckage began to appear, it was like entering a bombed-out museum. Thousands upon thousands of artifacts littered the rolling fields of sediment, many of them perfectly preserved. The entrails of the *Titanic* spilled across the ocean floor in seemingly endless quantity. In stark contrast to the grandeur of the broken bow, this was a grisly mixture of beauty and destruction.

(Top) A broken electric space heater, one of the 520 on board.

(Above) A similar "Promotheus" space heater stands in a first-class hallway.

As I snapped away on my Nikon, a *Titanic* buff's wildest dream-come-true passed by – chinaware, silver serving trays, pots and pans, wine bottles, boots, chamber pots, headboards, space heaters, bath-tubs, suitcases and porcelain sinks. Then, without any warning, I found myself looking into the eyes of a small, white smiling face. For a split second I thought a corpse had actually materialized – and it scared the hell out of me. Then I realized I was seeing a ceramic doll's head, its hair and clothes gone. My initial shock changed to sadness as the poignancy of the image sunk in. Who had owned this toy? Had the girl been one of the lucky survivors? Or had she clutched it tightly as she sank in the icy waters?

We moved on and I glanced at my two companions. They, too, were engrossed in the amazing scenery passing by our viewports. The contents of the *Titanic*'s kitchens were laid out on the sea floor, copper pots and pans (and lids) polished to a sheen by the current, serving dishes, plates, cups, and even a copper sink. One pan even had a big piece of pink floor covering sitting in it. There was a wine and spirit cellar that would have fetched a fortune laid out before us – including champagne bottles, many with the corks intact. Soon it became difficult to keep track: porcelain chamber pots, white-enameled metal bed headboards, ornate wrought iron supports from the wooden deck benches, rusting bathtubs, faucets marked hot and cold, sinks, brightly colored red-and-white floor tiles – even a spittoon. All the sundry accoutrements of shipboard life were on display; their very ordinariness making them all the more haunting.

Occasionally the juxtapositions were dramatic. In one instance, an ugly twisted piece of iron wreckage sat just inches away from a lovely glass window from one of the bays in the first-class lounge, still in one piece. In another instance, we were exploring the face of a boiler and there on top of it rested an upright rusty metal cup of the type used by the crew, as if placed there by a stoker moments before water had burst into the boiler room. Beside it was a doorknob; the wooden door itself long gone.

At first, we moved slowly around the debris field in systematic fashion using Al Uchupi's map as a guide. We looked and looked but couldn't find the ship's telegraph, so clear in the ANGUS stills. But as time wore on, we began to follow our instincts and our senses, turning to pursue objects caught in the outer edge of *Alvin*'s lights. Whenever something interesting appeared in my viewport, we'd slow down so I could snap a picture. The sheer scale of this "museum" was overwhelming.

Around noon, we spotted a safe. Quickly, I told Jim to bring the sub to a halt and immediately we were engulfed in a giant cloud of sedi-

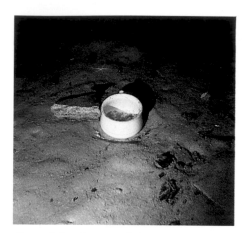

One of the dozens of chamber pots in the debris field.

The Doll's Head

(Right) The ghostly doll's head lying on the ocean floor caused a shudder when it was sighted from the *Alvin*. It has been identified by experts as a bisque head of either French or German origin. The proportions of the face indicate that it is from a lady doll rather than a round-cheeked baby doll. The eyes would have been made of glass and its ears are probably pierced for earrings. It had a swivel neck fitted into a bisque shoulder plate that allowed the head to tilt and turn realistically. The shoulder plate was sewn to a kid or cloth body and realistic hair and china hands would have been attached.

These lady dolls were most popular from the 1860s to the 1890s but were also made well into the twentieth century. The 1871 French doll pictured (**opposite, left**) shows how the doll in the debris field would have looked before all but the head was devoured by undersea organisms.

ment. Driving *Alvin* slowly across this muddy bottom was like driving a land rover at 70 miles an hour across salt flats with a rooster tail of dust streaming out behind. Visibility was good as long as we kept moving, but the minute we stopped, our dust tail caught up.

Since the current wasn't that strong today, I knew it was going to take a while for the mud cloud to clear. And I wanted to take a close look at that safe, which appeared to be in good condition. My first impulse was simply to photograph it. The safe was now about 65 to 100 feet behind us and to the right, so I told Jim to swing around 180° and move closer to its position, figuring we might as well stir up more mud now and then wait for it all to settle while we ate lunch. Soon our tiny cabin was filled with the smell of peanut butter, as we excitedly discussed our safe and what it might contain.

Lunch in *Alvin* was never three stars. In fact, it was more like half a sparkler. But working in the cold cramped sphere built up such an appetite you'd eat almost anything. The best underwater meals I'd ever eaten were with the French. Good cheese, fresh fruit, cold meats, fine French bread, and sometimes even a plastic cup of slightly chilled Beaujolais. But there was no booze allowed on *Alvin*.

Sixteen years before, when I'd first dived in *Alvin*, the traditional lunch was a bologna sandwich. In fact, those early lunches had become legend. In October 1968, *Alvin* had slipped its moorings with three people aboard, filled with water through the open hatch, and sunk in 5,200 feet of water. The crew just managed to escape in time. Ten months later when the sub was recovered, the bologna sandwiches were still edible. This triggered a whole new field of research in microbiology since this new evidence suggested that the rate of decay of organic material at these depths was much slower than previously assumed. It was because of this accident with *Alvin* that many people held out hope that the *Titanic* would be much better preserved than she turned out to be.

In 1977, during our dives off the Galápagos Islands, our Portuguese cook had sent us down to the bottom with pepper steak and onion

The champagne bottle on the right still has its cork in place. The wine bottle to the left of it has had its cork pushed into the center of the bottle by the pressure.

A doll such as the one shown (**left**) would have cost 40 dollars or more – a considerable amount in 1912. So it is likely that it belonged to one of the first-class passengers. Perhaps it was purchased in Europe by an adult collector. Maybe it was being taken to New York as a generous gift for a child in America. It may even have belonged to three-year-old Lorraine Allison of Montreal, the only child from first-class who did not survive the disaster. She clung to the skirt of her mother, Mrs. Hudson J. Allison, who chose to stay on the *Titanic* with her husband, although she put Lorraine's baby brother, Trevor, in a lifeboat with his nurse. Lorraine and Trevor are pictured (**right**). Except for Lorraine, all 29 first and second-class children were saved as compared to the 53 out of 76 children from steerage who died.

(A)

(B)

(A) A painted metal footboard from a first-class stateroom.

(B) These wooden stairs may have taken third-class passengers from the Well Deck to the Poop Deck. Probably made of teak, the stairs are in a remarkable state of preservation.

(C) A toilet bowl lies next to a liquor bottle.

(D) A grenadier fish and Alvin's arm inspect a third-class coffee cup bearing the White Star emblem.

(C)

(D)

The Debris Field

Like a silent underwater museum more than two miles down, debris lies scattered over the ocean floor near the *Titanic* wreck. Most of the debris is concentrated near the severed stern section which is 1,970 feet away from the more intact bow section. A map of the debris field near the stern appears on page 207.

(E)

(F)

(E) The cast-iron frame of a deck bench appears almost bronze in the light from Alvin. Although here, the wooden slats are gone, the wood on some of the other deck benches in the debris field has survived (see page 214).

(F) This plain third-class or crew headboard provides a strong contrast to the more elegant enameled footboard shown in (A).

(Below) Letters indicate the location of artifacts pictured above. The dark area represents a concentration of spilled coal. For contrast, the red, black and white paint on the wreck has been accentuated.

sandwiches. The smell was overwhelming when we unwrapped them in our tiny airtight ball. Now the standard fare was good old peanut butter and jelly sandwiches, apples, cookies, and candy bars.

By the end of a long day in a tiny submersible, the atmosphere can become, well, close. You pray that your diving companions have taken a nice long shower that morning and that they didn't eat garlic or beans for dinner the night before. And with no room for a toilet, we have to resort to facilities similar to those used by weightless astronauts. (Our plastic urine bottle is nicknamed HERE, an acronym for human endurance range extender.) At least, unlike astronauts, we don't have to spend days at a time in our capsule.

As we finished our repast, the safe began to emerge at the edge of the arc illuminated by our headlights. Very gently, so as not to disturb more mud than necessary, our pilot swung us around until the object of our interest was directly outside my starboard window. It sat with its door face-up. The handle looked like it was made of gold though it had to be brass. Right next to it, I could see a small circular gold dial and above both a nice shiny gold crest. I could make out figures facing one another – they looked like horses or unicorns rearing up on their hind legs – but the crest was too small for me to read the lettering.

I directed Jim to bring *Alvin*'s sample-gathering arm around for a picture. As he did so, I realized the claw was going to practically touch the safe's handle – why not try to open it? So I watched as the arm's metal fingers locked onto the handle and its wrist began to rotate clockwise. To my surprise it turned easily, then stopped. But the door wouldn't budge, its flanges apparently rusted shut. For a moment, I felt

When the safe was lifted by Alvin's *arm, we saw that its bottom was missing.*

a little like the kid caught with his hand in the cookie jar. It would be so easy to bring the safe back with us to the surface. We'd lifted heavier things with *Alvin*.

I looked at Jim and he looked back at me.

"What now?" he asked.

There was a long pause as I considered the possibilities, and imagined what the safe might contain. What would I have done if we'd opened it to discover something valuable – the bejeweled *Rubaiyat of Omar Khayyam*, for instance? I probably would have called the surface and told them to radio Woods Hole: "Have found priceless *Titanic* artifact. Please advise." Fortunately, my vow not to return with *Titanic* salvage wasn't put to the test. Probably the safe was empty, anyway. I remembered Bill Tantum telling me once that supposedly the ship's second-class safes had been opened by the crew and emptied during the final moments before the *Titanic* sank. Lawrence Beesley recalled in his account of the sinking that he had heard the door of the assistant purser's safe clang back shut after it had been emptied. Since it was apparent on closer examination that this was clearly one of the safes from the second-class purser's office, it was unlikely that it had ever held real treasure. Perhaps it contained some money and not-too-expensive jewelry. It would have been wonderful to find out.

"Let go of it and let me take some more pictures," I finally replied. If I could pass this souvenir up, I could pass up anything. (When I later examined the photos I took, I could see that the bottom of the safe had rusted out. Any contents ought to have been visible on the sediment underneath, but we saw no sign of them.)

Two days passed before I again descended to the *Titanic*. It was now time for one of the young Navy submarine officers (on board to gain experience piloting *JJ*) to have a turn down below while I took an inventory of what we'd found so far. Actually I was ready for a break. We'd reached the halfway point in the expedition and we'd already gone a long way toward getting the *Titanic* on film – both video and high-quality still images.

But Navy Lt. Jeff Powers had to wait an extra day for his trip because *Alvin*'s battery charger let us down. It had accidentally been left turned off overnight. So instead of heading for the bottom, *Alvin* spent July 19 aboard *Atlantis II* having its batteries juiced up. The next morning, July 20, dive number seven departed as planned with Lt. Powers on board and Jim Aguilar at the controls. Martin went along to help Jeff handle *JJ*. Despite a strong current on the bottom, the sub managed to land on the *Titanic* and take some pictures, but *JJ* again had problems: this time his video wasn't working. After performing beautifully in our early dives, *Jason Jr.* was becoming a problem child.

After two days' rest, I was raring to go as we again headed for the bottom – this time for the stern. Ralph Hollis was back at the controls and the third member of the crew was Ken Stewart, a graduate student working in the Deep Submergence Laboratory. Ken had been in charge of *JJ*'s development before Chris von Alt joined our team and he was looking forward to driving *JJ* in for a close-up look at the propellers – if they were there.

Today, I was determined to finally lay Jack Grimm's "propeller"

(Top) The second-class purser's office aboard the Olympic. *Three safes found in the debris field came from a similar office on the* Titanic.

(Above) This copy of the Rubaiyat of Omar Khayyam *was bought at an auction house for £405 and was being shipped to New York on the* Titanic. *The peacock design on the cover was done in gold and over 1,000 precious stones studded the binding.*

153

claim permanently to rest. We planned to land *Alvin* on the bottom directly behind the stern section and then send *JJ* in under the overhanging hull. Unless the propellers had fallen off during the descent, they ought still to be there. All eyewitnesses agreed that only the forward section of the *Titanic* had actually bashed the iceberg, although a number of the crew members who did not see the berg and had barely felt the collision assumed that the reason the ship stopped was that she had dropped a propeller blade, a rare, but not unheard of problem. If only it had been that simple. At any rate there was every reason to expect that the great blades were still fitted to their bosses and that the 101-ton rudder was still in its place. The *Titanic* had three huge propellers, the two three-bladed ones on each side measuring 23 feet, 6 inches, the smaller one in the center was 16 feet, 6 inches. Together they were capable of moving the ship at a speed of over 23 knots. In fact, her maximum speed was never known – Ismay later stated that her top speed test had been scheduled for Monday April 15. . . .

This was Ralph's third trip down to the wreck. Instead of skiing along the bottom, we made a breathtaking high-altitude approach over the debris field. Soon the Poop Deck gradually came into view through the eye of the *Argo* SIT camera. This aftermost piece of the *Titanic*'s stern was recognizable at least, rimmed by big fairlead rollers – spool-like guides for the mooring lines. But instead of landing on this deck, which was dangerously cluttered with debris, Ralph steered us aft and down beside the wall of the stern, hovering briefly while Big Bird searched in vain for some sign of the *Titanic*'s name or her home port, Liverpool. The rusticles were just too thick.

Then we dropped further and Ralph made a soft landing on the bottom, pumping ballast so that we could deploy *JJ* from a solid base. This was what Ken Stewart had been waiting for but he wasn't showing his excitement. I knew he felt it though – this wasn't his first dive in *Alvin*, but it was his first look at the *Titanic*. *JJ* was hardly out of his garage when it became apparent that something was wrong. He was going in circles. One of his motors, which had worked fine on the surface, was gone.

"Damn," I said. "We've come all this way. We are sitting right where we want to be and *JJ* won't work." Ralph wasn't smiling an "I-told-you-so" smile, but he might as well have been as we pulled our dead robot back home by the tether.

This was the only trip I'd scheduled to the heavily damaged stern section and it looked like a washout. I sat glumly staring out my viewport at the muddy bottom and feeling sorry for myself. Suddenly, the mud started to move! Ralph was slowly inching *Alvin* forward on its single ski in under the stern. Was he crazy? What if a piece of wreckage came crashing down? I looked at Ken, rolled my eyes and pointed my thumb at Ralph's back as if to say, "He's the pilot, we've got to trust his judgment." He rolled his eyes in silent assent. Ken was obviously thinking the same thing I was: Ralph was breaking the first rule of *Alvin* piloting; never go in under a man-made overhang. He was going to prove that *Alvin* could do anything *JJ* could do better. He still thought he could win the battle against unmanned robots.

Looking out my porthole, I could see ahead of us the line that marked the beginning of no-man's land: the area covered with the rust that had fallen from the stern above. Up to that demarcating line the

(Top) Fairlead rollers, once used to guide the ship's mooring lines, lie on the starboard side of the stern.

(Above) A stern view of the Titanic.

ocean floor was clear; beyond it was a pile of hundreds of foot-long rusticles. Crossing that line was like accepting a dangerous dare; once on the other side, there was no sure route of escape in an emergency. I prayed Ralph knew what he was doing, but I said nothing. I wanted to see those propellers. None of us spoke. The only sound in the sub was our breathing.

Quietly, I reached over to a point just by Ralph's right elbow – the control for *Alvin*'s arm – and began to maneuver Big Bird's camera to look upward. If a problem was going to occur it would come from the corroded hull hanging above us. I turned my back on the viewport and concentrated on the color video monitor in the rear of the sphere. At first, all I could see was a stream of particles, but slowly a massive black surface began to inch down toward the lens. Soon the entire monitor was taken up by a single giant section of steel plating, the rivets clearly visible. If we went much further, we'd wedge ourselves under the stern. I didn't usually feel claustrophobic in the sub, but this was different – the hull seemed to be coming in at us from all sides.

"I see the rudder, Bob, but I don't see any propellers," Ralph reported in a matter-of-fact voice. If he was nervous, he wasn't showing it. He had stopped *Alvin* dead.

I moved up to his viewport and gazed out into the dark. There directly in front of me and in every direction was the stern rising from the sea floor, its curved hull plating disappearing up and out of sight. From here, it looked in almost perfect condition, as if it were in dry dock to have its bottom cleaned – but the bottom was clean! There was hardly any rust and virtually no marine growth – apparently the steepness of the hull provided little purchase for rusticles.

Like the bow, the *Titanic*'s stern section was buried deep into the mud – 45 feet or so – with the mud-line resting well above the position of the propellers. Only about 16 feet of her rudder could be seen rising out of the ooze, as if the ship were floating on the surface of the sea. I was sure the propellers were down there, but I couldn't prove it. I could almost hear Jack Grimm's chuckle. I knew he wouldn't believe it.

There was nothing more we could do and Ralph had proven his

(Top) An A-Deck cargo crane – still fitted but lying askew on the stern section. This same crane can be seen in the 1912 photograph of the boy spinning his top on page 17.

(Above) Fuse boxes and other controls can be seen on this 1912 shot of a similar Titanic crane.

(Left) The giant screws from the Titanic's stern are now deeply buried in the mud.

155

point. "Let's get out of here," I said.

The pilot turned *Alvin* around, and ever-so-gently retraced the path left by our lone ski mark. *Alvin* recrossed the demarcating line of rust and passed out from under the stern. At last we could relax, our sense of relief almost palpable, though no one said anything. All of us, including Ralph, were glad our adventure was over.

In the time remaining on this eighth dive to the *Titanic*, I intended to complete one mission that had long been on my mind. I wanted to place a memorial plaque on the stern in memory of my friend Bill Tantum and to all those lost on the *Titanic*. More than anybody else, Bill had kept my *Titanic* dream afloat. And a memorial to him would also be a tribute to the members of the *Titanic* Historical Society, who have done so much to keep the memory of the ship alive. Bill's wife Anne had liked the idea, and on the day we sailed had presented me with a handsome bronze plaque.

It was a risky maneuver to get this picture of the ship's rudder under the Titanic's overhanging stern.

(Right) This painting of the Titanic's *stern section shows the Poop Deck peeled back and partly overhanging the stern under which* Alvin *is exploring. Moving forward, the after Well Deck has been torn away and shell plating and framing have peeled outward from the hull. The fallen main mast and the starboard A-Deck cargo crane are still fitted to the ship as is the second-class entrance deck house on the Boat Deck.*

The large piece of debris in the left foreground is a section of deck from the galley. In a trail of debris leading back to the ship are broken hull and deck sections, three cargo cranes, two lifeboat davits and many other items.

I had originally thought of putting the plaque on the more nobly preserved bow. But those who died on the *Titanic* had gathered on the stern as the ship tilted bow first. The stern had been their final haven.

We rose up the wall of steel and Ralph carefully maneuvered *Alvin* onto the edge of the Poop Deck next to two of the steel fairlead rollers. There was so little space that Ralph could only rest the forward part of the sub on firm decking while our tail hung out in space, like a rock teetering on the brink of a cliff. With great care, *Alvin*'s arm plucked the plaque from its quiver strapped to *JJ*'s garage. Then Ralph rotated the arm and gently released it. The three of us watched on the video screen as the plaque sank quietly onto the thin veneer of sediment covering the hull.

Now Ralph lifted off and we began rising upward, Big Bird's camera keeping the plaque in view as long as possible. As we rose, it grew smaller and smaller until finally it was swallowed up in the gloom as if

The plaque placed on the stern in memory of Bill Tantum and those who perished on the Titanic.

someone were dimming the lights on a movie set. I found myself fighting back feelings of sadness. Fading from our sight was a picture of the last spot where people had stood on dry *Titanic* deck, now peaceful and deserted. There was little talking in the sub. We were all emotionally drained as we headed back toward sunlight.

Time was now getting short and our next two dives proved especially frustrating. After working so well during the first half of the expedition, *Jason Jr.* had been plagued with recurring problems. Despite yeoman efforts by Chris von Alt and his team, *JJ* failed to work properly on either July 22 or July 23. That meant that for four days in a row we'd been without our swimming eyeball, and denied access to the other places inside the wreck I'd wanted to explore.

On July 22, we photographed the entire exterior of the bow and took a close look at the area where the iceberg supposedly tore a gash. From the bow to a point roughly even with cargo hatch number 2, the hull below the water line was buried in the mud. Aft of this point, we could begin to see the area where the gash should have been, but no tear was visible. Instead, as we moved aft, descending along the mud-line, we passed two large and dramatic vertical buckles in the hull plating. The one further aft was particularly interesting: there, the steel hull had folded out at an angle of almost 90 degrees and then back in on itself with no evidence of a torn seam or a popped rivet. These vertical buckles were clearly the result of the bow's crash into the bottom which had left the forward part of the ship bent down several degrees. Farther aft, however, about even with the bridge and just above the turn of the bilge, we could see some horizontal buckling and creasing of hull plates, the plates themselves slightly separated at the seams, and we could see the holes where rivets had popped out. We were now well within the area damaged by the iceberg. Were we looking at a fragment of the *Titanic*'s mortal wound? If so, where was the great gash we'd been led to expect? Perhaps there was an actual hole in the hull further forward, but from what we could see, it appeared perfectly possible that the famous gash had never existed.

On July 23, the two other Navy submariners on board, Lt. Mike Mahre and Lt. Brian Kissel, got their turn to dive. On the port side of the bow section at D-Deck level, they discovered a large, first-class gangway door that was wide open – probably jarred out on impact. They shone *Alvin*'s lights through the hatchway and into the entrance foyer beyond. All that could be seen was a bulkhead and the ceiling disappearing into the darkness. What lay beyond the limit of the headlights? This would have made a wonderful point of entry for *JJ*. He could easily have ventured into the first-class reception room, viewed the three elevators, traveled forward into passenger companionways or aft into the first-class dining saloon. But once again our little robot petulantly refused to cooperate.

On the eve of our final day and final dive, I was determined that *JJ* would have one more successful deployment. So I asked Chris and his troops to work through the night in an effort to find and fix the problems. Then, just before midnight, Chris came into my cabin and handed me a piece of smashed wire. Emile had found it tucked up inside the tether take-up reel. Apparently, during the original assembly,

(Top) The Titanic's *D-Deck gangway doors in 1912. (Above) An open gangway door in 1986. The worm gear that opened and closed the windows is clearly visible.*

this small wire had been damaged just enough to break its protective plastic jacket without severing the actual wire. On the surface nothing had shown up; but at the tremendous pressures on the ocean floor the wire had sometimes grounded. So the problem would be there one day and not the next, and so on: a technician's nightmare. We'd caught and killed the gremlin, but that piece of smashed wire had cost us three dives worth $60,000 in total.

Now, finally convinced that all was well, I slept soundly and bounced out of bed on the morning of July 24 ready for our final dive and what I knew would be my last look at the *Titanic*. Will Sellars, who'd piloted us on our banner fourth dive, was to take us down, and Martin Bowen was on board to take a final turn with *JJ*. Miraculously, the weather still held, our spirits were good, but within seconds of a perfect launch euphoria turned into despair. Martin Bowen gave me the bad news. "Bob, I have a hard ground on *JJ*."

"You've got to be kidding. Tell me you're kidding," was my only response.

I couldn't face another dive without my little R2D2. *JJ* was going inside the A Deck first-class promenade if I had to throw him in there with *Alvin*'s arm. There was no choice but to resurface and see if we could fix the problem. Today, we had even less flexibility than usual. Before the morning's launch, Captain Baker had stressed the importance of being back in time for our scheduled departure for home. The powers that be wanted us to arrive at Woods Hole for a carefully orchestrated welcoming ceremony and the captain didn't want to be late.

For an hour, Martin, Will, and I baked inside the pressure sphere as it sat on the gently rolling deck of *Atlantis II*, while Chris and his cohorts attacked *JJ* once more. As the heat rose inside our tiny compartment, I couldn't tell which was its main source: the hot sun on our metal hull or my rising annoyance. Mercifully, the delay turned out to be a false alarm – minor electrical grounds in each of *JJ*'s four motors that added up to a seemingly serious ground when taken together. *JJ* should work fine when we got to the bottom.

Finally, shortly after 10 a.m., we were back in the water and headed toward the bottom as fast our descent weights would take us. At noon, as we neared our destination, we ate the last peanut butter sandwiches of the 1986 *Titanic* expedition. Just after 12:30, we approached our now familiar forecastle landing site. We placed a second plaque (given to us by the Explorers' Club of New York, of which I am a member) on one of the bow's beautiful bronze-topped capstans. The inscription asked all those who follow to leave the ship in peace.

As we lifted off and headed for the port A-Deck promenade, Martin reported that *JJ* seemed fine. On previous trips along the port side, I'd noted an opening on B Deck I thought was big enough for *JJ* to enter – just abeam of the bridge. It was a gangway opening in the bulwark railing, its door now missing, two decks below one of the remaining lifeboat davits.

After we'd spotted the opening, I directed Will to land *Alvin* on the Boat Deck just above it, at a landing spot on the port side I'd first noticed on our second dive, beside the collapsed officers' cabins. Once over the rail, we moved forward along the Boat Deck, passing the windows on the port side of the Grand Staircase until we were beside the expansion joint, just aft of the number 1 funnel opening and the

(Above) The forward expansion joint on the port side through which the interior of the ship was visible to us.

(Below) The still-shiny worm gear that was turned to lower the forward davit arm for lifeboat No. 2.

159

officers' quarters. The superstructure of the ship had actually cracked open along the expansion joint and I could see all the way through and out the starboard side; there were tantalizing glimpses of the interior. Inside one cabin, I could see a small coal-burning stove, which appeared to be coated in a green ceramic glaze. Perhaps it had warmed the officers' pantry.

We moved slowly forward toward the forwardmost davit on the port side, the davit for lifeboat No. 2, where we intended to land, right beside First Officer Murdoch's cabin. It was the only davit still standing on the port side. Will could see the davit now – and quite a bit of wreckage ahead to the right, where the wall of the officers' quarters had collapsed outward. Landing near there would be tricky. Just aft of the davit, a few metal stanchions, which had once lent support to a short bulwark rail along the side of the ship, jutted up a couple of feet. But Will landed safely and brought *Alvin* in as close as he could.

This would be *JJ*'s last hurrah. In all likelihood none of us would ever sit on the deck of the *Titanic* again. "Let's go for it Martin. It's now or never," I said.

With accustomed skill, but some nervousness, Martin maneuvered *JJ* down the two decks and then back and forth, scanning the opening I'd chosen. Would it prove big enough? Martin thought so and cautiously inched forward, clearing the railing on either side of the gangway opening into B Deck and carefully going in. Unfortunately, there was nothing much to see. Sediment and falling rusticles filled the water and Martin soon gave up.

Stymied in our first attempt to enter promenade space, Martin flew *JJ*

(Above) A sign which reads, "This door for use of crew only." (Below) The arched windows of the port-side Boat Deck foyer to the Grand Staircase.

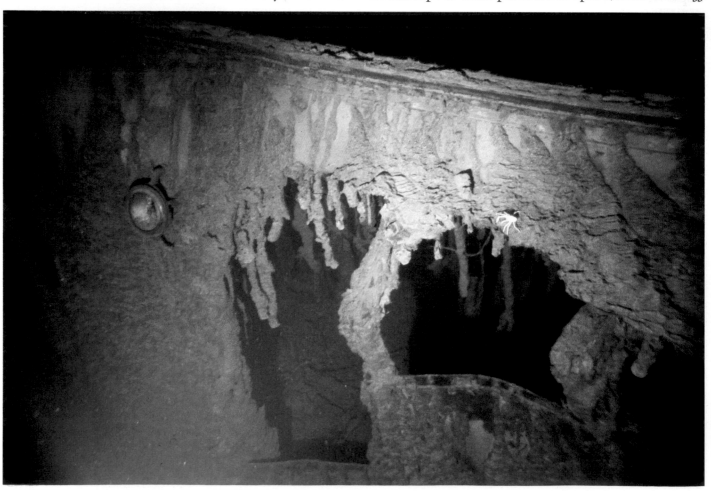

back up onto the Boat Deck to inspect boat davit number 2, taking some wonderful close-up stills that show marvelous detail. Its worm gear was as bright and new as the day it was made. Both lifeboat No. 2 and collapsible D were launched from this spot. Collapsible D, the very last one to be launched from the ship, was the one Lightoller had protected with a ring of crew members who had locked arms around it to prevent a stampede. Among those who had left in this boat were the two little Navratil boys, kidnapped by their father from his estranged wife. When the *Carpathia* arrived in New York, it had taken days before their identity was known. (The father, who went down with ship, had been listed on the passenger roster as a Mr. Hoffman.) Many other children were not so lucky.

Martin now took *JJ* over the rail again to search for a way into A Deck, steering him into an ''open promenade'' enclosure at the forward end of the first-class promenade just above the disappointing B-Deck gangway. Here there were doorways leading in two directions. On the outboard side of the large door in the bulwark separating us from the enclosed promenade, there was a sizeable window. Rusticles dangled down menacingly over both so Martin moved toward a second open door, apparently leading to the interior of the ship. As he did so, I spotted a brass plate to the right of it and he zoomed in for a closer look. It read, ''This door for crew use only.'' As it turned out, the door opened into an inner stairway that led to the Boat Deck just above, next to the bridge, or down to B Deck – not to interior cabins.

As *JJ* rose up for an even closer look, he banged into a large rusticle suspended from the overhanging deck and suddenly his eye went blind

(Above) The brass plate from over the first-class entrance door on the port side of the Boat Deck (below) now hangs slightly askew.

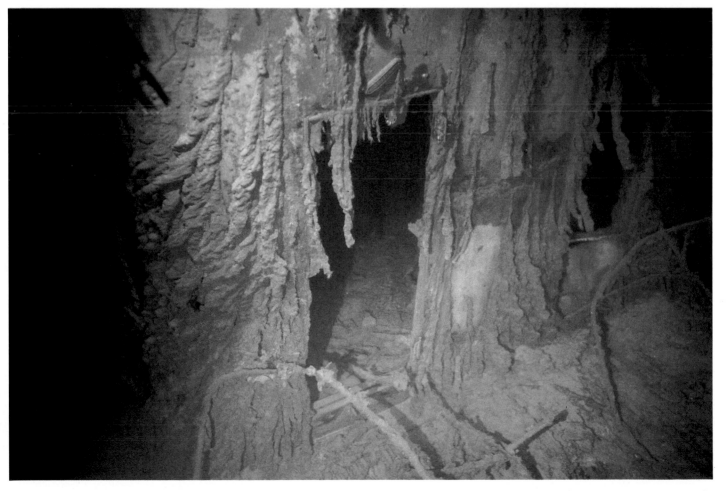

161

– *JJ* was spinning around and we became disoriented. Then *JJ*'s tether got hung up on something. I thought of Stan Laurel's famous line: ''Well, Ollie, you really have us in a fine fix now.'' And now Will Sellars decided to remind me that it was almost time to head back to the surface.

Finally *JJ* was able to see his own tether in the rusty water. It was hung up on a jagged piece of steel. Martin brought *JJ* up, freed the cable, and we all breathed a sigh of relief as I gave my final command.

''Bring him home, Martin. We have proven our point. All final objectives have been reached. Now get him back in his garage and let's go home.'' As *JJ* maneuvered out of the open promenade and rose back up to the Boat Deck, he spied a little hose plug (hydrant) at the edge of the deck near the stanchions. The red paint was still visible.

With *JJ* safely home, Will lifted off from the deck and moved slightly away from the ship so that our ascent weights would drop harmlessly into the mud. The sub paused for a moment, as if reluctant to leave the *Titanic* for the last time. Then we began to drift upward, accelerating toward the surface. I watched the video screen as the Boat Deck of the ship faded into the gloom; the last things I saw were the squashed roof of the officers' quarters and that lonely lifeboat davit. . . .

Suddenly it was over. The *Titanic* disappeared from view as Will turned off the incandescent headlights, and we floated silently upward in the blackness. For once, I didn't put the *Flashdance* tape on the stereo – instead I played something soft and classical – there was none of the usual talking and joking, none of the customary unwinding after hours of intense concentration. Each of us sat quietly with our own thoughts.

I knew I had visited the ship for the last time. In the unlikely event I ever did return, it would not be in *Alvin*. *Argo* and *Jason*, my remotely controlled underwater imaging system, would replace our sub. Certainly it would be an advance for science, but I knew something would be lost – gone would be the immediacy, the intimacy that I had known over the last 12 days.

A melancholy feeling of emptiness came over me. How could I be experiencing this sense of loss, I wondered? After all the *Titanic* was, in the final analysis, only a big wreck in deep water. Our mission had been a technological success. I should be feeling jubilation. Instead, I felt like a high-school senior saying goodbye to his steady girlfriend before heading off to college. I wanted to look to the future, but I couldn't help looking back.

Two and a half hours later, when we reached the surface, there was no time for celebration or reflection. Everyone had a job to do as we recovered the transponders, stowed the sub, made sure *JJ* was comfortable, and prepared to head for home. Later that night there would be a party in the lab, but through it all I would still be thinking about the *Titanic*: of the people who had built her, sailed on her, and died when she went down.

The Royal Mail Steamship *Titanic* had yielded up many of the secrets she had guarded for 74 years. Our two expeditions had been a remarkable accomplishment. The *Titanic* had been found, and now she had been paid a respectful visit. But had we put the ship finally to rest, or merely opened a whole new era of speculation about her fate and attempts to rob her grave?

The small hose plug (hydrant) that we spotted on the Boat Deck.

R.M.S. *Titanic* – Then and Now

Although the sumptuous Edwardian furnishings have vanished, the funnels gone and the hull broken, the wreck and debris field of the *Titanic* reveal fascinating glimpses of the great ship that was.

(Right) The port-side Boat Deck of the Titanic *in a photograph taken at Queenstown by Miss Kate Odell. In the left foreground can be seen one of the "Sirocco" ventilation fans and its motor. (Below) The fan and motor housings still rest in their original position after 74 years. The tall cowl vent shown above was wrenched away in the sinking. Only a few feet from this point, the deck collapses downward, plunging at a precipitous angle.*

Marschall '87©

The new White Star Liners "Clympic" and "T
2,500 passengers, besides a crew of 860

Inside the *Titanic*

(Above) This cross-section was created by the White Star Line, while the *Olympic* and *Titanic* were under construction, as part of a brochure advertising the new liners. The copy at the bottom proudly states the dimensions and cost of "the largest vessels ever built." While not a technically accurate rendering of the interior of the *Titanic*, it is a helpful reference for understanding the general layout of the ship. From the Boat Deck at top, the

The Bow Section

A rear view seen from the port side

When the *Titanic*'s bow section hit the bottom, the decks nearest the tear collapsed down on top of each other.

1. *Missing gangway on B Deck where JJ briefly entered on final dive.*
2. *Where "This door for use of crew only" sign was found.*
3. *Forward davit for lifeboat No. 2.*
4. *Telemotor from wheelhouse.*
5. *Officers' quarters.*
6. *Remains of after part of number 1 funnel.*
7. *Electric winch for raising lifeboats.*
8. *After davit for lifeboat No. 8.*
9. *Vent for first-class elevator shaft.*
10. *First-class entrance.*
11. *Collapsed first-class Grand Staircase area.*
12. *Open D-Deck gangway door.*
13. *Remains of number 2 funnel.*
14. *Collapsed roof over gymnasium.*
15. *Fallen first-class lounge roof.*
16. *Number 3 funnel casing.*
17. *Bilge keel.*
18. *Plating torn open at first-class dining saloon.*

decks proceed downward as follows: Promenade Deck A; Bridge Deck B; Shelter Deck C; Saloon Deck D; Upper Deck E; Middle Deck F; Lower Deck G; Orlop Deck and Tank Top. Note the two first-class staircases, the gymnasium, and the first-class lounge, dining saloon and smoking room.

(Below, left) An overlay of markings has here been applied to the original Olympic/Titanic *plan from* The Shipbuilder *to compare the present condition of the wreck to the ship as her builders conceived her.*

1. *Rudder buried 45 feet.*
2. *Poop Deck peeled back over stern.*
3. *After Well Deck torn away.*
4. *Decks collapsed and compressed.*
5. *Starboard A-Deck cargo crane wrenched but still fitted.*
6. *Second-class entrance and elevator housing remain.*
7. *Decks collapsed down.*
8. *Deck rests on cylinder heads of reciprocating engines.*
9. *Shell plating remains partially upright although Boat Deck is angled down in center.*
10. *One-foot gap in expansion joint.*
11. *Hull buckled below expansion joint.*
12. *Possible iceberg damage here.*
13. *Bow angled downward.*
14. *Buckling caused by angle of bow.*
15. *Level of original keel.*
16. *Bow plowed in over 60 feet.*

THE LARGEST STEAMERS IN THE WORLD

ts. contain nine steel decks, and provide accommodation for ...essel when completed will have cost £1,500,000

(Left) This photograph from the Olympic, *shows how the starboard second-class entrance on the* Titanic *once looked. (Above, left) The second-class entrance and elevator housing still stand on the stern section (see painting on pages 156-157). The port-side arched windows have fallen inward (above, center) and the curved weather cover from the entrance (above) is still attached.*

The First-Class Lounge

The first-class lounge of the *Titanic* is described in a 1911 issue of *The Shipbuilder* as "...a noble apartment in the Louis Quinze style, the details being taken from the Palace of Versailles. Here passengers will indulge in reading, conversation, cards, tea-drinking and other social intercourse."

(Above) The glass remains intact inside some of the panes of this first-class lounge leaded window. In the upper left of the picture of the lounge, (right) light can be seen coming through just such a window.

(Below, left) This window from the Olympic's first-class lounge helped identify the one in the Titanic's debris field (above). This photograph was taken at the White Swan Hotel in Alnwick, England which is furnished

with fittings taken from the Olympic. (Below) The outline of one of the candelabra-style wall sconces from the lounge (above) can be seen in this photograph taken by ANGUS in the debris field.

(**Far right**) *This statuette once adorned the mantelpiece (**above and in inset**). It is a reduced copy of the classical statue the "Artemis of Versailles" which is now in the Louvre. It shows Artemis, the Greek goddess of* the hunt, drawing an arrow from her quiver while grasping a stag. The grayish tone of the statuette indicates that it was probably made of a zinc alloy known as spelter and then painted bronze.

The First-Class Lounge on A Deck

This plan of the first-class lounge shows the positioning of the statuette on the fireplace and locations of the leaded glass windows. The dotted line indicates where the tear occurred when the ship broke up.

The Aft First-Class Staircase

Although not as long or as grand as the forward first-class staircase, the aft Grand Staircase was decorated in a similar style and boasted the same oak carving and elaborate wrought-iron balustrades. Since the tear which occurred while the *Titanic* was sinking went directly through the aft Grand Staircase, many more artifacts from it have been discovered than from its more celebrated forward counterpart.

(Above) The brass base, fittings, and even part of the cord remain on this light fixture that is similar in style to those on the ceiling of the A-Deck foyer.

(Left) The A-Deck foyer of the Olympic's aft Grand Staircase.

(Above) This section of a four-foot-long piece of carved oak matches the newel post carving on the staircase shown above. It was found floating near the scene of the disaster in April 1912 by the Minia, one of the ships dispatched from Halifax by the White Star Line to search for the *Titanic's* victims.

(Above) Nine wrought-iron balustrades from the aft Grand Staircase were found in the debris field. Two of the angled, descending sections are shown *(above)*. The gilt floral decorations are still there, reflecting the strobe of the camera.

The First-Class Dining Saloon

The largest room afloat, the *Titanic*'s first-class dining saloon could seat more than 500 people in Jacobean-style splendor. Recessed bays at the sides of the 114-foot-long room provided private dining areas and the white walls and richly molded ceiling created a light but elegant atmosphere.

(Top, right) The frame and shattered glass of one of the room's windows.

(Above) One of the side dining areas of the first-class saloon.

(Right) A fragment from the leaded glass windows shown *(above)* and in the bay window *(below)*.

(Below, right) Although bent and missing most of its glass panes, the leaded-paned grill from the dining-saloon door was still clearly recognizable when photographed in the debris field. Later, its more intact partner was also discovered in footage from one of the ANGUS runs (inset, right).

In the dining-saloon illustration from The Shipbuilder *(above) the two door grills can clearly be seen.*

This menu for the last first-class dinner served aboard the Titanic *on the night of April 14, 1912, reveals the elaborate and extensive fare enjoyed by upper-class diners. The menu card was enclosed within a folder which pictured the symbolic figures of Europa and Columbia linked above a radiant white star, and a picture of the reception room which adjoined the saloon.*

R.M.S. "TITANIC."

APRIL 14, 1912

HORS D'ŒUVRE VARIÉS
OYSTERS

CONSOMMÉ OLGA   CREAM OF BARLEY

SALMON, MOUSSELINE SAUCE, CUCUMBER

FILET MIGNONS LILI
SAUTÉ OF CHICKEN, LYONNAISE
VEGETABLE MARROW FARCIE

LAMB, MINT SAUCE
ROAST DUCKLING, APPLE SAUCE
SIRLOIN OF BEEF, CHATEAU POTATOES

GREEN PEAS   CREAMED CARROTS
BOILED RICE
PARMENTIER & BOILED NEW POTATOES

PUNCH ROMAINE

ROAST SQUAB & CRESS
COLD ASPARAGUS VINAIGRETTE
PÂTE DE FOIE GRAS
CELERY

WALDORF PUDDING
PEACHES IN CHARTREUSE JELLY
CHOCOLATE & VANILLA ECLAIRS
FRENCH ICE CREAM

(Left) Although subject to 6,000 pounds of pressure per square inch, this champagne bottle has its cork still in place. Even the lead wrap around the neck remains in recognizable condition.

(Right) Battered but still shiny, a silver-plated soup tureen lies next to a broken steam pipe.

(Inset, above, right) This silver-plated platter may once have served up the salmon in mousseline sauce featured in the first-class menu *(left)*.

The Kitchens

"The culinary departments in these ships are among the most complete in the world," enthused *The Shipbuilder* of the kitchen facilities aboard the new *Olympic* and *Titanic*. The combined first-and-second-class kitchens which included pantries, bakeries, and sculleries were located on D Deck between the first-and-second-class dining saloons and were outfitted with all the latest culinary equipment. During the sinking of the *Titanic*, thousands of pots, pans, dishes, and kitchen utensils hurtled to the ocean floor.

(Top, right) A plate from the third-class dining saloon (two decks below the first-class saloon) bears the emblem of the White Star line on its rim.

(Above) This copper sink no doubt came from one of the sculleries or may have been used in the kitchen for washing pots and pans.

Corrosion seems to have had little effect on the copper saucepan and stock pot *(below, left, and center)*. A broken piece of sub-flooring has lodged itself inside the saucepan.

Pots similar to these can be seen in use in the Olympic's first-class galley in the photograph *(below, right)*.

One of the 96-foot range tops can be seen in the pantry picture *(opposite, top)* which shows jugs hanging from the ceiling and plates stacked on shelves.

A section of one of the range tops, showing oval openings where burner covers once sat, can be seen in the picture *(opposite, bottom, left)*.

(Above) This jug is like one of the many dozens suspended from racks in the pantry seen above.

(Below) Rows of serving bowls are still neatly stacked although the shelves that carried them to the bottom have been eaten away. *(Left)* Another set of kitchen shelves, probably made of metal, has survived.

The Smoking Rooms

When the *Titanic* collided with the iceberg on the quiet Sunday night of April 14, 1912, most of the passengers who had not gone to bed were enjoying a nightcap or cigar in the first-class smoking room on A Deck. With its Georgian-style mahogany paneling inlaid with mother-of-pearl, open fireplace, and large, stained-glass windows, it had the cozy atmosphere of a London men's club.

(Below) A fragment of stained glass from the debris field matches the lower left-hand quadrant of the stained glass window with the sailing ship in its center **(right)**.

(Right) This photograph from the Olympic *reveals how the first-class smoking room on the* Titanic *would have looked.*

(Right) A well-preserved decorative door panel from the second-class smoking room lies on the ocean floor. It appears in the door at the right of the photograph **(bottom, right)**.

(Below) A spittoon that may have come from one of the smoking rooms.

(Above, left) A piece of linoleum tile from the smoking room.

(Above, right) This light fixture is similar to those pictured on the ceiling except that it held five globes and was positioned along the side of the room.

(Left) A section of a baseboard vent similar to the one shown in the bottom right of the first-class smoking room. Metal floor vents with differing patterns were used throughout the ship.

Funnels

During the plunge to the bottom, the *Titanic* was shorn of her towering funnels. It was difficult to even locate evidence of them in the debris field. After examing ANGUS footage, the base of the number 4 funnel was found near the stern and parts from two other funnels were also identified.

(Above) The Titanic's *third and fourth funnels. Note the whistles at top similar to those (below).*

(Left) The base of the number 4 funnel. The inset diagram shows how it once appeared.

(Below) A water-main pressure pipe from the side of one of the funnels.

(Above) The last of the Olympic's *giant funnels leaving the shop.*

(Right) The four-foot-high steam whistles on the Titanic's *funnels were blown automatically once each minute during foggy weather.*

Staterooms

One of the goals of the White Star Line in building the *Olympic* and the *Titanic* was to make their passenger accommodations superior to anything previously seen afloat. From the period decor of the special B and C-Deck suites to the brass and mahogany of the berths in the second-and-third-class cabins, White Star brought a whole new world of passenger comfort to the transatlantic crossing.

(Top, right) Light from Alvin *gleams off brass fitted to one of the windows of the starboard B-Deck suites.*

(Above) The bed in this 1912 photograph of suite B-57 has a brass and enamel footboard identical to the one photographed (right).

(Below) This plan shows the layout of suite B-57.

(Above) Although not quite as luxurious as a first-class suite, this stateroom still has two marble-topped sinks, a porthole for ventilation, and a space heater next to the bed.

(Right) These taps on a broken piece of sink top match those shown (above).

(Below) This space heater closely resembles the one attached to the wall next to the bed (above).

(Above) Although surrounded by rusticles, the porthole for stateroom C-10 is unbroken and its brass fittings remain shiny.

(Right) Lacking a porthole, this two-berth, third-class cabin was provided with a ceiling fan similar to the one found by ANGUS (inset, right).

(Middle, right) This cabin wash basin matches the one in the third-class cabin (right). It is still attached to part of the stand that was tipped to drain the water.

(Right) *Shot from below on board the tender embarking passengers at Queenstown, this side view of the* Titanic *shows passengers and crew peering from over the side. At the very top is Captain Smith, looking down from the starboard wing of the bridge, photographed here for the last time.*

(Above, right) This sink tank surrounded by a chamber pot and a wash basin came from a four-berth third-class room like the one shown (above).

(Below) The white porcelain of this iron bathtub has been almost completely overtaken by rust, in stark contrast to its pristine appearance when new (right).

(Below) The sink of this first-class bathroom has a soap dish similar to the one shown (inset, right).

(Bottom, left) A tangle of faucets and pipes and an overturned toilet tank create an abstract sculpture on the ocean floor.

The Gymnasium

In its description of the gymnasium, *The Shipbuilder* notes that "...passengers can indulge in the action of horse-riding, cycling, boat-rowing etc. and obtain beneficial exercise, besides endless amusement." Situated on the Boat Deck near the starboard first-class entrance, the gymnasium provided a warm refuge on the night of the disaster for the Astors and others while they waited for the lifeboats to be loaded.

(Above) This photograph of the Olympic's gymnasium shows a mechanical horse on the left by the window.

(Below) In his white flannels, the Titanic's gym instructor T.W. McCawley demonstrates the rowing machine.

(Above) Lawrence Beesley (who was later the author of a survivor's account of the sinking), and a female friend try out the stationary bicycles.

The Gymnasium (cont'd)

(Below) An unidentified man stands by the large arched windows of the gym with the doorway and first-class entrance sign behind him.

(Right) The bracket that held the first-class entrance sign, the doorway (center), and a rusticle-encrusted gym window.

(Left) A girl rides the gym's electric camel. A fragment of the protective mesh that surrounded the machinery of this and other gym equipment can be seen in the window (bottom, left).

(Below, right) The arched windows of the gym are draped in rusticles in the three pictures at bottom.

The lever, at top, that operated one of the electric horses (right) still stands upright in the gym window pictured (center, right).

Lifeboats

Among the most powerful reminders of the *Titanic* tragedy seen from the *Alvin* were empty lifeboat davits still standing on the Boat Deck, providing a poignant recollection of the night they were in service for the first and last time.

*The same lifeboat davit pictured **(right)** can be clearly seen holding lifeboat No. 8 directly behind the passenger at the rail **(above)** in this picture taken aboard the* Titanic *at Queenstown.*

*A crab scuttles along the arm of a lifeboat davit **(right)** that last saw use at 1:10 a.m. on April 15, 1912 as it lowered lifeboat No. 8. Behind the still-intact block can be seen the outline of the upper Promenade Deck.*

The Story of Lifeboat No. 8

(Above) The Countess of Rothes, who took the tiller of lifeboat No. 8.

(Right) This photograph shows one of the Titanic's *lifeboats approaching the* Carpathia *in the early dawn.*

Lifeboat No. 8, the second port-side lifeboat to be lowered, carried 24 women and four crew members. It could have held Mrs. Isidor Straus, wife of the founder of Macy's department store, but she chose to stay with her elderly husband. Second Officer Lightoller loaded it with all the women and children he could see but there were still many empty places. The women on board begged Captain Smith to let some of the husbands come into the lifeboat to row. But "women and children only" was the order.

Lightoller put Seaman Jones in command and instructed him to row for the light that could be seen in the distance. Jones put the Countess of Rothes in charge of the tiller. "She had a lot to say so I put her to steering the boat." They rowed toward the light they assumed was a ship but it never seemed to get any closer. Mrs. J. Stuart White testified at the American investigation that "the women in our boat all rowed...the men did not know the first thing about it."

After the *Titanic* sank, Seaman Jones pro-

posed that they row back and try to rescue some of the people struggling in the water. But he was greeted with a wail of protest from most of the very women who earlier pleaded for their husbands. Seaman Jones is quoted as having said, "Ladies, if any of us are saved, remember I wanted to go back. I would rather drown with them than leave them."

Finally at around 3:30 in the morning the flash of a rocket was seen in the distance – the *Carpathia* was steaming to their rescue.

(Above) This illustration shows life-boat No. 15 nearly being lowered on top of lifeboat No. 13, which had drifted underneath while a crew member was trying to cut the tackle

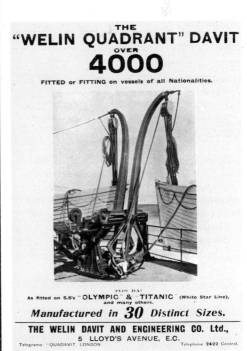

(Above) The Welin davits on board the Titanic *were designed to carry 32 lifeboats, but instead they held only 16 – the number legally required by the British Board of Trade.*

Boilers

For years, many historians assumed that the *Titanic*'s massive boilers broke loose and went crashing through the hull when the ship was upended. In fact, only five single-ended boilers from the boiler room closest to where the tear occurred were located in the debris field. The remaining 24 boilers presumably are still within the bow section of the wreck.

(Above) A man standing in Harland & Wolff's boiler shop is dwarfed by a row of 17-foot-high boilers. *(Far right)* A tin cup and a doorknob assembly rest by a circular furnace door on one of the boilers. *(Right)* This ANGUS photograph shows the full face of another of the five boilers.

(Below) This plan shows where the keel broke when the ship sank. The missing area in between is now in the debris field. The rectangles in boiler room No. 1 indicate the original locations of the five single-ended boilers.

(Inset, above, right) Lumps of coal from the breached coal bunkers are heavily strewn over areas of the debris field.

(Right) This photograph of stokers at work in another ship of the Titanic era gives an impression of the appearance of the Titanic's boiler rooms. A stoking shovel similar to the one found on the ocean floor by ANGUS *(left)* leans beside a pile of coal.

Passengers and Crew

"Did you see any bodies?" is one of the questions asked most often of those who took part in the 1986 *Titanic* expedition. Although any human remains have long since disappeared, the many poignant personal relics photographed by ANGUS are a strong reminder that the *Titanic* wreck is indeed a gravesite.

(Right) Expectant passengers prepare to board the Titanic at Queenstown, (now Cobh) Ireland, on a tender piled with mail bags.

(Below) This farewell message scribbled on a sheet torn out of a pocket calendar was handed to a woman entering one of the lifeboats.

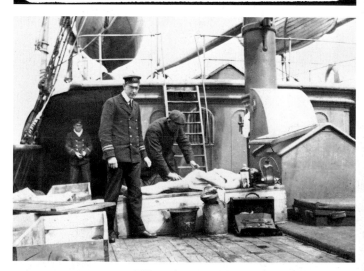

(Above) One of the 328 bodies recovered from the disaster site, by ships dispatched by the White Star Line, is here embalmed on the deck of the Mackay-Bennett.

(Right) A pair of shoes lying side by side is all that remains where a body once lay. Several pairs of shoes like these were photographed by ANGUS.

(Right) The April 27, 1912 issue of The Illustrated London News *used this crowd photograph of over 1500 people to demonstrate the horrifying loss of life represented by the* Titanic *disaster.*

(Below) Passengers walking on the second-class promenade three days before the disaster.

(Above, middle) This illustration shows a passenger with her luggage in a second-class cabin. (Left) The remains of an open suitcase, (above, left) a hairbrush and (above, right) a hand mirror were found among the Titanic's *debris.*

Aboard the Atlantis II, *I try to recreate what must have happened during the* Titanic's *sinking.*

CHAPTER 10
Titanic Reconsidered

PART OF MY ORIGINAL FASCINATION WITH THE *TITANIC* WAS THE SIMPLE FACT she was there. This vanished ship was the Mount Everest of my world – the deep ocean – a peak that no one had scaled. In the course of my long quest, the ship came to represent other things. As I became familiar with the story of her building and her fateful first voyage, I was caught in the grip of the story of human tragedy and by the larger morality tale of technological arrogance leading, as if inevitably, to disaster. It still seems an extraordinary coincidence that this particular ship – the largest and the finest passenger ship yet built – should have sunk on her maiden voyage. And the events of that night are so tantalizingly studded with what-ifs and might-have-beens. What if the ship had been traveling more slowly? What if the lookouts had been issued with binoculars? What if the moon had been out or the night had been less calm, the collision head-on instead of a glancing blow? What if the radio operator on the *Californian* had not gone to bed minutes before the *Titanic* sent out her first distress signal?

The *Titanic's* place in history and imagination is secure. In reflecting on our efforts, I find it interesting that in one key respect the *Titanic's* tragedy and our success in finding her are linked: technology. The technological achievements of the time made it possible to build this "practically unsinkable" ship. In turn, it was sophisticated technology in our day that allowed us to find and then photograph her in such stunning detail. In a sense our discovery of the *Titanic* brought one chapter of history to a close while at the same time opening another. After the *Titanic* sank, the world was never quite the same again. As a result of finding her, I believe the exploration of the deep ocean has moved into a new era.

The past and the future merged into one another two-and-a-half-miles beneath the waves. As our state-of-the-art robot peered down the *Titanic's* Grand Staircase, we were acutely aware of the human beings who had gone before. Finding and photographing the ship enabled us to test our new deep-sea imaging technology, which will allow us to explore many new submarine frontiers. It also gave us new information that allows us to reconsider some of the circumstances of the *Titanic's* final hours and to reconstruct what happened after she disappeared from sight – not to be seen again for almost three-quarters of a century.

The "Gash"

We'll probably never know for sure the exact nature of the damage inflicted by the iceberg on the starboard side of the *Titanic's* bow. Too much of it is buried too deep. But what we did see confirmed that the damage was nothing like the gash many had believed resulted from the impact with the ice. Of course, as some serious *Titanic* buffs knew – and

A 1912 artist's conception of the ice field the Titanic encountered on her last night.

as Walter Lord points out in his book *The Night Lives On* – a continuous gash or tear in the ship's hull was virtually a physical impossibility.

There were enough eyewitness accounts of where the water had entered the ship to conclude that damage to the hull extended from the first through the fifth of the ship's 16 watertight compartments, and slightly into the sixth – a distance of as much as 249 feet. At the British Inquiry in 1912, Edward Wilding, one of Harland & Wolff's naval architects, made some calculations on the damage. On the basis of the evidence given at the Inquiry about the times at which the water had reached various decks within the hull spaces affected, he figured that the ship took in about 16,000 cubic feet of water during the first 40 minutes. He then used a formula to calculate the total area of the openings and came up with about 12 square feet. Assuming a continuous gash about 200 feet in length (enough to account for all the evidence of damage), he divided this figure into the 12 square feet, yielding an average width of about three-quarters of an inch. This result naturally struck Wilding as highly unlikely. He therefore concluded that the damage to the hull was probably intermittent, not continuous.

Our examination of the wreck tends to confirm Wilding's conclusion – at least in part. But the ship as it now lies is buried deeply in the mud from the bow to just aft of the forward Well Deck, so we couldn't see most of the damaged area. All we can say with certainty is that the damage we were able to observe and photograph seemed quite minor: a number of separated and horizontally creased hull plates, the openings ranging from less than an inch to six inches in width. On the basis of the portion of the damaged hull we were able to see – from a point just aft of the Well Deck to its furthest aft point a couple of feet into boiler room No. 5 (roughly between hull frames 58 and 80 forward) – Wilding's hypothesis that the damage was intermittent seems to be supported.

His theory that the damage probably consisted of a number of punctures in the hull is not. What we were able to see was plates knocked apart at their riveted seams. If this was all that happened – a number of ruptures, not punctures, at the joints between the hull plates – it could still account for the water seen by the various witnesses. Of course, we couldn't see the bottom of the hull or the forward part of the bow where much damage occurred, so we'll never know for sure. But it seems likely that the outright punctures, if any, were few, and that the impact of the iceberg simply caused the riveted plates to separate, water rushing in through the resulting cracks.

A metallurgical engineer has written to me to suggest that the *Titan-*

(Above) The hull of the Olympic *looms in the graving dock, its riveted steel hull plates and bilge keel clearly visible.*

(Below) A mosaic constructed from stills taken from Alvin's *video footage shows what may be iceberg damage to the* Titanic's *starboard hull. Popped rivets can be seen as well as open seams.*

ic's steel hull may have been particularly susceptible to high stress at cold temperatures. Professor H. P. Leighly of the University of Missouri suggested that some turn-of-the-century steel became brittle below a certain temperature and would have begun to crack under pressure from the weight of the berg. This cracking would have progressed "catastrophically" – an apt word – causing rivets to pop from their sockets. It might even have contributed to the fact the ship broke in two. It's an intriguing theory and, indeed, some of our photos show portions of the hull that have cracked like an eggshell and blown apart – rather than tearing along the plate joints as one would expect.

Whatever the exact nature of her ice wound, it was enough to sink the ship – barely enough, given a design which allowed for the simultaneous flooding of the first four, but not all of the first five watertight compartments. It is important to stress that the tragedy should not be allowed to overshadow the fact that the *Titanic* was a relatively safe ship, not only according to the standards of her time but of ours. According to English naval architect K. C. Barnaby in his book *Some Ship Disasters and Their Causes*, "It is very doubtful if modern subdivision rules make present-day liners any safer than the *Titanic*." Indeed, from Barnaby's accounts of the sinking of the *Andrea Doria* in 1956 and the *Shillong* in 1957, it appears that damage fatal to these two ships would have proved no more than a nuisance to the *Titanic*. The fault lay not in her construction but in her failure to avoid hitting an iceberg at almost full speed. In defense of the ship's builders, it must also be said that no ship before had ever experienced a glancing blow such as the iceberg gave, running over a quarter of the ship's length. (Unless, of course, in the age before wireless when ships sank without a radioed distress call, none survived to tell the tale.) Nor has such an accident occurred since. The odds against this particular kind of collision happening were extremely high.

The True Position of the *Titanic* and the Question of the *Californian*

There is no longer any reason to keep the exact position of the *Titanic* wreck a secret. Originally I hoped to protect the wreck from treasure seekers, but too many people now know where it is, or could figure it out. Many of those associated with our two expeditions know the location and a number of aircraft equipped with navigational equipment flew over the site as we were working in 1986. And, if we are to give a thorough accounting of our findings, we are bound as responsible

(Above) Was this the iceberg that inflicted the fatal wound on the Titanic? *It was photographed near the scene of the sinking on April 15 (the next day) from the German ship* Prinz Adalbert. *Observers noted a scar of red paint along the berg's waterline.*

(Below) Here, the hull plates have been bent outward and separated by the passage of ice. (The pipe visible on the right fell during or after the impact with the bottom and lodged in the open seam.)

scientists to give out enough information so that another serious expedition could find the wreck with relative ease. But until that happens, the main interest the true position of the wreck holds is the possible insight it can provide into the controversy that still surrounds Captain Lord and his ship the *Californian*, believed by some to have been close enough to the scene that night to have rescued most if not all of those on board the *Titanic*.

Those who support Captain Lord and feel that the British and American inquiries made him into a convenient scapegoat are known in *Titanic* circles as "Lordites." They believe that the ship seen by some people aboard the *Titanic* while she sank was not the *Californian*, and that the ship the officers and men on the *Californian* saw was not the *Titanic*.

For readers unfamiliar with this aspect of the *Titanic* story, it can be briefly recapitulated. Around 10:20 p.m. (*Californian* time) on the night of April 14, 1912, the 6,000-ton steamer *Californian* stopped after being blocked by a large field of ice. She remained with her engines stopped, drifting with this ice for the rest of the night. Based on dead reckoning after a celestial sighting taken at sunset, Captain Lord calculated his position as 42°5'N, 50°7'W – or 19 miles north-northeast of the *Titanic*'s CQD position. It was not long after stopping that the radio operator on the *Californian* contacted the *Titanic* and attempted to give her an ice warning, but was rudely brushed off by Phillips who was busy "working Cape Race."

Around 11:00 p.m. the *Californian*'s third officer, Charles Groves, saw the lights of a steamer coming up from the southeast. At 11:30, the ship's radio officer went to bed, exhausted after a long day. At about 11:40, the stranger stopped. After midnight, white rockets were seen, just above or beyond the stopped ship. Both *Californian*'s Second Officer Stone and Apprentice Officer Gibson suspected that the strange ship was in trouble. Stone, now on watch, remarked to Gibson: "She seems to look queer now." Gibson took a look through the bridge binoculars and concurred: "She looks rather to have a big side out of the water." At 1:40 a.m., an eighth and final rocket was observed. Sometime after 2 a.m., the stranger disappeared completely, appearing to have steamed away to the southwest.

Despite various discrepancies between the testimony of those on board the *Titanic* and the *Californian* – for instance as to the times at which the rockets were fired – both the British and American inquiries

Captain Stanley Lord, master of the Californian, *as he looked at the time of the British Inquiry.*

Crew members of the Californian *pose outside the British Inquiry. Fourth and fifth from right, respectively, are Second Officer Stone and Apprentice Gibson, who were on watch when the white rockets were sighted.*

April 14, 11:00 p.m.

April 14, 11:40 p.m.

April 15, 2:20

held that the ship sighted from the *Californian* was indeed the *Titanic* and condemned Captain Lord's inaction as verging on criminal negligence. Lord had gone below after the ship steamed into view, but before the first rockets were sighted. When informed of the rockets, he had done nothing except to ask what color they were and tell his men to attempt to signal the vessel by Morse lamp. They received no answer. The radio operator was not wakened.

Captain Lord maintained to his dying day that a third ship, not the *Titanic*, was the one sighted from the *Californian*. He claimed that she didn't look like a passenger ship (one of the officers on board the *Californian* disagreed on this point) – and that she disappeared still afloat. Of course, even if he was right – and no mystery ship has ever been positively identified (although the Lordites claim to have turned up all sorts of ships in the vicinity that night) – the presence of a third ship does not change the fact that rockets were seen around the time the *Titanic* was firing them – rockets corresponding in character to distress rockets – and that no move was made to rouse the *Californian*'s sleeping wireless operator in order clarify the situation. (To justify the skipper's inaction, the Lordites point out that all sorts of rockets and flares were used in 1912, that procedures covering distress signals at sea were in a state of flux, and that some company signals were white.)

Until now, the two great unknowns in the tale were the actual position of the *Titanic* and the actual position of the *Californian*. At least now the *Titanic*'s final position can be stated with reasonable certainty – assuming the wreck lies pretty well directly below it. Since the stern and boilers likely fell almost straight down, these probably are closest to the ship's surface position at the time of sinking. The stern section sits on the ocean bottom at 49° 56' 54'' W, 41° 43' 35'' N and the center of the boiler field is at 49° 56' 49'' W, 41° 43' 32'' N. (The center of the bow section is located at 49° 56' 49'' W, 41° 43' 57'' N.) This means the *Titanic* sank roughly 13.5 miles east-southeast of her CQD position. She is just south of her calculated course, but well to the east. So the navigators on board overestimated the *Titanic*'s speed by roughly 2 knots: instead of traveling at 22.5 knots as Fourth Officer Boxhall had supposed, she was moving at about 20.5 knots. This position therefore puts the *Californian*'s logged position 21 miles to the north-northwest.

An interesting sidelight here – and part of the reason Jack Grimm didn't find the wreck – is that the actual position of the ship is five and a half miles northeast of where the first lifeboat was picked up by the

The *Titanic* and the *Californian*

Could the *Californian* have come to the *Titanic*'s rescue? Here are the main events in the story keyed to the illustrations at bottom.

April 14, 11:00 p.m. Steaming westward, the *Titanic* approaches a barrier of field ice and bergs several miles wide and stretching north and south some 400 miles. A half hour earlier the *Californian*, on a course slightly to the north, has encountered the ice barrier and stopped for the night.

April 14, 11:40 p.m. Traveling at a speed her navigator mistakenly believes to be more than 21 knots, the *Titanic* hits an iceberg and, as she begins to sink, radios a distress call giving her estimated position (pink cross). Shortly after midnight, the *Titanic* begins sending up white distress rockets. About the same time, officers on the *Californian* see white rockets fired, apparently from the ship they have observed steam up from the east. Defenders of Captain Lord have long propounded the theory that there may have been a mystery ship between the *Titanic* and the *Californian* and that it was this ship the *Californian* actually saw. (The large arrow indicates the direction of the *Californian*'s drift.)

April 15, 2:20 a.m. The *Titanic* sinks while the Cunard liner *Carpathia*, which had picked up the first distress call 58 miles to the southeast of the distress position, races to the rescue.

April 15, 4:10 a.m. Just after dawn, the *Carpathia* encounters the drifting lifeboats, but well to the southeast of the official position. Meanwhile, the *Californian* has learned of the sinking and headed for the reported position, arriving there about the same time as the *Mount Temple* and other ships. Captain Lord now steams for the *Carpathia*'s position, arriving after all the survivors have been rescued. The mystery ship, if it ever existed, has vanished.

Mount Temple

Carpathia

April 15, 4:10 a.m.

Carpathia. If the *Carpathia*'s lifeboat position was correct – and it too must be questioned in light of the inaccuracy of the *Titanic*'s own reckoning – then the lifeboats drifted, rowed, or were blown (by the wind that came up before dawn) southwest from the site of the sinking. Grimm, Spiess, and Ryan worked with the assumption that the wreck was very likely no further east than the lifeboat position, which was 50°W longitude. In fact, it was well to the east.

After she struck the iceberg, the *Titanic* undoubtedly drifted somewhat south and west in the current, but so likely did the *Californian*, already stopped in field ice. And since the *Californian* stopped sooner, she would already have drifted south from her course, given the current, nearer to the course the *Titanic* was on when she actually struck the berg. The drift that night was noted by, among others, Third Officer Groves.

The true position of the *Titanic* does cast the *Californian*'s stated position in a new light – but does not decisively weight the scales for or against Captain Lord. All witnesses on board the *Californian* agreed that the ship they saw "disappeared" to the southwest. But we now know that the *Californian*'s stated position was west, not east, of where the *Titanic* went down. As long as the old CQD position was accepted, this put the *Titanic* west of the *Californian* so that her sinking could have been mistaken as sailing off to the west. This appears to give the Lordites a boost.

But the *Titanic* was so far east of where she thought she was – at least in part because of the current that night – that we must consider the strong possibility that the *Californian* was also roughly on course, though south of it – but well east of her calculated position. In sum, given the new evidence, the weight of probability is that the *Californian* was not more, and probably less, than 21 miles from the *Titanic*'s position. Equally probable is that she was considerably further away than the five or six miles estimated by Boxhall and Lightoller on board the *Titanic* when they saw the lights of a ship to the north – causing them to send up distress rockets.

The Californian *seen from the* Carpathia *as she steams up from the southwest. After finding no trace of the* Titanic *in the area of the distress position, she had to sail south to get around the ice barrier before heading northeast to the* Carpathia's *position.*

This chart shows all we know for sure of the whereabouts of the Californian *and the* Titanic *during the crucial hours. The only reasonably certain positions are that of the* Titanic *wreck and that of the lifeboats when they were picked up. All else remains speculation.*

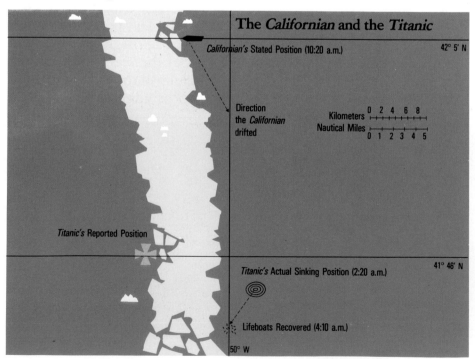

The *Californian* and the *Titanic*

Californian's Stated Position (10:20 a.m.)   42° 5' N

Direction the *Californian* drifted

Kilometers 0 2 4 6 8
Nautical Miles 0 1 2 3 4 5

Titanic's Reported Position

Titanic's Actual Sinking Position (2:20 a.m.)   41° 46' N

Lifeboats Recovered (4:10 a.m.)

50° W

All of this only supports the likelihood that the white rockets seen by the officers on board the *Californian* were indeed the same ones sent up by the *Titanic*. Whether the two ships were 21, 19, or even fewer miles apart, rockets could certainly be seen on a calm night over that distance. Later that morning, the *Californian* spotted rockets that almost surely came from the *Carpathia* as she raced to the rescue – considerably further away than the *Titanic* could ever have been.

Of course, the *Californian*'s true position will never be known and Captain Lord's case will never be settled. Even if he had wakened the radio operator at the first sighting of rockets, learned the *Titanic* was in distress, fired up his boilers, headed for the ship he could see, and discovered that it was indeed the sinking liner, he might have arrived in time only to fish a few half-dead bodies from the water. But the telling fact remains that he and his officers failed to act when action was called for.

The Break-Up

On the basis of many previous wrecks that have been found in shallow water – including large ships, older and more poorly built – most people held considerable hope that the *Titanic* was lying on the bottom in one piece. Certainly, until we discovered the *Titanic*, most people believed that she had left the surface intact. Although several witnesses testified to the contrary, this was the finding of the two inquiries in 1912, that's how she was pictured in the movies made about the tragedy and, until very recently, that's how all authors including Walter Lord have described the sinking. But Walter Lord changed his mind after examining in more detail the testimony given at the British and American inquiries, testimony ignored in the official reports. The inquiries gave particular credence to the testimony of Second Officer Lightoller, Colonel Archibald Gracie, and Third Officer Herbert Pitman, all of whom described the vessel as sinking whole. Lightoller, Gracie, and Lawrence Beesley (who also backed this version) also published authoritative accounts of the disaster. None of them, however, was in a good position to

(Left) On the way to New York aboard the Carpathia, *Jack Thayer described the ship breaking up while sinking to L.D. Skidmore of Brooklyn, who rendered this sketch. Although inaccurate in many ways, the sketch is interesting in that it shows the stern pivoting around before sinking.*

(Below) Jack Thayer as he looked in 1912 at age 16.

see the ship's final moments (Gracie was actually underwater and didn't see it at all). On the other hand, many eyewitnesses agreed that the ship in fact had broken in two, the bow plunging down while the stern briefly righted itself before turning almost vertical and sinking a few moments later.

Young Jack Thayer was one of these eyewitnesses. The drawings reproduced here were based on his description of the final plunge and executed from memory on the *Carpathia* as she carried the survivors toward New York.

Given the facts – a 1,970-foot distance between the two main pieces of the hull on the bottom, the cluster of additional wreckage in the vicinity of the stern, the absence of a skid mark between the two pieces, and the fact they are pointing in different directions and upright on the bottom – it does seem almost certain that the ship broke apart at or near the surface. As the bow sank and the stern rose ever higher out of the water, the pressure on the keel became increasingly unbearable until it finally snapped at a weak point in the structure between the third and fourth funnels in the area of the reciprocating engine room hatch. It was weak there because of the large open spaces in the decks above – the aft Grand Staircase and the air shaft from the reciprocating engine room. The ship did not break at either expansion joint – these were part of the superstructure and did not continue down into the hull of the ship. But the hull does show vertical buckling below the forward expansion joint, which therefore may have been a factor when the bow hit the bottom. The after expansion joint had nothing to do with the tearing of the hull below – that was caused when the keel bent and snapped – but as this happened the after expansion joint was probably the place where the superstructure first gave way.

The bow and stern sections that now lie on the bottom of the ocean account for most of the keel. The seven hull segments, 130 feet to 260 feet northeast, east, and southeast of the stern – which include at least one stack and possibly a second one – represent a V-shaped chunk of the hull and superstructure at a point just aft of amidships. The Boat Deck area aft of the number 2 funnel – where the large brass ship's compass platform stood – is still there but collapsed down at an angle. The compass itself has not been found.

(Top) A view of the port-side forward expansion joint at the edge of the Boat Deck.

(Above) The bilge keel with traces of red anti-fouling paint visible.

The Final Plunge

About 2:15 a.m., the stunned passengers of the *Titanic*'s lifeboats watched in horror as the ship's bow sank ever more deeply and the stern lifted further and further up out of the water until it reached an angle of at least 45° (according to eyewitness accounts). Then the bow broke off or split down (perhaps remaining for a few moments attached at the keel) ''with a sound like thunder,'' in the words of one survivor, and soon began its plunge. It was closely followed by various pieces of the ship that crashed into the ocean as the hull and superstructure pulled apart. The heavier these were the more quickly they fell. The keel definitely snapped right under the forward part of the reciprocating engine room (between stacks 3 and 4); and the two forward low-pressure cylinders, ahead of the break, must have fallen straight to the bottom like bombs, along with all the single-ended boilers from boiler room No. 1. The two high-pressure cylinders and the rest of the engines, aft of the break, remained bolted to their bedplates and survived the plunge and the impact with the bottom. The heaviest piece of all was the intact bow section, which had slowly filled with water over the previous two-and-a-half hours and now planed down and away from the surface still upright and at a slope, gathering speed. (Given enough depth to stabilize, all shipwrecks should rest on the bottom on their keels, since these are the heaviest parts of the ship.)

Some people have theorized that when the bow reached a certain angle the boilers broke loose from their fittings, crashed through the bulkheads and fell forward, possibly piercing the bow and dropping ahead of it down to the bottom. If this were even possible (naval architects generally have scoffed at the notion of boilers bursting through the *Titanic*'s hull) it now seems unlikely this occurred. Assuming the bow broke off at or close to the surface, it never reached the extreme angle of the stern and apparently never exceeded the maximum tilt it had when it left the surface. We know this because the condition of the bow indicates it didn't crash nose first almost vertically in the mud. Therefore the boilers couldn't have ended up in the forwardmost part of the bow. If they had crashed through the hull, we would certainly have found some of them on the ocean floor. (We found only five single-ended boilers which all came from the boiler room nearest to where the ship broke in two.)

Shortly before 2:20 a.m., while the bow began its descent, the stern temporarily righted itself, then turned sternmost straight up in the air before it too disappeared. What some people assumed was the whole ship standing almost on end was actually the stern alone. When the stern turned up, whatever was loose fell into the water – and can now be found in the debris field. Mysteriously, not much of what we found there can be definitely linked to the stern. What can be includes "Orex" spring and chain mattresses from third-class berths and metal-slat or ribbon mattresses from crew and steerage areas. The engine-room equipment we saw also came from the stern section, and we found cranes, bench supports and cowl vents from the stern decks.

All sorts of lighter debris from the damaged midsection floated down at various speeds, some of it taking several hours to reach the bottom. Some of it we found, some we didn't, but a sampling of the items included the following: tons of coal from the two breached boiler rooms and the bunkers on G Deck along with stoking shovels, pails, and other tools; pots, pans, and utensils from the kitchens; stacks of plates and casserole dishes; thousands of bottles of wine, champagne, and other beverages (including 15,000 bottles of ale and stout); patterned linoleum floor tiles from many different rooms; many sections of wrought-iron and gilt-bronze balustrades from the after Grand Staircase; crumpled sections of the leaded glass windows from the first-class dining-room and stained glass from the first-class smoking room; a wall sconce from the first-class lounge, light fixtures, bathtubs, washbasins, toilets, bedsprings, head and footboards, deck benches, dustpans, chamber pots, stateroom fans, milk containers, baseboard-vent grills, silver serving trays, hairbrushes, hand mirrors, and all sorts of passengers' effects – from items of clothing to toys and suitcases. If any of the cargo left its holds, the rain of debris may have included 30 cases of golf clubs and tennis rackets for Spalding, 800 cases of shelled walnuts, a cask of fine china for Tiffany's, a case of gloves for Marshall Field (the department store), 30,000 fresh eggs, and 76 cases of something called

Three ANGUS shots of debris. (Top) Two bathtubs sit side by side. (Middle) Some of the many thousands of wine bottles. (Bottom) An "Orex" spring and chain mattress from a third-class berth.

The Break-Up and the Final Plunge

These drawings represent a likely scenario – based on a careful study of the evidence – of the *Titanic*'s break-up and fall to the ocean floor.

STEP 1

By around 1:00 a.m. ship's time, about an hour and a half after the collision, the *Titanic* is well down at the bow. Water floods one compartment after another, spilling aft over the top of bulkheads.

STEP 2

At about 2:17 a.m., the rate of flooding suddenly increases dramatically, and the ship takes a lurch downward. As the bridge plunges under, a wave washes aft. The number 1 funnel collapses forward and the bridge and forward officers' quarters collapse under the water pressure. Shortly after, water washes over the forward Grand Staircase roof and the weight of it causes the roof to implode.

STEP 3

According to Jack Thayer and other witnesses who watched the *Titanic*'s final minutes, the stern rose ever higher out of the water until it was at an angle of 45° or more. Like all ships, the *Titanic* was designed to easily withstand normal seagoing stresses. Now with her stern high out of the water, the *Titanic*'s keel suffers a prolonged stress of much greater force than the hull was designed to withstand. To make matters worse, the force is concentrated at the structurally weakest position – in the area of the reciprocating-engine-room hatch.

STEP 4

Just before sinking, amidst a great noise, witnesses see the stern appear to right itself. Almost certainly this is when the hull breaks in two between the third and the fourth funnel. The stern settles back temporarily. As the bow tears away, it rips off some of the lower hull of the stern section. Perhaps the bow hangs on for a short while at the keel before separating. As the ship breaks, the upper decks pull in on each other and begin to collapse downward. Number 3 funnel breaks off. Number 4 funnel falls aft as the first-class smoking room is pulled apart.

STEP 5

The stern settles deeper as it floods. Debris from the break filters down – boilers, pieces of the hull, funnels, etc. The bow, now completely broken off from the stern, levels slightly as it begins its descent and accelerates toward the bottom. The force of water rushing past wrenches the foremast aft and sweeps the forecrane jibs off their crutches and aft against the superstructure. (The mast bends very neatly at the Forecastle Deck level, but breaks where it falls on the port bridge area.) On the bridge, the wheelhouse is swept away, probably after being knocked loose by either the mast or the falling funnel.

STEP 6

As the stern rights itself, it pivots around. The heavy engines forward cause the hull to assume an increasingly steep angle until it eventually points nearly straight up. Remarkably, it remains in this attitude for a minute or more, before slowly descending out of sight.

STEP 7

During the initial plunge – as the stern sinks rapidly – the force of water scooping under the Poop Deck causes it to tear up and peel backward on itself. Perhaps the cranes are torn away by the rush of water. After the stern glides beneath the surface, it soon assumes a more level attitude, its heavy lower hull leading the way to the bottom.

STEP 8

While the stern falls more or less straight down like a lead weight, possibly rotating slowly as it falls, the bow probably planes gently away at a slight downward angle while accelerating at a much faster rate toward the bottom. (The line of the bow's descent is at a 12° angle from the vertical descent path of the stern.) Of course, it's possible the bow didn't plane continuously away from the surface while speeding downward, but waffled back and forth like a falling leaf, seeking equilibrium between the point of minimum drag (the forward knife edge) and the point of maximum weight (the heavy mid-section). But the fact that it seems to have hit the bottom at a slight forward incline argues against this theory. No one will ever know.

STEP 9

(A) The bow must have plowed into the bottom at a shallow angle with enough forward momentum to cause a "stubbed toe" effect, buckling the hull downward in two places. It could not have struck the bottom at a very steep angle or the superstructure would have sheared off.) As this happens, the bow assumes an approximate 6° bend just forward of the bridge and another 3-1/2°-to-4° buckle under the expansion joint. The braking action of the bow digging deep into the sediment (over 60 feet at the anchors) causes the anchor crane to swing around forward. Huge clouds of silt billow up as the bottom is plowed away and chunks of soft mud are thrown aside.

(B) As the after part of the bow section now slams down into the mud, the decks near the tear in the hull collapse further.

(A)

(B)

STEP 10

The stern comes crashing straight down, with other heavy debris such as engine cylinders and boilers in close proximity. It slams into the bottom with such force that the decks compress one upon another and the shell plating and framing crumple and splay out from the hull. The stern section buries itself 45 to 50 feet at the rudder. It has landed disoriented from the bow by some 180°. For the next several hours, lighter debris drifts down to settle in the vicinity of the wreck and to the south where it is carried by the current.

dragon's blood (probably a patent medicine).

These items all fell or drifted in the wake of the plummeting stern – which most likely fell straight down. Unlike the bow, the stern hadn't filled with water before it began its plunge. After the break, water began to pour in, probably crushing the weaker bulkheads and wreaking considerable havoc in the interior. Air escaping from the stern may have contributed to the fact that the Poop Deck peeled up and over onto itself. But this may have been the result of the force of the water rushing aft and scooping under the deck as the stern plunged into the ocean. As the stern accelerated straight down, it probably turned slowly (something subs like *Alvin* do during their free-fall descent), accounting for its orientation away from the bow on the bottom.

Any estimate of the maximum speed of the *Titanic*'s descent is largely speculative. There are simply too many variables involved. Based on the evidence of a later ship that was scuttled and clocked during its fall, the two large hull sections may have reached a speed of as much as 25 or 30 miles an hour. Depending on how quickly that speed was reached they could have fallen in as little as six minutes. We simply don't know enough about the weight of the two big hull pieces or the way their shape and surface area would have slowed or aided the speed of the plunge – but it probably took at least several minutes for these huge hull pieces to reach their terminal or maximum falling velocity.

The port-side officers' quarters just aft of the "peel."

The bow probably hit before the stern, prow first and at a slight angle, its tremendous forward and downward momentum driving it deep into the mud to a depth of over 65 feet at the anchors, the plowing action bending and buckling the forward part of the bow section downward. Seconds later, after the bow had dug in, the part aft of the forward expansion joint slammed down into the bottom, possibly accounting for some additional "tweaking" in the hull at a point beneath the expansion joint. The impact worsened the damage caused by the surface break-up of the hull, the decks inside the aftermost part of the bow section collapsing on top of each other like a stack of pancakes.

Writer Charles Pellegrino, who has been working on his own book about the *Titanic*, has a plausible theory that may help to account for the devastation of the area around the bridge, which, when I first saw it, looked to me as if it had been squashed by a giant's fist. A large, heavy object accelerating through water at the speed of the bow would create a sort of slipstream effect similar to an airplane passing through air. When the bow abruptly stopped dead, the water following it would have come crashing down, most powerfully at the center of the bow section – exactly where the bridge was. This "down blast" of water may partly explain the current state of the wreck.

Alternatively, the damage in the area of the officers' quarters may have happened near the surface. Some eyewitnesses noted a sudden lurch just as the bridge was dipping under the water. If the bow sank rapidly for a few seconds when this lurch occurred, the wave of water rushing aft might have flattened the bridge area fairly symmetrically – the walls peeling outward, the roofs of the still water-free cabins smashing down.

A few minutes after the bow came to rest on the bottom, the stern hit even harder, about 1,970 feet to the south, sinking about 45 feet into the mud. Since it had already been weakened by the havoc caused by the water rushing in at or near the surface, the effect of the impact of the stern with the bottom was more devastating as the upper decks all pancaked down. (Any down blast would have abetted this process.) The entire deck area of the stern is now utter devastation. Most of that damage happened both at the start of the plunge and at the moment of impact.

For the next several hours, pieces of debris fell; the lighter ones carried by the below-surface current southeast, but most settling near the stern. First, the low-pressure cylinders, the boilers, and the other heavier pieces of wreckage crashed into the bottom mud – then, a shower of medium-heavy debris; and, finally, the lightest items such as shoes, tea cups, perhaps a pack of waterlogged playing cards fluttering down. By the time the survivors were all on board the *Carpathia* six hours later, most of the falling objects had settled on the muddy bottom. Some objects, including bodies (which sink once the lungs fill with water), may have floated awhile before falling to the sea floor far from the original wreck site. But some human beings, those without lifevests who drowned quickly or were trapped inside the sinking hull and escaped too late, would have sunk down to join the debris. (In cold deep water, gas cannot form and lift the body back to the surface.)

The trail of debris and wreckage that we actually found on the bottom represents in fact two overlapping debris fields – one trailing southeast from the bow to the area of the stern; one trailing southeast from the area of the stern. Each of these fields is between 2,000 and 2,600 feet long – less than the mile I was expecting. When you add them together they are about a mile long, however. Because the two fields overlap in the area of the stern, you get a combination of heavy and light debris there.

The Passing Years

The deep ocean is a quiet and relatively stable place. After the *Titanic*'s tumultuous final hours she found herself at a depth of 12,460 feet in an environment where most changes happen over decades rather than days. First to disappear would have been any soft organic material such as food – then human bodies, the flesh and bones rapidly devoured by bottom-feeding fish and crustaceans (any bones they missed would soon have been dissolved by the salt water). Clothing would have taken much longer, probably years. In some cases leather shoes have survived, sitting side by side where once a body rested. Perhaps the chemicals used in the shoe-tanning process are unappetizing to bacteria.

At some point, weeks or months later, wood-boring molluscs, the larvae of which were probably borne by the submarine currents, found their way to the wreck. They settled, metamorphosed and then dined on the soft pine wood of the *Titanic*'s decks and gradually migrated inside the openings in the hull. Within a few years, the decks were mostly eaten away and, inside the ship, the lavish wood furniture, fine carvings, elaborate tapestries, and Axminster carpets were all but gone, along with the wood paneling and the oak banisters of the grand staircases.

These molluscs play an important role in deep-submarine ecology, breaking down wood and thus increasing the cycling of nutrients. But by the time we visited the ship, these creatures were likely dead and gone; all that was left were the calcareous tubes characteristic of a particular species of wood-borer – the one that likely played the major

The Debris Field
Where debris is located near the severed stern section

Stack of davits

Stern

Well-Deck section

Possible funnel section

Galley section

Base of number 4 funnel

Meters
0 20 40 60 80 100

▲ Low-Pressure Cylinder
● Crane
■ Safe
○ Boiler
⌀ Large Debris

role in devouring the ship. While these molluscs thrived, so did the species of fish and crustaceans that prey on them, making the ship an underwater oasis.

We can only speculate as to why some of the wood on the *Titanic* and in the debris field remained intact. Teak, being a very dense wood, is generally resistant to the borers, and teak has survived rather well on the *Titanic*. All teak railings, topcourses, and roof trim appeared to be in almost mint condition. But these creatures don't generally respect wood that has been treated with anti-weathering material; so why was that set of stairs we saw so well preserved? Perhaps it, too, was teak. Not long ago, an ancient ship buried under Mediterannean bottom mud was found with much wood intact. Once uncovered, the wood remained impervious to wood-borers while fresh wood left nearby was devoured. Apparently something happens when the wood is buried, but we don't know what. And since the wood on the *Titanic* was never covered, this can't explain the selective preservation there.

Other types of organisms, such as bacteria and other tiny animals, would have attacked the remaining organic material on the ship. Unlike the wood, most of these items – such as clothing – would have deteriorated very slowly: mattresses (probably made of horsehair), bed linen, the cloth body of a doll. Thus, as the years passed, most of the organic contents of the ship and the debris field gradually disappeared and the *Titanic* became an even quieter place. But she continued to be a haven for a few deep-ocean creatures, mainly galathean crabs, starfish, and various bottom-dwelling rat-tail fish, who found shelter in the roomy wreck.

The main exception to all this was and will continue to be the iron-eating bacteria responsible for the rusticles. These are tiny organisms that use ferrous iron as an inorganic source of energy; they oxidize the iron and leave rust particles behind as a waste product. Because conditions in the deep ocean are not acidic enough to suit these bacteria, they manufacture a more favorable environment in which to live. They do this by secreting a highly viscous slime that protects them from the surrounding seawater. As the slime is produced, it flows outward and away from the metal surface, carrying with it dead cells and ferric oxides (rust) and hydroxides. These are what form the rusticles. They grow and grow until, if left undisturbed, they eventually fall off from own weight.

Since these rusticles are very fragile – they broke off when touched by *JJ* or *Alvin*, or even when disturbed by the wake of our little sub – they are testimony to the stability and tranquility of the deep-ocean environment. It is unclear just how much damage the iron-eating bacteria have done over the years. When we brushed them away, the steel underneath seemed in quite good shape – but this is partly because, unlike chemical oxidation, bacterial oxidation actually "cleans" the metal, leaving a smooth surface. Woods Hole's expert on iron bacteria, Dr. Holger Jannasch, thinks the ship has probably already corroded to the point that any attempt to raise her would result in the hull breaking into many pieces.

On November 18, 1929, 17 years after the sinking, the general area where the *Titanic* rests was rocked by the Grand Banks Earthquake. This far from the epicenter, whatever mudslide the tremor set off was blocked by *Titanic* Canyon, saving the wreck from possible burial. We

(Top) Rusticles formed by iron-eating bacteria now grace the hawsepipe opening for the center anchor at the tip of the bow.

(Above) Most of the wood on the Titanic *had disappeared by the time we found her. This asbestos-backed board placed in the ocean for slightly over a year shows what can happen in such a short time. Wood-borers have gnawed much of it away leaving only their hard kernels, or tubes, behind.*

have no way of knowing what damage, if any, the quake did to the ship, but it does not seem to have done much. We do know that we could see many things that looked "as if" they hadn't moved since the day of the sinking. The cup that still rests on the boiler is a good example.

Since the earthquake, apart from the rust bacteria (and perhaps bacteria that have gradually worked their way deep inside the ship), the *Titanic* has remained undisturbed and virtually a dead place. Only a few creatures of the dark lurk in her corners and crevices.

Remaining Questions

We now know a great deal about the *Titanic*. We can plausibly reconstruct what happened as she sank and settled. But mysteries remain. A number of artifacts that we should have found easily either escaped our notice or were hidden from view. Where, for instance, is the big brass compass platform that must have fallen off the top deck between number 2 and number 3 funnels? It ought to have survived in good shape, yet we found no trace of it. And while we found numerous sections of wrought-iron and gilt balustrade from the aft Grand Staircase, along with floor tiles from that area, where is the famous large bronze statue of a boy holding a light standard that stood at the B-Deck landing? It was one of two nearly identical statues, the other on the A-Deck landing of the forward staircase. Also missing was any sign of the ship's bells, bridge instruments, first-class chinaware, or small silver items such as knives and forks. Surprisingly, we saw very little that came from the first-class smoking room, which was right under the fourth funnel. And there is precious little from the stern, which ought to have emptied all sorts of articles when it turned end up before it plunged.

Who knows what we might find if we could walk the corridors of the wreck at will? Perhaps the wrought-iron grillwork of the first-class elevator doors is still in place. And maybe in the first-class dining saloon on D Deck we might still see the remnants of the breakfast settings scattered on the floor. The innards of the piano that graced the first-class reception room are probably still there though badly out of tune. And down inside the forward cargo hatches are the remains of the Renault and all sorts of other freight – maybe even the fabled *Rubaiyat* with its cover studded with emeralds and rubies. Maybe fish now swim in the *Titanic*'s small swimming pool; perhaps the tiles still gleam inside the Turkish Baths. Likely no one will ever know.

The Future – Sanctuary or Salvage?

As long as the wreck is left unmolested by treasure-hunters, the *Titanic* won't appear to change much in my lifetime. The prevailing currents, which gave us so much trouble on some dives, will continue to build up a sediment around the "windward" sides of the large pieces of wreckage, but complete burial under sediments falling from above would take less than a thousand years for the smaller pieces, nearly one million years for the two large hull sections. Before then, iron-eating bacteria would have finished their demolition work. Sedimentary deposition this far out in the ocean is very slow and even the smallest objects we saw, such as the doll's head, showed very little evidence of burial despite the passage of 75 years. Since the ship sits in an area of underwater sand dunes, the surrounding terrain will shift as the dunes migrate, revealing currently buried pieces of debris and covering up things we saw.

(Top) Just behind young Jack Odell rises the impressive compass platform.

(Above) The bronze cherub statue from the Grand Staircase as it looked in 1912.

In the longer term, the rusticle-forming bacteria will continue to do their work. Gradually, the ship will be eaten away until its remaining structural integrity is threatened. My colleague Holger Jannasch predicts that in another 75 years, perhaps a little longer, the R.M.S. *Titanic* will likely be a jumble of rubble, its noble bow section only a memory. Certain things will still be there to see – mostly in the debris field: ceramic, bronze, and brass remains; lumps of coal. But it will not be a pretty sight.

For now, the greatest threat to the *Titanic* clearly comes from man, particularly in the form of crude dredging operations. There are all sorts of fishing boats and drill ships that could be hired to go out to the site and attempt to bring up pieces of wreckage. But most artifacts of any value lie scattered in the debris field and would have to be salvaged by a sub with a mechanical arm. But apart from *Alvin* there are only two submarines that could dive this deep – the U.S. Navy's *Sea Cliff*, and France's *Nautile*.

The legislation passed by the United States Congress and signed into law by the President, calling for the wreck to be made an international memorial and left unmolested, should discourage most treasure-seekers. At least it guarantees them bad publicity. My simple wish is that any who do mount new expeditions to visit the wreck will respect the site as I have.

Now that the wreck's true position is known, its ownership could well become an issue. It lies within the offshore waters claimed by Canada, a claim not recognized by the United States. Fortunately, the Canadian government has strongly indicated it would oppose salvage. But in whatever jurisdiction the wreck falls, the *Titanic* belongs to all of us.

Looking Back

With the advantage of hindsight we can see that the sinking of the *Titanic* came to represent an historical turning point. It's easy to imagine the first-class passengers gathered in the smoking room during the ship's maiden voyage contemplating the state of the world and the progress of science with a rather self-satisfied air. Their world was at peace and man had seemingly triumphed over nature. The very ship they were sailing on was physical justification for their optimism, the perfect backdrop for their Edwardian smugness.

The loss of the *Titanic* was as traumatic to the people of that time as the assassination of John F. Kennedy was to ours. Some kind of innocence seemed lost for good. People's faith in the natural order of things was shaken. The most recent and closest parallel of our day is unquestionably the loss of the space shuttle *Challenger*. In both cases, there was unjustified overconfidence in technology. In both, the power of the natural environment was underestimated. And, in both cases, this led to negligence by those in high command. Apparently, we still have something to learn from the *Titanic*.

Finding and filming the *Titanic* doesn't compare in historical importance with the tragedy of 1912, but it represents a turning point of another sort. For one thing, it demonstrated the effectiveness of a visual search in deep water. As a result of our success, it seems likely that future searches for sunken wrecks will at the very least combine acoustic and visual imaging. Sonar search works best on a flat featureless bottom. But the ocean floor is complex, full of mountains and valleys which present

This portrait of Alvin *taken by* Jason Jr. *two and a half miles down, points to the future of video exploration of the deep ocean.*

many false acoustic targets. In order to ensure complete coverage with sonar, you must overlap ground covered and, even then, you can't be a hundred percent sure about what you've seen or missed. Only a camera's eye can tell you that a particular sonar target is really the thing you're looking for.

More important than any contribution to underwater search techniques, however, the video exploration of the *Titanic* was a pioneering super hi-tech job done in the deep sea. For the first time, a remotely operated vehicle was crucial to the success of a deep undersea mission. Seventy-five years from now, I'd like to be around to find out just how important this scientific achievement appears. Will we look back and see the *Titanic* expedition as the beginning of genuine exploration of the deep? So far, man has barely visited the two-thirds of the earth covered with seawater and these regions remain mysterious at best.

The oceans represent the last truly unexplored areas of our planet. With the exception of a few obscure tracts of tropical rainforest and a few remote mountain peaks, human beings have pretty thoroughly visited the earth's exposed and dry surface. Climbing Mount Everest – though still dangerous enough – has practically become routine. If you've got the money, you can take a daytrip to the North Pole. But our knowledge of the deep ocean remains primitive. For true adventure we must look either to outer space or inner space, that unknown world beneath the waters.

We've expended so much scientific energy and money on the exploration of outer space in comparision to the discovery and exploration of our own planet. In part, we've taken the seas for granted. In part, oceanography has never captured the public's imagination in the way the conquest of space has – and it will likely never be as glamorous. But there are very good reasons for increasing our knowledge of the oceans.

The most obvious of these is that water is both the most abundant and the most precious substance on earth, the blood of our planet. Understanding the whole ocean system is increasingly essential because of the rapid dissemination of pollutants. We are poisoning that life blood. The oceans determine our weather, affect the amount of oxygen we breathe, and conceal beneath them the dynamic forces that shape and modify our planet.

There are other reasons. As long as there are global rivalries between superpowers, the seas will be of great strategic importance and deep-sea exploration will have military significance. Also, the sea may one day become a major source of resources, although this possibility seems to be receding as we become less dependent on primary metals.

Our *Titanic* expeditions also demonstrated to the doubters that science and showmanship can make a successful mix. Traditionally, scientists have been interested in science, not publicity. Sometimes it has seemed that they've gone out of their way to keep their discoveries from the public. But I believe showmanship – properly exercised – can help science achieve its goals. If you can get the public interested, and get their support, then it's much easier to raise the money for your research.

Perhaps in a few generations the *Titanic* will be forgotten by all but a few – but somehow I doubt it. Long after her hull has decayed to rubble, I have a feeling people will still be drawn to the events of the night of April 14, 1912.

CHAPTER 11

Epilogue to the 1989 Edition

W HEN I SAILED FROM THE *TITANIC* WRECK SITE IN AUGUST 1986, I DID SO with the reasonable hope that the ship's last resting place would be left undisturbed. In the first edition of this book, I wrote: "My simple wish is that any who do mount new expeditions to visit the wreck will respect the site as I have." However, the lure of *Titanic* "treasure" proved even stronger than I guessed. And now a new chapter of *Titanic* history must be written. As it has always been with this most mesmerizing of lost ships, this latest episode is full of contradictions and human foibles — not to mention the competing demands of science and sensationalism.

The 1987 *Titanic* Expedition
In August 1987, an impressive new expedition arrived at the *Titanic* site. A number of American investors had formed a consortium with France's IFREMER, my partners in the 1985 discovery. This organization's declared purpose was to salvage artifacts from the wreck. IFREMER provided their deep submersible *Nautile*, as well as their video and salvaging technology and considerable oceanographic expertise. The Americans provided the money — an enormous amount of money, roughly $6 million according to George Tulloch, one of the organizers.   In 1986, we had one ship, the *Atlantis II*, and could afford a mere 12 days on the site. During our 11 dives in *Alvin*, we had a total of 33 hours to investigate the wreck and the debris field. The 1987 *Titanic* expedition had two ships and stayed 54 days on site, making 32 dives in all and spending well over 200 hours on the ocean floor. In short, the 1987 expedition had more than six times as many hours on the bottom, but most of this was used up in the laborious process of deep-ocean salvage.

If you're a *Titanic* buff, you probably watched the news reports of the salvage with very mixed emotions. On the one hand, each new object that was raised from the deep carried strong associations with the 1912 tragedy: a ship's telephone (was this the one used by the lookouts to call the bridge when the iceberg was sighted?); an officer's megaphone (did Captain Smith use this bullhorn to issue the order to "abandon ship" or to admonish his crew, "Be British"?); the ship's bell from the crow's nest (this sounded three clangs when the iceberg was sighted). On the other hand, each relic removed from its deep-sea resting place lost some of its meaning and mystery and diminished the dignity of the wreck we had found.

I have argued long and hard that the *Titanic* is a gravesite that should have been left undisturbed, except by visitors with even better video cameras who would come to explore and wonder. Whether or not one agrees that salvage was wrong, it has to be admitted that a teacup brought to the surface and restored to "mint condition" with its red

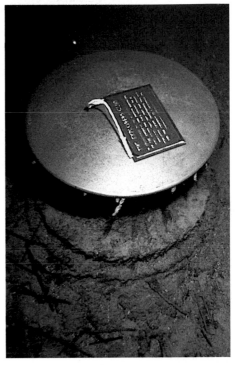

This is the Explorers' Club plaque we left on a bow capstan. We have no way of knowing if it was disturbed during the 1987 Titanic *expedition.*

White Star Line insignia gleaming as good as new is little more than a teacup. However, a teacup resting on a boiler at the bottom of the ocean, as if set there moments ago, is a moving reminder of the *Titanic*'s fate. Personally I'd rather see that teacup left where it is.

The *Titanic* is a place of historical importance but not archeological significance. Sure, people would pay handsomely to own a *Titanic* fork or plate or silver tray — but their interest is sentimental, not scientific. The objects raised revealed precious little that was new or thought-provoking. And the act of raising them altered the site irrevocably. It will never again be as we found it.

Worst of all, the 1987 salvagers did serious physical damage to the hull in their eagerness to bring back booty. This, despite the promises from those involved that the ship itself would not be harmed in any way. Yet as we watched the television special aired from Paris, ''Return to the *Titanic*... Live,'' the damage was obvious. The mast light that lay on the table of artifacts next to host Telly Savalas had been ripped from the foremast (it was firmly attached when I last saw it), and the section of the foremast that used to continue above the Boat Deck (see painting on page 127) has been crushed flat — presumably in this effort. Rigging hanging from the forecastle was cut, perhaps so the *Nautile* could get close enough to clean the *Titanic*'s name on the port bow. A block that was still dangling forlornly from a davit lying on the bridge is missing, as is part of the port Boat Deck bulwark. Most tragic of all, the crow's nest is now gone, utterly destroyed, perhaps in the act of getting at the ship's telephone that was inside. All this was visible to us in just the few minutes of video that have been made available. Who knows what damage was done that we haven't seen?

This cartoon by James Morin appeared in the Miami Herald *when the 1987 expedition began raising artifacts from the wreck site.*

New Discoveries

When it was finally over, the French and their American colleagues had raised something like 900 artifacts from the bottom. And their cameras had discovered some new facts about the state of the wreck. The story of the 1987 expedition is not all bad. Alongside the damage and the disrespect, these discoveries must also be given their due.

Most of the items brought to the surface were things we had seen and photographed in 1986. But a few of them our cameras had missed. And some were quite startling. One of the most exciting finds was the bronze cherub — according to one account only its foot was visible sticking above the bottom mud. This engaging little fellow, who held a lamp in his right hand, presumably graced the B-Deck landing of the aft first-class staircase (see page 172). But this cherub, approximately 18 inches tall, is considerably smaller than those on *Titanic*'s sister ship *Olympic*, which were over three feet tall. Perhaps the *Titanic*'s cherubs were scaled down by the ship's decorators. Possibly there was an additional smaller cherub on the C-Deck landing. In any event, this may be further evidence that the *Titanic* was not as identical to the *Olympic* as has generally been thought.

Another surprise was the cache of elegant first-class Spode Copeland's china with its blue and gold pattern. Historians had no idea until now that this beautiful pattern was used on the ship.

Of greatest interest to those hoping for genuine valuables was the leather Gladstone bag stuffed with jewelry, U.S. banknotes and gold coins, in all worth several thousand dollars even without their *Titanic*

41° 43′ 55″ N.

Depth 3795 m.

Bow Section

Depth 3790 m.

Depth 3795 m.

41° 43′ 45″ N.

⑩

⑦

41° 43′ 35″ N.

⑨

⑤

⑧

⑥

Stern Section

④

⑨

②

Depth 3800 m.

⑪

①①

①

⑥

②

Depth 3785 m.

②

②

④

③

⑩

49° 57′ 00″ W.

⑤

②

⑩

Scattered Coal

Depth 3795 m.

Scattered Coal

Depth 3790 m.

49° 56′ 45″ W.

NORTH

The Wreck Site

This painting depicts the Titanic
*wreck site as we found it, spread out on a
gently sloping area of ocean floor (the slope is right
to left in the illustration). The numbers indicate the
original locations of debris objects, although many of them were
removed in 1987.*

association. From the initials "RLB" found on several of the items inside. it was initially theorized that this satchel belonged to first-class passenger Richard L. Beckwith, a socially prominent executive at a New York real estate firm. But the finders now believe that whomever the satchel belonged to, it wasn't Beckwith. The items found inside, which include a bracelet bearing the name "Amy" in small diamonds and a member's badge from a London Masonic temple, are simply too varied to have belonged to one person. Besides, if it was Beckwith's, why didn't he bring it with him when he left the ship? It seems more likely that the bag was used by a thief who took advantage of the confusion as the ship was sinking to loot the first class staterooms, or possibly one of the ship's safes.

Reportedly, three ship's telegraphs were also salvaged, instruments used to communicate between the bridge and the engine room. Only one of these came from the captain's bridge; the other two are from the docking bridge at the stern and were not in use at the time of the accident. Much was made of the fact that the engine room response indicator arrows of all three telegraphs were discovered to be in the "slow ahead" position. This, the finders say, may be the true reason why the *Titanic* was found so far from where she was expected to be — she never completely stopped! But this is a far-fetched theory that flies in the face of common sense and all eyewitness accounts. Lifeboats would never have been launched if the ship were still moving.

Actually, this type of telegraph worked on a system of pulleys and sprockets, and the arrows were surely yanked from their last positions

① *Cargo cranes (see p. 223).*
② *Boilers (see pp. 82, 190, 191, 223).*
③ *Foundation for number 4 funnel (see pp. 180 and 216).*
④ *Other funnel sections.*
⑤ *Low-pressure cylinders.*
⑥ *Well Deck section with bitts (bollards) attached.*
⑦ *Single set of davits.*
⑧ *Tangle of davits (see p. 223).*
⑨ *Ship's wheel pedestal (see p. 222).*
⑩ *Telegraph (see pp. 222, 223).*
⑪ *The safe (see pp. 152, 216, and 219).*

215

The Stern From Starboard

This new painting by Ken Marschall shows the massive destruction of the *Titanic's* stern section as viewed looking aft on the starboard side. The stern appears to have struck the bottom with such force that the decks collapsed down on each other and the hull literally blew apart. Particularly striking are the two high-pressure cylinders from the reciprocating engines that are still upright and in position despite the fact the ship broke in two at this spot. Underneath the folded back Poop Deck, where the *Titanic's* passengers huddled in the final moments of the tragedy, the interior remains of the third-class smoking room and staircase now lie open to view.

1. *Second-class purser's safe discovered in 1986 and raised in 1987 (see pp. 152, 219).*
2. *Hull shell plating.*
3. *Foundation for No. 4 funnel (see p. 180).*
4. *High-pressure cylinders of reciprocating engines (see p. 224).*
5. *Boilers (see pp. 190-91 and p. 223).*
6. *Underside of decking peeled back aft.*
7. *Exposed interior decks where shell plating has blown away from hull.*
8. *Turbine engine room.*
9. *Aft davit for boat No. 16, lying down on the deck.*
10. *Second-class entrance deck house (see p. 169).*
11. *Main mast.*
12. *Underside of Boat Deck above A-Deck promenade, now peeled up and aft and hanging over the side.*
13. *A-Deck cargo crane (see p. 17 and p. 155).*
14. *Windows of second-class enclosed promenade.*
15. *Poop Deck peeled back and over on itself.*
16. *Evaporator from turbine engine room (see p. 224).*
17. *A main condenser from the turbine engine room.*
18. *Funnel remains.*
19. *Steel decking*
20. *Large section of D-Deck shell plating.*

when the instruments were torn from the deck. The identical indicator positions are nothing more than coincidence.

Many other surprisingly well-preserved objects were floated up to the surface in large salvage baskets, including the following: a jar of skin cream, according to reports still fragrant and showing the finger imprint of the last person to use it; a wallet; a pair of eyeglasses still in their leather case; sterling silver cutlery, several cut-glass carafes and a complete leaded-glass window from the first-class dining saloon; a five-globed ceiling fixture from the first-class smoking room; a cut-glass decanter from a first-class stateroom; over one hundred white ceramic egg dishes; a coffeepot and a teapot; a silver tray; a vase; at least one bottle of champagne with the cork still in place; and various shipboard paraphernalia including a binnacle (this would have held one of the ship's compasses) along with the remains of its wooden stand, and a ship's wheel pedestal, both probably from the captain's bridge.

One of the *Titanic*'s safes was also raised and opened with great fanfare at the climax of the television special. This was the same second-class purser's safe we had examined so carefully the year before (see page 152). We knew then that the back had rusted away and that the safe was empty. Its contents as revealed on television came from somewhere else.

To my mind, the only real treasure the 1987 *Titanic* expedition brought back was on videotape. For instance, *Nautile* filmed a gaping hole in the starboard bow. However, there is no evidence to suggest this

The Hole in the Starboard Bow

This painting shows the starboard bow area that includes the hole discovered by the 1987 expedition. A lot of nonsense has been spoken and written about this hole, above all the claim that it is due to an explosion and that this explosion was the real cause of the sinking. Seductive as it must be to concoct a theory that contradicts all the eyewitnesses on the scene, there is no evidence to support it. The hole is surely not the result of a coal-gas explosion. The British inquiry unequivocally established that the fire that had been burning in one of the coal bunkers was extinguished more than a day before the disaster. And even if the coal fire were still smouldering, the coal bunker in question is somewhat aft of and well below the hole's position. Nor was there any way for coal gas to get trapped belowdecks and build up before being ignited. Finally, since the hole's position is considerably above the waterline, it could have played no part in causing the sinking.

was the result of an explosion or was the real cause of the sinking.

The hole in the starboard bow is located some twenty feet below the Well Deck level, just about even with the forward cranes, and appears to measure approximately 15 by 30 feet. Although we had missed this in *Alvin* — our main pass along the starboard bow was at the mudline to look for iceberg damage — we suspected the existence of major damage in this area because of what happened when the bow collided with the bottom (see p. 205). There is a natural weak spot in the hull just below the forward end of the C-Deck superstructure. Forward of this point, the bow section angles down sharply, and there is a rippling, buckling and tearing of the hull plates, which we observed on the port bow. This damage on the port bow has a similar blasted look and clearly has the same origin, as the hole on the starboard bow.

The major video find was of the port propeller sitting close to its original position at the stern. Readers may well ask how we could have missed such a massive object when we came within a few yards of it on our own white-knuckle foray under the starboard side of the stern. But investigating the wreck in a deep submersible was very much like exploring a haunted house at night with nothing more than a flashlight. We could only see what the arc of *Alvin*'s "flashlight" revealed. (It was only months after we'd returned to Woods Hole and, with the help of Ken Marschall, analyzed the 75,000 ANGUS images that the overall condition of the wreck began to take shape. In fact, we learned more about the ship after we'd returned to port than during our 11 dives.) When we found no evidence of the starboard propeller, we mistakenly assumed that the port one was buried also.

Although *Nautile*'s video footage shows the propeller seemingly in its proper position, it has clearly been wrenched up, probably on

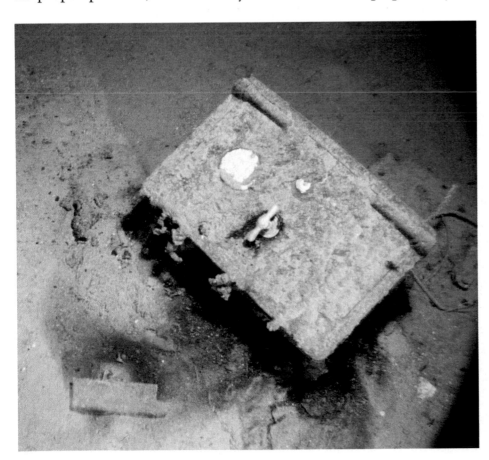

The backless second-class purser's safe that was raised in 1987 and "opened" during a live U.S. television special.

impact. The mudline at that part of the stern is above the ship's waterline, and all the propellers were, of course, well below water. Nonetheless, seeing one of Jack Grimm's missing propellers still almost in place at the stern provided me with one of the few moments of satisfaction from the 1987 *Titanic* enterprise.

The Future

At this writing, it remains unclear what will happen to the salvaged artifacts or to the wreck itself. A travelling display of *Titanic* treasure is promised once Electricité de France has finished the arduous process of electrolytic treatment to preserve objects that have spent 75 years two-and-a-half miles down and would soon disintegrate upon exposure to air.

Will there be another *Titanic* salvage expedition? One, scheduled by the same IFREMER team for the summer of 1988, never materialized, but by the time this edition of *The Discovery of the Titanic* is published the wreck may have been visited again. The consortium is planning further descents, either by deep submersible or deep-towed vehicle. They want to bring back more artifacts, but they swear they won't remove objects from inside the hull. One of their goals is to settle once and for all the question of exactly what kind of damage was done by the iceberg. Presumably this would mean excavating the mud along the starboard bow, although it seems likely that below the mudline the damage done on impact with the bottom will have erased the evidence. So the *Titanic* may be visited again and again, and her carcass and entrails gradually picked clean.

This possibility makes an international agreement to protect the *Titanic* site and control its use of even more pressing importance. Although the *Titanic* lies within Canada's declared 300-mile territorial limit, and the Canadian government has gone on record stating that it has a legal interest in the wreck, the Canadians did nothing to prevent the 1987 salvage of artifacts. But pressure from concerned citizens is mounting and perhaps an agreement between France, Canada and the United States will be possible.

I hope and pray that no more plunder is taken from the ship and that future visitors will be able to tour the wreck and the debris field almost as we found it. As our 1986 expedition proved, and as the 1987 expedition inadvertently confirmed, the images that can be brought back are far more compelling than a scattering of salvaged objects removed from their emotional and historical context.

The Jason Project

If I ever return to the *Titanic*, it will be to demonstrate the wonder of "telepresence" in the ocean depths. From a technological point of view, our two *Titanic* expeditions were important steps in the development of the *Argo/Jason* system (see page 53), which will permit unmanned exploration of the deepest parts of the ocean. In 1985, *Argo* — our underwater video eyes — found the *Titanic* wreck and participated in mapping the wreck site. In 1986, *Jason Junior*, the prototype for *Jason*, explored inside the ship, proving the effectiveness of a seeing-eye robot on an electronic rope.

Now it has all come together. As of this writing, the spring of 1989 will see the culmination of our development of the *Argo/Jason* system

The remotely operated vehicle Jason *will take part in our live broadcast from the Mediterranean seabed.* Jason *can travel at speeds of up to one knot and has a specially designed tray that can carry up to 250 pounds of equipment or samples it has collected. It can be fitted with one or two robot arms and is attached to* Argo *by a 500-foot cable.*

as it takes part in the first-ever live television broadcast from the ocean floor — the Jason Project. This will also be the first time high-quality color television images will be transmitted live to a network of museums for viewing by students and the general public. From May 1 to 14, more than 200,000 schoolchildren visiting museums in the United States and Canada will peer over our shoulders at the very moment *Argo* and *Jason* are exploring the Mediterranean seabed.

In 1988, we explored large areas of the Mediterranean with *Argo,* looking for the deep wrecks of ships from ancient times and investigating the undersea geology. In 1989, we will return to explore, with *Jason*'s help, two of the most fascinating discoveries we made in 1988: the Pliny Seamount, an active underwater volcano located in the Tyrrhenian Sea southwest of Naples, and the remains of a wrecked fleet of ships that sank in the waters northeast of Carthage during the heyday of the Roman Empire.

And this is only the beginning. Our new 6,000-meter fiber optic cable, specially developed for *Argo,* has suddenly placed 98 percent of the world's oceans within our reach. *Jason,* which can operate at depths of up to 6,000 meters (20,000 feet), will be able to peer into crannies and crevices previously accessible only by dangerous and time-consuming manned deep-submersible travel. *Jason*'s still and video cameras will be able to send to the surface even better pictures than we took in *Alvin,* and it will be able to bring back samples for scientific study. And who knows what lost ships we will now be able to find and explore?

I had hoped some day to return to the wreck of the *Titanic* with *Argo/Jason* and to broadcast live to the world as we revisited that majestic and tragic place. Now I don't know whether there will be any wreck left to visit. And knowing what ravages have already been wrought, I am reluctant to return. I would rather, I think, hang onto my memories of the grand old lady just as we found her, and left her.

This peaceful picture of the Titanic*'s bow is the way I would like to remember the wreck.*

My second glimpse of the *Titanic* is the one that will stay with me forever: a huge black shape looming up out of the darkness, the knife-edge of her bow plowing the bottom mud into a gigantic wave as it came straight for me....

Despite the efforts of salvagers, the *Titanic* is truly gone for good, home-ported at last. She'll never be raised, but her fate is now known. Although she is still awesome in her dimensions, she is no longer the graceful vessel that sank five days into her maiden voyage in April 1912. Her beauty has faded; she is broken in two and age has withered her. Her massive steel plates have begun to melt into rivers of rust. Her once-proud bulkheads are squashed and buckled. Her ornate wooden elegance has been eaten away and almost obliterated by armies of wood-boring molluscs. Her innards are scattered unceremoniously across the muddy ocean floor.

The bottom of the ocean is a quiet place, a peaceful place, fitting for a memorial to all the things that sank when the *Titanic* went down. The wreck we found and photographed should be left to stand as a monument to a mistake of arrogance, to a lost age, and to a kind of innocence we can't recover — and to the people, both guilty perpetrators and innocent victims, who figured in the drama.

In future, when I think of the *Titanic,* I will see her bow sitting upright on the bottom, dignified despite the decay and desecration and, finally, at rest.

An Inventory Of The Debris Field

Recorded on miles of ANGUS film are thousands of *Titanic* artifacts. Pictured here are some of the highlights. On this page, the debris items are keyed to the *Olympic* Poop Deck photograph at center.

A telegraph, used to send signals to the engine room, identical to the two shown on the docking bridge, below.

This Poop Deck telephone was contained in the box that juts above the docking bridge railing at center.

This binnacle is similar to the one that held the docking bridge compass at center, below.

The pedestal for the ship's wheel stands directly behind the binnacle, above.

This bench, with some of its wooden sluts intact, is similar to those shown above.

A cowl vent like those standing on the Poop Deck, above.

This steam valve wheel and pedestal can be seen on the deck opposite, center.

The helm indicator quadrant from the wheelhouse telemotor (see page 126).

This bridge telegraph may be the one seen behind Captain Smith on page 126.

One of the five single-ended boilers from boiler room No. 1.

A rectangular piece of metal debris has landed on the face of this boiler.

A boiler on its side. (For the two other boilers see pages 190-191.)

A tangle of davits forms an abstract pattern on the ocean floor.

An arched bronze window from the Verandah Café (see page 17).

One of the three safes from the second-class purser's office.

A Gibbs extractor ventilator from the roof of the second-class entrance.

The tower and boom of a stern crane lies near some ladders.

A metal pantry cabinet with cupboards at the bottom.

An Inventory of the Debris Field (cont'd)

The plan below shows the layout of the *Titanic*'s two large engine rooms. Numbers indicate the location of engine parts discovered and the jagged line shows where the break-up occurred.

(Right) The reciprocating engines for the three White Star sister ships were the largest ever built. Over 30 feet high, they extended up as high as E Deck. Here, the Britannic's engines are assembled at Harland & Wolff.

(Left) This catwalk was fitted next to the starboard intermediate-pressure cylinder.

(Above) A tube plate from one of the main condensers. *(Above, left)* A condenser with its casing partly removed.

(Left) A gear shaft from one of the watertight doors (see page 22) lies across the cross-connection valve from between the steam separators.

(Below) One of the three evaporators, each of which could process 60 tons of water per 24 hours. *(Below, left)* An evaporator before installation.

The high-pressure cylinder from the starboard reciprocating engine, still fitted within the ship.

The port low-pressure cylinder in the debris field. It weighs about 50 tons and is over eight feet in diameter.

One of the four main feed filters, two of which were photographed by ANGUS in the debris field.

(Right) A feed filter identical to the one shown above, stands next to its casing. They were located next to the forward engine room bulkhead as shown in the diagram (left).

(Above) The direct-contact heater.
(Above, right) The direct-contact heater before being mounted in the ship.

(Below) A vertical direct-acting feed pump which was part of a pair. One-half of a set of these feed pumps is shown (below, right).

225

An Inventory of the Debris Field (cont'd)

This may be a woman's high-button shoe.

Two shoes lying side by side.

A boot that may have belonged to a stoker.

A stack of buckets.

A dust pan showing little sign of rust.

Wine bottles still stacked in the remains of their cases.

Floor tiles similar to those in the gymnasium.

Floor tiles used in many areas (see cabin photo page 183).

A floor tile from the aft Grand Staircase (see page 135).

A Summary of Debris Field Highlights

5 single-ended boilers.
4 cargo cranes plus 3 still on ship.
2 forward low-pressure cylinders and crankshaft parts; 2 high-pressure cylinders visible in wreck; 2 eccentrics; many sections of catwalks.
3 second-class purser's office safes.
9 aft first-class staircase balustrades.
3 telegraphs, 2 from docking bridge, 1 from captain's bridge; 4 binnacles, 1 from captain's bridge, 1 from wheel-house, 1 from compass platform and 1 from docking bridge; 2 ship's wheel pedestals; 1 docking bridge telephone and pedestal.
Base of number 4 funnel, pieces from other funnels and 2 sets of funnel whistles.
6 cowl vents; 1 squirrel cage for stokehold fan; 1 steam separator; 1 evaporator; 2 main feed filters.
4 bathtubs, 4 intact deck benches; 2 gangway doors; 2 sections of galley range tops. 3 pairs of shoes, assorted single shoes, boots and hairbrushes. Countless toilets, chamber pots, wash basins, metal ribbon and spring and chain mattresses, wine bottles, floor tiles and refrigeration coils. Assorted white enamel footboards, Promotheus space heaters, silver-plated serving dishes, window fragments from dining saloon; baseboard vent grills and china dishware.

A *Titanic* Chronology

The following chronology of dates and events constitutes the main highlights of the story of the R.M.S. *Titanic*. (N.B. Times noted during night of April 14 and morning of April 15, 1912, are approximate and based on testimony recorded in the British Inquiry into the disaster in 1912.)

1867 — Thomas Henry Ismay purchases the White Star Line, a line of sailing vessels, originally founded about 1850 – and mainly engaged in trade centered on Australian goldfields.

1869 — Ismay forms the Oceanic Steam Navigation Company in order to establish White Star as a high-class steamship service in the Atlantic passenger trade.

1869-1870 — First ships built for White Star by Belfast shipbuilders Harland & Wolff.

1891 — J. Bruce Ismay admitted to partnership of the White Star Line. He takes over after his father's death in 1899.

1894 — William J. Pirrie becomes chairman of Harland & Wolff.

1898 — American author Morgan Robertson publishes the novel *Futility* in which a British passenger liner called the *Titan* hits an iceberg and sinks on her maiden voyage without enough lifeboats in the month of April in the North Atlantic. The fictional ship is eerily similar to the yet-to-be conceived *Titanic* in size, speed, equipment, numbers of passengers (both rich and poor), and those lost.

1902 — The White Star Line purchased by the International Mercantile Marine Company, a shipping trust headed by U.S. financier J. Pierpont Morgan. While White Star ships will still fly the British flag and carry British crews, the company is essentially controlled by American interests.

1904 — J. Bruce Ismay, age 41, with Morgan's full support, becomes president and managing director of International Mercantile Marine with complete control. As well, Harland & Wolff chairman William J. Pirrie becomes a director of Mercantile Marine.

1907 — At a dinner party in William J. Pirrie's London mansion, Ismay discusses the construction of two huge ships (a third to be added later) to compete with the luxury, size, and speed of rival lines. These ships are to be known as the Olympic class of liners, and are intended specifically to beat out the Cunard Line for the Atlantic luxury passenger trade.

1908 — July 29: White Star owners, including Ismay, approve in principle the design plan for the Olympic class ships prepared by builders Harland & Wolff under direct supervision of Lord Pirrie, with the assistance of his nephew Thomas Andrews.

1908 — July 31: A contract letter is signed for construction in the Belfast shipyards of the *Olympic*, the *Titanic*, and a third sister ship *(Britannic)* to follow. Ultimate decisions of design, equipment, and decoration are to be made by J. Bruce Ismay. The size of the *Titanic* will be 882 feet 9 inches long, 94 feet wide, and 100 feet high to the bridge level. Final cost: £1,500,000 or approx. $7,500,000. New docks have to be built on either side of the Atlantic to accommodate the size of these ships. Harland & Wolff build specially strengthened slips to take their weight, and a new gantry under which they will be built.

1908 — December 16: Keel laid down for Harland & Wolff yard number 400 – *Olympic* construction begins.

1909 — March 31: Keel laid down for Harland & Wolff yard number 401 – *Titanic* construction begins.

1910 — October 20: *Olympic* hull successfully launched.

1911 — May 31: *Titanic* hull successfully launched, witnessed by more than 100,000 people. At the time, (together with the *Olympic*) she is the largest man-made object ever moved. Twenty-two tons of tallow, soap, and train oil are used to grease the slipway bed to coat and protect against the enormous three-tons-per-square-inch pressure of the freshly painted hull. The *Titanic* towed by tugs to fitting-out basin. Outfitting begins.

1911 — June: The *Olympic* leaves on her maiden voyage.
July: First projected date agreed on by White Star and Harland & Wolff for the *Titanic*'s maiden voyage – March 20, 1912.
September 20: The *Olympic* (with Captain Edward J. Smith who would later captain the *Titanic*) has her hull badly damaged in collision with Royal Navy cruiser *Hawke*. The *Titanic*'s maiden voyage delayed due to necessary diversion of workers and materials to repair the *Olympic*.
October 11: White Star officially announces new date for the *Titanic*'s maiden voyage in the London *Times* – April 10, 1912.

1912 — January: Sixteen wooden lifeboats are installed on the *Titanic* under Welin davits (designed to handle two to three boats). The original designer, Alexander Carlisle (who was no longer in the employ of Harland & Wolff) had suggested davits capable of carrying more boats, but presented it as an economy measure, and not in the interests of increased safety. Outdated British Board of Trade regulations mean that the *Titanic*'s 20 lifeboats (including four "collapsible" lifeboats) actually exceed requirements by ten percent capacity.

1912 — February 3: The *Titanic* successfully drydocked at Belfast's Thompson Graving Dock.
March: Engineering crew begins to assemble in Belfast, some actually living on board ship.
March 25: Lifeboats are tested; swung out, lowered, and hoisted back into position under davits.
March 31: Except for a few minor details in some passenger staterooms, the outfitting of the *Titanic*

is complete. Her capacity includes a size of 46,328 gross tons, with approximately 52,250 tons of displacement, 46,000 horsepower with 29 boilers, 159 furnaces, and funnels 73 feet above Boat Deck. She has three propellers and is estimated to be able to make some 24 knots full speed (although this is never put to the test). Although the *Titanic* and her sister ship the *Olympic* are identical in dimensions, more staterooms and suites were added to the *Titanic* (plus other structural additions), making her the heavier of the two. The *Titanic* is now the largest ship in the world.

1912 — **April 1:** Sea trials delayed due to high winds.

April 2, 6:00 a.m.: Sea trials begin. The *Titanic* assisted by tugs through Victoria Channel to Belfast Lough. All equipment tested, including wireless. Speed and handling trials undertaken, including various turning and stop-start maneuvers. Major stopping test conducted: runs full ahead at 20 knots and then stops full astern.

2:00 p.m.: Running test conducted. She travels for about two hours (about 40 miles) out into the open Irish Sea at an average speed of 18 knots, and then returns in two hours to Belfast. All tests meet Board of Trade standards. Trials have lasted less than a day.

8:00 p.m.: Leaves Belfast (under Captain Bartlett) for overnight trip to Southampton, her port of embarkation (about 570 miles).

1912 — **April 3:** Arrives port of Southampton just after midnight to begin provisioning and staffing for maiden voyage.

April 5, Good Friday: The *Titanic* is "dressed" in panoply of flags and pennants for a salute to the people of Southampton. Only occasion she is ever "dressed."

April 6: Recruitment day for remainder, and majority, of crew. General cargo begins to arrive. The final total cargo includes 559 tons and 11,524 separate pieces. As well, 5892 tons of coal are loaded on board.

April 8: Fresh food supplies taken on board. All final preparations overseen by ship's builder Thomas Andrews down to the tiniest detail.

April 10, Wednesday – Sailing Day:

7:30 a.m.: Captain Edward J. Smith boards the *Titanic* with full crew. Officers have spent the night on board. Smith receives sailing report from Chief Officer Wilde.

8:00 a.m.: Entire crew mustered, followed by brief lifeboat drill using only two starboard boats, No.'s 11 and 15.

9:30 to 11:00 a.m.: Second-and-third-class boat-trains arrive and passengers board ship.

11:30: Arrival of first-class boat-train from London at dockside. First-class passengers board and are escorted to cabins.

noon: The *Titanic* casts off and is towed from dock by tugs. During downstream passage into River Test under her own steam, the water displaced by the *Titanic's* movement causes all six mooring ropes on

the *New York* to break and her stern to swing toward the *Titanic*. Quick action narrowly averts a collision by only four feet. Departure delayed for an hour. This incident (together with the *Olympic-Hawke* collision) indicates unfamiliarity with ships of this size by those handling them.

1912 — **April 10, 1:00 p.m.:** The *Titanic* resumes 24-mile trip downstream to English Channel en route to Cherbourg, France.

4:00 p.m.: Boat-train from Paris arrives Cherbourg. Late arrival of ship announced.

5:30 p.m.: Cherbourg – passengers finally board tenders and wait to be ferried out to the *Titanic*.

6:30 p.m.: The *Titanic* rides at anchor in Cherbourg harbor, all lights ablaze. Twenty-two cross-Channel passengers disembark, and some cargo is unloaded.

8:00 p.m.: 274 Cherbourg passengers are all aboard and tenders return to shore.

8:10 p.m.: Anchor raised and the *Titanic* leaves for Queenstown, Ireland, taking her through the English Channel and around England's south coast.

April 11, Thursday morning: Captain Smith takes the *Titanic* through some additional practice turns en route to Queenstown to test maneuverability.

11:30 a.m.: The *Titanic* rides at anchor in Queenstown harbor, about two miles from land. 113 third-class and seven second-class passengers board from tenders with 1385 bags of mail. Seven passengers disembark.

1:30 p.m.: The starboard anchor is raised for the last time and the *Titanic* departs on her first transatlantic crossing for New York. Estimated total number of crew and passengers on board: 2227. (Exact total unknown due to discrepancies in passenger/crew lists.)

April 11 to 12: The *Titanic* covers 386 miles in fine, calm, clear weather.

April 12 to 13: The *Titanic* covers 519 miles. Fine weather continues. Various ice warnings received, which is not uncommon for April crossings.

April 13, 10:30 p.m.: Heavy ice pack warning signaled by passing *Rappahannock*, which has sustained damage coming through ice field.

April 14, Sunday: 9:00 a.m.: The *Titanic* picks up wireless message from the *Caronia* warning of field ice and icebergs in 42° N, from 49° to 51° W.

10:30 a.m.: Divine service held in first-class dining saloon.

11:40 a.m.: Dutch liner *Noordam* reports "much ice" in about same position as the *Caronia*.

noon: As usual, ship's officers gather on the wing of the navigating bridge to calculate daily position with sextants: "Since noon Saturday, 546 miles."

1:42 p.m.: Iceberg warning received via the *Baltic* and "large quantities of field ice" in latitude 41° 51' N, longitude 49° 52' W about 250 miles ahead of the *Titanic*. Message delivered to Captain Smith. Smith later gives it to J. Bruce Ismay, who puts it in his pocket.

1:45 p.m.: "Large iceberg" warning received via German liner *Amerika* (41° 27' N, 50° 8' W). Message not sent to the bridge.

5:30 to 7:30 p.m.: Air temperature drops ten degrees to 33°F.

5:50 p.m.: Captain Smith alters ship's course slightly to south and west of normal course – possibly as a precaution to avoid ice.

6:00 p.m.: Second Officer Lightoller relieves Chief Officer Wilde on the bridge.

7:15 p.m.: First Officer Murdoch orders forward forecastle hatch closed to stop the glow from inside interfering with crow's nest watch above.

7:30 p.m.: Three warning messages concerning large icebergs intercepted from the *Californian* (42° 3' N, 49° 9' W). Message delivered to bridge. Captain attending dinner party below. Ice now only 50 miles ahead.

8:40 p.m.: Lightoller gives order to look after ship's fresh water supply, as outside seawater is now close to freezing.

8:55 p.m.: Captain Smith excuses himself from dinner party, goes directly to bridge, and discusses calm and clear weather conditions with Lightoller, as well as visibility of icebergs at night.

9:20 p.m.: Captain Smith retires for the night with the order to rouse him "if it becomes at all doubtful …."

9:30 p.m.: Lightoller sends message to crow's nest to watch carefully for icebergs until morning.

9:40 p.m.: Heavy ice pack and iceberg warning received from the *Mesaba* (lat. 42° N to 41° 25', long. 49° W to 50° 30' W). Message overlooked. Wireless operators busy with passenger traffic. Altogether the day's six ice warnings show a huge field of ice some 78 miles long directly ahead.

10:00 p.m.: Lightoller relieved on bridge by First Officer Murdoch. Lookouts in crow's nest relieved. Warning to watch for icebergs passed between the watches. Temperature is 32° F, sky cloudless, air clear.

10:30 p.m.: Sea temperature down to 31° F.

10:55 p.m.: Some 10 to 19 miles north of the *Titanic*, the *Californian* is stopped in ice field, and sends out warnings to all ships in area. When the *Californian*'s wireless operator calls up the *Titanic*, his ice warning is interrupted by a blunt "Keep out! Shut up! You're jamming my signal. I'm working Cape Race." The *Californian*'s sole operator listens in to the *Titanic*'s wireless traffic and then at 11:30 turns off his set and retires for the night, as is the custom.

11:30 p.m.: Lookouts Fleet and Lee in crow's nest note slight haze appearing directly ahead of the *Titanic*.

11:40 p.m.: The *Titanic* moving at 20½ knots. Suddenly, lookouts see iceberg dead ahead about 500 yards away towering some 55-60 feet above the water. They immediately sound the warning bell with three sharp rings and telephone down to the bridge: "Iceberg right ahead." Sixth Officer Moody on bridge acknowledges warning, relays message to Murdoch who instinctively calls "hard-a-starboard" to helmsman and orders engine room to stop engines and then full astern. Murdoch then activates lever to close watertight doors below the waterline. Helmsman spins wheel as far as it will go. After several seconds the *Titanic* begins to veer to port, but the iceberg strikes starboard bow side and brushes along the side of the ship and passes by into the night. The impact, although jarring to the crew down in the forward area, is not noticed by many of the passengers. Thirty-seven seconds have elapsed from sighting to collision.

11:50 p.m.: During first ten minutes after impact, water rises 14 feet above the keel, forward. First five compartments begin to take on water. Boiler room No. 6, five feet above keel, is flooded in eight feet of water.

12:00 a.m.: Mail room, 24 feet above keel, begins taking enough water to float mail bags. Following reports to Captain Smith, now on the bridge, of water pouring into number 1, 2, and 3 holds, and boiler room No. 6, and his own rapid tour to inspect damage with Thomas Andrews, Smith asks Andrews for his assessment. Andrews calculates the ship can stay afloat from one to one-and-a-half hours only. This is based on the mathematical certainty that if more than four holds are flooded, once a compartment fills with water, the water will spill into the next compartment and so on. The *Titanic*'s bow begins to sink. The ship is doomed. Captain Smith orders CQD distress call for assistance sent out over ship's wireless. The *Titanic*'s estimated position: 41° 46' N, 50° 14' W. Boilers shut down and relief pipes against funnels blow off huge noisy clouds of steam.

1912 — April 15, Monday, 12:05 a.m.: Squash court, 32 feet above keel, is awash. Orders given to uncover lifeboats and muster the crew and passengers. Only enough room for 1178 out of the estimated 2227 on board if every boat is filled.

12:10 to 1:50 a.m.: Several crew members on the *Californian*, some 10 to 19 miles away, see lights of a steamer. A number of attempts to make contact with the ship with Morse lamp fail. Rockets are observed, but as they appear so low over the ship's deck, and make no sound, they do not seem like distress rockets, and no great concern is taken. Distance between ships seems to increase until they are out of sight of each other.

12:15 to 2:17 a.m.: Numerous ships hear the *Titanic*'s distress signals, including her sister ship the *Olympic*, some 500 miles away. Several ships, including *Mount Temple* (49 miles away), *Frankfort* (153 miles), *Birma* (70 miles), *Baltic* (243 miles), *Virginian* (170), and *Carpathia* (58 miles) prepare at various times to come to assist.

12:15 a.m.: Band begins to play lively ragtime tunes in first-class lounge on A Deck, later moving up to

Boat Deck near port entrance to Grand Staircase.

12:20 a.m.: Water floods seamen's quarters, 48 feet above keel, on E Deck forward.

12:25 a.m.: Order given to start loading lifeboats with women and children. The *Carpathia*, southeast some 58 miles, receives distress call and immediately heads full speed to rescue.

12:45 a.m.: First boat, starboard No. 7, safely lowered away. It can carry 65 people, but leaves with 28 aboard. First distress rocket fired. Eight rockets will be fired altogether. Fourth Officer Boxhall observes vessel approach the *Titanic* and then disappear despite attempts to contact her with Morse lamp. Boat No. 4 begins loading between 12:30 and 12:45.

12:55 a.m.: First port-side boat No. 6 lowered with only 28 aboard, including Molly Brown and Major Peuchen.

Starboard No. 5 is lowered. Ismay is chastised by Fifth Officer Lowe for interfering with his command. (41 aboard – room for another 24.)

1:00 a.m.: Starboard boat No. 3 is lowered with only 32 aboard including 11 crew.

1:10 a.m.: Starboard No. 1 is lowered (capacity 40) with only 12 aboard, including Sir Cosmo and Lady Duff Gordon, and seven crew. Port-side No. 8 loaded and lowered carrying only 39 people. It is steered in the water by the Countess of Rothes.

1:15 a.m.: Water reaches the *Titanic*'s name on the bow and she now lists to port. Tilt of deck grows steeper. Boats now begin to be more fully loaded.

1:20 a.m.: Starboard No. 9 leaves with some 56 people aboard. The *Titanic* has now developed a noticeable list to starboard.

1:25 a.m.: Port-side boat No. 12 is lowered, with 40 women and children on board. Two seamen are put in charge of boat. After the *Titanic* sinks, this boat is tied together with boats 4, 10, 14 and collapsible D. Later on, survivors are moved from boat 14 to the other boats by Fifth Officer Lowe so he can return to pick up swimming passengers. Boat 12 is subsequently overloaded with 70 passengers, many rescued from collapsible D.

1:30 a.m.: Signs of panic begin to appear among some passengers on the ship. As port-side boat 14 is lowered with 60 people, including Fifth Officer Lowe, a group of passengers appears ready to jump in the already full boat, and Lowe fires shots into the air to warn them away.

The *Titanic*'s distress calls now near desperation. "We are sinking fast" and "Women and children in boats. Cannot last much longer."

1:35 a.m.: Port-side boat No. 16 is lowered with over 50 people. Starboard boat No. 13 leaves with 64 people, mostly second and third-class women and children.

Starboard boat No. 15 is lowered 30 seconds later with 70 aboard and barely avoids collision with boat 13 as it is lowered on top of No. 13. The latter pulls away in water in the nick of time.

1:40 a.m.: Most of the forward boats are now away, and passengers begin to move to the stern area. Ismay leaves on collapsible C (39 aboard), the last starboard-side boat launched. The forward Well Deck is awash.

1:45 a.m.: Last words heard from the *Titanic* by the *Carpathia* on her way to the rescue – "...Engine room full up to boilers...." Port-side boat No. 2 is lowered and leaves with only 25 people. She can carry 40.

1:55 a.m.: John Jacob Astor, refused entry to port-side boat No. 4 by Lightoller, sees his wife off safely as the boat is lowered with 40 women and children and some crew aboard. In the rush, 20 places in the boat are left empty.

2:00 a.m.: Water now only ten feet below Promenade Deck.

2:05 a.m.: There are now still over 1500 people left on the sinking ship. Collapsible D is one of the last boats left. It has room for 47 people. To prevent a rush on the boat, Lightoller waves (and possibly fires) his pistol into the air and crew members form a circle around it, with arms locked together, and allow only women and children aboard. The boat is lowered with 44 aboard.

The *Titanic*'s forecastle head sinks under water, the tilt of her decks growing steeper.

2:10 a.m.: Captain Smith releases wireless operators Bride and Phillips from their duties.

2:17 a.m.: Phillips continues to send last radio message. Captain Smith tells crew members, "It's every man for himself," and returns to the bridge to await the end. Thomas Andrews, the ship's builder, is seen alone in the first-class smoking room staring into space.

The *Titanic*'s bow plunges under, enabling the ensnared collapsible B to float clear upside down. Father Thomas Byles hears confession and gives absolution to over one hundred second and third-class passengers gathered at the aft end of the Boat Deck.

The ship's band stops playing. Many passengers and crew jump overboard. The *Titanic*'s forward funnel collapses, crushing a number of swimming passengers. Collapsible A now floats free and about two dozen people in the water grab hold of it. It clears right side up, but is swamped and dangerously overloaded. Lowe, in boat No. 14, saves them just before dawn. Probably as many as half, however, have died.

2:18 a.m.: A huge roar is heard as all moveable objects inside the *Titanic* crash toward the submerged bow. The ship's lights blink once and then go out. Many survivors witness the ship break in two. The bow half sinks.

2:20 a.m.: The *Titanic*'s broken-off stern section settles back into the water, righting itself for a few moments. Slowly it fills with water and again tilts its stern high into the air before slowly sinking into the sea. Over 1500 souls are lost in the "greatest maritime disaster in history."

3:30 a.m.: The *Carpathia*'s rockets sighted by lifeboats. Her normal speed is 14¹/₂ knots, but she has raced to the rescue at a shuddering 17¹/₂ knots.

4:10 a.m.: First boat, No. 2, is picked up by the *Carpathia*. Ice floats all about the disaster area amid debris from the *Titanic*.

5:30 a.m.: The *Californian* advised by the *Frankfort* of the loss of the *Titanic* and makes for the disaster area.

5:30 to 6:30 a.m.: Collapsible A survivors rescued by boat No. 14, and collapsible B by boats 4 and 12.

8:30 a.m.: Last boat, No. 12, picked up by the *Carpathia*. Lightoller is the last survivor to come on board.

The *Californian* arrives at side of the *Carpathia*, and then steams through disaster area to undertake final check for survivors.

8:50 a.m.: The *Carpathia* leaves area bound for New York. She carries 705 survivors. An estimated 1522 souls have been lost.

Ismay wires White Star New York offices: "Deeply regret advise you *Titanic* sank this morning after collision with iceberg, resulting in serious loss of life. Full particulars later."

April 17: Hired by White Star, the *Mackay-Bennett* leaves Halifax to search for bodies at disaster site.

April 18, 9:00 p.m.: The *Carpathia* arrives New York. She outruns hordes of newspaper reporters in boats clamoring for news. As the *Carpathia* passes Statue of Liberty, 10,000 people are on hand to watch. The *Titanic*'s lifeboats hang at her sides. She passes the Cunard pier (no. 54) and steams on up-river to the White Star piers, there to lower the *Titanic*'s boats. The *Carpathia* then returns to the Cunard pier to finally unload the survivors.

April 19 to May 25: Inquiry into the *Titanic* disaster undertaken by United States Senate Inquiry, headed by Senator William A. Smith. Eighty-two witnesses are called.

April 22: White Star sends the *Minia* out from Halifax to help overtaxed *Mackay-Bennett*, which has picked up 306 bodies. The *Minia* finds only another 17 after a week-long search.

April 24: As the *Titanic*'s sister ship *Olympic* is about to leave Southampton, her "black gang" (stokers) go out on strike. They will not work on a ship that does not carry enough lifeboats. 285 crew desert ship, and the *Olympic*'s voyage is canceled.

May 6: White Star sends out the *Montmagny* from Sorel, Quebec, to help search for bodies. Recovers four.

May 15: White Star sends out the *Algerina* from St. John's, Newfoundland. Recovers only one body. Altogether, the White Star-commissioned ships find a total of 328 bodies.

May 2 to July 3: British Board of Trade Inquiry is conducted. 25,622 questions are asked of 96 witnesses, including such expert witnesses as the inventor of radio, Marconi, and the explorer Sir Ernest Shackleton regarding ice and icebergs. The only passenger witnesses are Sir Cosmo and Lady Duff Gordon and J. Bruce Ismay. Other witnesses include Captain Lord of the *Californian*, Lightoller, who endures 1600 questions alone, members of the crew, the ship's owners, and members of the British Board of Trade. The final judgement recommends "more watertight compartments in ocean-going ships, the provision of lifeboats for all on board, as well as a better lookout."

1913 — **April:** International Ice Patrol created to guard sea lanes of North Atlantic under direction of U.S. Coast Guard.

1914 — **February:** The *Titanic*'s second sister ship, the *Britannic* is launched.

1916 — **November:** The *Britannic*, converted to a hospital ship, is sunk by German mines.

1929 — **November 18:** The Grand Banks Earthquake is thought to have triggered a huge underwater mudslide which some feel may have buried wreck of the *Titanic* in same vicinity.

1935 — After 24 years of service, including war service carrying troops, and four major refittings, the *Olympic* is retired. She has crossed the Atlantic 500 times, steamed a million and a half miles, and earned the nickname "Old Reliable."

1980 — **July:** U.S. entrepreneur and explorer Jack Grimm funds scientific expedition which sets out to locate wreck of the *Titanic*. Dogged by bad weather and equipment malfunction, expedition fails to find the *Titanic*.

1981 — **June:** Jack Grimm's second expedition sets out to locate the *Titanic*, but again fails to find the wreck.

1983 — **July:** Third and final expedition funded by Jack Grimm fails to find the *Titanic*.

1985 — **September 1:** Franco-American scientific expedition led by Dr. Robert Ballard finally discovers and photographs remains of the wreck of the *Titanic* at a depth of 12,460 feet on the ocean floor.

1986 — **July:** Dr. Robert Ballard returns to the *Titanic* with a second expedition. Landing the submersible *Alvin* on her decks, he explores and photographs the entire wreck and debris field in detail.

1987 — The U.S. Congress moves to make the *Titanic* an international memorial. A French expedition recovers approximately 900 artifacts from the *Titanic* wreck.

Acknowledgments

Where does one start? While Jean-Louis Michel and I received much of the glory for discovering the *Titanic*, literally hundreds of others played crucial roles in the making of a historic event or contributed to the writing of this book.

There were those who fought beside us in the trenches of at-sea exploration: the crews of *Le Suroit*, *Knorr*, and *Atlantis II*; the technical teams that operated SAR, *Argo*, ANGUS, *Alvin*, and *Jason Jr.*; and all those ashore who supported us through the many long months of planning and preparation.

In addition to these highly professional troops, there are a number of people who deserve particular credit. Bill Tantum of the *Titanic* Historical Society never lost faith in me and our dream, but died before it could be fulfilled. Admiral Brad Mooney, Admiral Dwaine Griffith, and Admiral Ron Thurman of the U.S. Navy believed in *Argo* and *Jason* and in our team's ability to make these technological wishes into realities. The Navy's Dr. Eugene Silva gave us constant support. Navy Secretary Melvyn Paisley sheltered us under his protective wing. Lt. George Rey and Hugh O'Neil were there when the going got tough. And above all, Navy Secretary John Lehman Jr. risked the most to make the dream possible.

The *National Geographic* Society deserves special thanks for the faith they have had in my work over so many years: Bill Garrett for his constant support of our efforts; Sam Matthews and Bill Graves for teaching me how to write; Jan Atkins for pulling my 1985 press conference out of the fire; Susan Eckert for showing me how to determine my priorities; and Emory Kristof for taking many thousands of beautiful photographs.

My most loyal and long-suffering supporters are the members of my family. For 22 years I have gone to sea, spending months and months away from home on one expedition after another. Meanwhile, my wife Marjorie and sons Todd and Douglas have kept the home fires burning. I know it has been hard and that much has been lost that can never be regained, but their quiet support has given me the strength to keep going.

When *Atlantis II* returned to Woods Hole in July of 1986, the *Titanic* Project was over but the book had just begun. As I soon discovered, a publication of this complexity requires almost as many people and skills as a scientific expedition. Their collective contribution affected every page of *The Discovery of the Titanic*. Michael Levine introduced me to Madison Press Books, who shepherded the project from idea stage through to the finished book. David Weil helped me organize my plans. Rick Archbold asked a million questions and, with editor Patrick Crean, skillfully shaped the text. Hugh Brewster and the staff at Madison worked overtime making sure that no details were overlooked. Ken Marschall, whose support and enthusiasm for the book never flagged, painted and drew superbly and spent countless hours identifying *Titanic* artifacts, matching them with archival photographs, and commenting expertly on the manuscript. In addition to providing us with a splendid introduction and photographs from his personal collection, Walter Lord gave much help and guidance from his vast store of *Titanic* knowledge. Alasdair McCrimmon also gave freely of his time and expertise, carefully checking the text for accuracy.

I'd also like to thank a number of other individuals who made valuable contributions: Stu Harris for details regarding the preparation of *Argo* in 1985; Charles Pellegrino for his "down blast" theory; Bill Ryan of the Lamont-Doherty Geological Observatory for reminiscing at length about Jack Grimm's three *Titanic* expeditions and for providing numerous pictures; Fred Spiess of the Scripps Oceanographic Institute for recalling his role in the Grimm adventure; author Bill Stevenson for his recollections of Jack Grimm's first voyage; Anne Tantum for helping me recreate her late husband's role in our *Titanic* quest, and for providing photographs of Bill and film of the White Star liner cross-section; cartographer Marie Tharp (1 Washington Ave., South Nyack, NY 10960) for her map of the ocean floor; and Dr. Ruth Turner of Harvard University's Museum of Comparative Zoology for scientific detail about wood-boring molluscs and slides of these creatures.

At the Woods Hole Oceanographic Institution: Dr. Holger Jannasch for providing scientific details about iron-eating bacteria and the formation of rusticles; Bill Lange for his expertise and assistance, especially in finding and identifying ANGUS images; John Porteous for processing miles of film and for his work on the mosaic; my secretary Terri Nielsen for typing and retyping and for efficiently fielding innumerable requests; Ann Rabushka and the staff of the Public Information Office for finding slides and diagrams; Dr. Elazar Uchupi for reviewing the manuscript and suggesting helpful changes; and Tom Dettweiler and Bob Squires for helping me recall details of our 1985 expedition.

For reviewing the manuscript for historical accuracy and providing photographs: Charles Haas and John Eaton, authors of *Titanic: Triumph and Tragedy* (Patrick Stephens Ltd. / W.W. Norton). For advice on specific historical questions: Cory Keeble and Janet Holmes of the Royal Ontario Museum; and Don Lynch and Bill Sauder.

At the *National Geographic* Society: Rob Hernandez, Bill Allen, Virginia Miller, and Laura Mink for providing slides; artists Davis Meltzer, William H. Bond, Richard Schlecht, and Pierre Mion for their illustrations; and photographers Perry Thorsvik and Joseph Bailey for their pictures.

Finally, my thanks to those not already mentioned who provided photographs for the book: Roger Barrable; George Buckley of the Sea Rovers; Joe Carvalho and the *Titanic* Historical Society; Margaret Campbell of the Nova Scotia Archives; Eric Sauder; Janet Homfeld of the Margaret Strong Museum; Sangorski and Sutcliffe Bookbinders; and Roy Varley. A special thanks to Jeremy Nightingale for the 1912 Odell photographs, published here in book form for the first time.

Dr. Robert Ballard
Woods Hole, Massachusetts
May 1987

Madison Press Books would also like to thank the following people for their help and encouragement: Larry Ashmead; Ian Ballantine; Jane Baird; Carolyn Brunton; Peter Benchley; Alexandra Chapman; Peter Elek; Sharon Gignac; Ed Kamuda; Teri Koenig; Eva Koralnik; Joe Macinnis; Aaron Milrad; photographer Thomas Moore; Tom Mori; Ute Korner de Moya; Nick Noxon; Charles Sachs; Roberto Toso; and Peter Williams.

Photograph and Illustration Credits

Every effort has been made to correctly attribute all material reproduced in this book. If any errors have unwittingly occurred we will be happy to correct them in future editions.

Front Cover: Painting by Ken Marschall
Back Cover: (Top) Painting by Ken Marschall
(Bottom, left) Robert Ballard/WHOI
(Bottom, right) Perry Thorsvik ©*National Geographic* Society
Back Cover Flap: WHOI
Half-Title Page: The Bettmann Archive
Title Page: Robert Ballard/WHOI
Table of Contents: Robert Ballard/WHOI
Introduction: Harland & Wolff

Chapter One
8   Emory Kristof ©*National Georgraphic* Society
9   Emory Kristof ©*National Geographic* Society
10 Painting by Ken Marschall, Rustie Brown Collection
11 The Bettmann Archive

Chapter Two
12 Eric Sauder Collection
13 *The Illustrated London News*
14 (Astors and Straus) *The Illustrated London News* (*Titanic* at sea) Beken of Cowes
15 Harland & Wolff
16 (Top) Kate Odell, courtesy of Jeremy Nightingale
(Middle) *The Cork Examiner*
(Bottom) Kate Odell, courtesy of Jeremy Nightingale
17 (Top) Father Francis M. Browne, S.J., Charles Haas/John Eaton Collection
(Middle) Harland & Wolff
(Bottom, left) *The Illustrated London News*
(Bottom, right) Byron Collection, Museum of the City of New York
18 (Top) *The Illustrated London News*
(Bottom) Father Francis M. Browne, S.J., Charles Haas/John Eaton Collection
19 (Top) *The Illustrated London News*
(Bottom) Joseph Carvalho Collection
20 (Top) Ray Lepien Collection
(Bottom) The Bettmann Archive
21 *The Illustrated London News*
22 (Top) *The Shipbuilder*
(Bottom) *The Illustrated London News*
23 (Top and Middle) *The Illustrated London News*
(Bottom) Painting by Ken Marschall, Kenneth Smith Collection
24 (Top) *The Illustrated London News*
(Bottom) Donald Lynch Collection
25 (Top) *The Illustrated London News*
(Bottom, left) Harland & Wolff
(Major Butt) *The Illustrated London News*
(Ben Guggenheim) *The Illustrated London News*
26 (Top) Ken Marschall Collection
(Bottom) Painting by Ken Marschall, Charles Heebner Collection
27 (Top) *The Cork Examiner*/Ken Marschall Collection
(Middle) Ken Marschall Collection
(Bottom) From *The Truth About the Titanic*, Charles Haas/John Eaton Collection
28 Painting by Ken Marschall, David Hobson Collection
29 (Left and right) Walter Lord Collection

Chapter Three
30 Dann Blackwood, WHOI
32 Leonard Pinaud/Dr. George Buckley, Sea Rovers
33 WHOI
34 *Alvin* Diagram by Davis Meltzer, *National Geographic* Society
35 (Left and right) Emory Kristof ©*National Geographic* Society
36 (Top and bottom) John D. Donnelly/WHOI
37 (Top) WHOI
(Middle) Anne Tantum
(Bottom) Joseph Carvalho Collection
38 (Top and bottom) WHOI
39 WHOI
40 WHOI
41 Robert Ballard
42 Robert Ballard/WHOI

Chapter Four
44 From World Ocean Floor Map by Bruce Heezen and Marie Tharp, ©1977 Marie Tharp.
45-51 All photographs in Chapter 4 are by Anita Brosius courtesy of Lamont-Doherty Geological Observatory.

Chapter Five
52-53 Illustrations by Davis Meltzer/*National Geographic* Society
54 Emory Kristof ©*National Geographic* Society
55 (Photo of *Argo*) Emory Kristof ©*National Geographic* Society (*Argo* diagrams and screen photo) WHOI
56 Emory Kristof ©*National Geographic* Society
57 Emory Kristof ©*National Geographic* Society

Chapter Six
58-85 All photos in Ch. 6 are by Emory Kristof ©*National Geographic* Society unless otherwise noted.
63 Two charts, Robert Ballard/WHOI
64 Sketch at bottom, WHOI
66 All three charts, WHOI
72 Chart at bottom, WHOI
82 (Boilers in shop) Harland & Wolff (Boiler on screen) Robert Ballard/WHOI
83 Chart, Robert Ballard/WHOI

Chapter Seven
86-144 All photos in Ch. 7 are by Emory Kristof ©*National Geographic* Society unless otherwise noted.
91 Three ANGUS photos, Robert Ballard/WHOI
97 (Top, *Olympic* forecastle,) Harland & Wolff Two ANGUS photographs, Robert Ballard/WHOI (Bottom, the *Olympic* in New York,) Joseph Carvalho Collection
98 (Top) *The Toronto SUN*
99 Joseph H. Bailey ©*National Geographic* Society
100 WHOI
101 Stephen St. John ©*National Geographic* Society

Chapter Eight
102 In Chapter 8 all photographs taken from or on *Atlantis II* are by Perry Thorsvik ©*National Geographic* Society. All *Argo*, ANGUS, and *Alvin* underwater photographs are by Robert Ballard and Martin Bowen/WHOI.
106 Illustration of *Alvin* and *JJ* by William H. Bond/ *National Geographic* Society
111 (Top) Harland & Wolff
120-122 Painting by Ken Marschall
123-125 (Mosaic) Robert Ballard/WHOI Diagram by Richard Schlecht/*National Geographic* Society & Ken Marschall
126 (Telemotor) Bill Sauder Collection (Captain Smith), British Newspaper Library
127 (Top) Painting by Ken Marschall (Bridge photo) *The Illustrated London News*
129 Walter Lord Collection
133 (Top) Painting by Ken Marschall (Bottom, left) Diagram by Richard Schlecht/ *National Geographic* Society (Bottom, right) Joseph Carvalho Collection
135 (Top) Joseph Carvalho Collection (Bottom, left and right) Stills courtesy of *National Geographic* Society

Chapter Nine
136-162 All photographs in Chapter 9 on or from *Atlantis II* are by Perry Thorsvik ©*National Geographic* Society. All *Alvin*, *Argo* and ANGUS underwater shots are by Robert Ballard and Martin Bowen/WHOI.
139 (Telemotor, archival) Bill Sauder Collection
140 (Top) *The Cork Examiner*
142 (Top) Ken Marschall Collection
143 (Top) *Syren and Shipping Magazine*, *Titanic* Historical Society
144 Painting by Ken Marschall
145 (Bottom) Harland & Wolff
147 (Bottom) Harland & Wolff
149 (Doll) The Margaret Strong Museum (Lorraine Allison) Donald Lynch Collection
150-151 Illustration by Richard Schlecht/*National Geographic* Society
153 (Top) Nelson Arnstein Collection (Bottom) F. Sangorski & G. Sutcliffe Ltd.
154 (Bottom) The Mariner's Museum
155 (Bottom) Harland & Wolff (Crane) *The Cork Examiner*
156-157 Painting by Ken Marschall
158 (Top) Kate Odell, courtesy of Jeremy Nightingale
163 (Top) Kate Odell, courtesy of Jeremy Nightingale
164-166 Painting by Ken Marschall
167-169 *Titanic* cross-section courtesy of Anne Tantum (*Olympic* 2nd-class entrance) Joseph Carvalho Collection
170 (White Swan Hotel window) Roy Varley
170-171 (Lounge) Harland & Wolff

171 (Statue) Howard Holtzman Collection (Plan) *The Shipbuilder*
172 (Staircase) Harland & Wolff (Carved wood) Joseph H. Bailey ©*National Geographic* Society
173 (Dining saloon) Ken Marschall Collection (Bay window) *The Shipbuilder*
174 (Dining saloon) *The Shipbuilder* (Menu) Walter Lord Collection
176 (*Olympic* chefs) Ken Marschall Collection
177 (Pantry) Ken Marschall Collection
178 (Second-class smoking room) Harland & Wolff
178-179 (First-class smoking room) Byron Collection, Museum of the City of New York
180 (Funnels), Courtesy of Jeremy Nightingale (Funnel diagram) Ken Marschall (Funnel leaving shop) *The Shipbuilder*
181 (Suite B-57) Harland & Wolff
182 (Stateroom photo) Byron Collection, Museum of the City of New York
183 (Third-class cabin) Byron Collection, Museum of the City of New York (Lower right) Father Francis M. Browne, S.J., Charles Haas/John Eaton Collection
184 (Upper left) Byron Collection, Museum of the City of New York (Middle, left) Harland & Wolff (Bathtub) Harland & Wolff
185 (Top) Harland & Wolff (Bottom) Father Francis M. Browne, S.J., Charles Haas/John Eaton Collection (Right) *The Illustrated London News*
186 (Top, left) Father Francis M. Browne, S.J., Charles Haas/John Eaton Collection (Middle, left) Charles Haas/John Eaton Collection (Bottom) Ken Marschall Collection
188 (Top, left) *The Cork Examiner* (Countess of Rothes) *The Illustrated London News* (Lifeboat) Walter Lord Collection
189 (Top, right) The Bettmann Archive (Bottom, right) *The Shipbuilder*
190 (Top, left) Harland & Wolff (Bottom) *The Shipbuilder*
191 (Bottom, right) Ken Marschall Collection
192 (Top, left) Walter Lord Collection (Bottom, left) The Nova Scotia Archives (Top, right) *The Cork Examiner*
193 (Top, left) *The Cork Examiner* (Top, right) *The Illustrated London News* (Middle, left) Harland & Wolff

Chapter Ten
194 Perry Thorsvik ©*National Geographic* Society
195 *The Illustrated London News*
196 (Top) Harland & Wolff
196-197 (Bottom) Robert Ballard/WHOI, mosaic by Ken Marschall
197 (Top) Walter Lord collection
198 (Top) *The Illustrated London News* (Bottom) Illustration by Pierre Mion/*National Geographic* Society
199 (Top) *The Illustrated London News*
200 (Top) Walter Lord Collection (Bottom) Chart by Elaine Macpherson
201 From *The Doomed Unsinkable Ship*
202-203 Robert Ballard/WHOI
204-205 Drawings by Ken Marschall
206 Robert Ballard/WHOI
207 Diagram by Ken Marschall
208 (Top) Robert Ballard/WHOI (Bottom) Ruth Turner, Museum of Comparative Zoology, Harvard University
209 (Top) Kate Odell, courtesy of Jeremy Nightingale (Bottom) Walter Lord Collection
210 Robert Ballard/WHOI

Chapter Eleven
212-213 Robert Ballard/WHOI

An Inventory of the Debris Field
214 (*Olympic* Poop Deck) National Maritime Museum, Greenwich, U.K., Eric Sauder Collection
214-215 (ANGUS photos) Robert Ballard/WHOI
216 (*Britannic* reciprocating engines) Harland & Wolff
216-217 (ANGUS photos) Robert Ballard/WHOI (Remaining archival photos) *The Shipbuilder*
232 Kate Odell, courtesy of Jeremy Nightingale

Glossary

abaft: toward or at the stern of a ship (nearer the stern than aft of).

aft: near, toward, or at the stern of a ship.

altimeter: instrument for measuring distance from the ocean floor.

ANGUS: acronym for Acoustically Navigated Geological Underwater Survey. Unmanned underwater exploration technology consisting of a sled-like assembly of steel tubing and underwater still cameras, used for visual photographic survey of ocean floor as device is towed from ocean surface on a non-conducting steel cable.

aqualung: portable underwater breathing apparatus.

Argo: underwater exploration device consisting of a steel sled equipped with video cameras that takes moving television pictures, which are transmitted through cable to surface, as it is pulled at the end of a long cable 60 to 100 feet above the ocean floor.

ballast: weight added in ship's bottom to improve stability.

bathyscaphe: manned undersea craft used for deep-sea exploration with a spherical watertight cabin attached to its underside.

Big Bird: nickname for color television and still-camera system mounted on *Alvin*'s mechanical arm.

bilge: curved part of a ship's hull where bottom meets the side, in which water is likely to collect and from which it can be pumped out.

bitts: pair of posts on a ship for securing various ropes.

black smokers: underwater hydrothermal vents (q.v.) that belch mineral-rich fluids from newly formed volcanic terrain with a temperature of 350° to 400°C, hot enough to melt lead.

Boat Deck: deck of a ship on which lifeboats are carried in davits (q.v.). In the case of the *Titanic*, this was the topmost deck.

bollards: stout metal posts on a ship or wharf to which mooring lines are secured.

bow: forward end of a ship.

bridge: raised (and usually enclosed) platform or structure toward the forward end of a ship, having a clear view ahead and from which the ship is navigated.

bulkhead: upright partition dividing interior of ship into compartments.

bulwark: barrier built from steel plating and capped with wooden handrail.

calcareous tubes: one to two inches in length, these tubes are the protective homes of wood-boring molluscs (q.v.).

capacitor: device for storing electric charges.

capstan: upright revolving barrel or drum mounted at the bow and stern of a ship to aid in docking by winding a rope or cable around it.

collapsibles A,B,C,&D: squat wooden-bottomed lifeboats with canvas sides. The canvas sides were collapsed for stowing and raised when in use. The *Titanic* carried four of these Englehardt "surfboats," loosely called "collapsibles."

continental shelf: shallow submerged plateau surrounding most continents.

CQD: Morse code distress call used by ships at sea in first years of wireless telegraphy.

cycloidal propulsion system: state-of-the-art seagoing technology that enables ships to maintain precise stationary position in rough seas. System consists of two cycloid propellers (like giant egg-beaters) under the bow and stern of ship which can rotate ship in a tight stationary circle, or move forward or backward – and allow for optimum maneuverability.

davits: crane-like arms on board ship used for lowering lifeboats.

dead reckoning: estimating location of a ship at sea from last reliable navigational fix at sunset by simply extrapolating from estimated speed and direction of travel.

Deep Tow: deep-towed near-range side-scan sonar (q.v.) used for searching and mapping deep ocean – developed by Dr. Fred Spiess of Scripps Institute of Oceanography.

deep-towed vehicle: vehicle towed at end of long cable just above ocean floor.

diving tables: tables which show amount of time a diver can spend at various depths and return to surface without getting diving illness.

docking bridge: platform on the Poop Deck with instruments used to assist navigation while in port.

echo sounder: sounding apparatus for determining depth to sea floor beneath ship.

expansion joint: built-in seam in superstructure of a ship that allows some flexibility in heavy seas as the hull (q.v.) bends upward or downward.

fairlead rollers: spool-like guides for ship's mooring lines.

fantail: fan-shaped deck which overhangs the stern of a ship.

fathometer: device used for determining ocean depths by measuring time taken by sound waves to reach the bottom and return (same as an echo sounder).

fiber optics: transmission of information by light pulses along hair-thin glass fibers.

field ice: large expanse of ice covering surface of ocean.

forecastle: short raised deck at bow of ship; also forward part of a ship where crew lives.

foremast: on the *Titanic*, the mast which stands foward of the bridge (q.v.).

forepeak tank: a small watertight compartment in the bow of a ship that may be flooded or pumped out in order to adjust the ship's attitude in the water. There is a similar trimming tank at the after end of a ship's hull.

forward: toward the front or fore part of a ship.

galley: ship's kitchen.

gangway: passageway onto a ship.

geophysics: study of the physics of the structure, composition, and dynamic changes of the earth and its atmosphere.

growlers: small, low, flat icebergs.

hard-a-starboard: in 1912, this order required the man at the wheel to turn the wheel to port, not to starboard, and the rudder and hence the ship would turn to port. This practice was a survival of the days when ships were steered by a helm or tiller bar rather than by a wheel. The helm or tiller bar was directly connected to the rudder post so that if you wanted the ship to go to port you had to put the helm to starboard. The use of these old "helm orders" began to die out after the First World War and was obsolete by the middle 1930s.

hawsepipe: heavy metal sleeves which guide the anchor chains through the Forecastle Deck and over the ship's side.

hull plates: metal plates joined together and covering ship's hull framing (on the *Titanic* generally less than one inch thick).

hydrothermal vent: opening in bottom of ocean from which issues heated and altered seawater.

IFREMER: acronym for the French national institute of oceanography (Institut Français de Recherches pour l'Exploitation des Mers).

International Ice Patrol: created in 1913, as a direct result of the sinking of the *Titanic*, to guard sea lanes of North Atlantic under the direction of the U.S. Coast Guard.

Jason: an unmanned ROV (remotely operated vehicle), now under construction, which will be attached to *Argo* (q.v.) on a tether, this self-propelled underwater exploration robot will be equipped with lights and stereo cameras and will be able to maneuver into difficult and dangerous areas – as well as gather specimens from the ocean floor.

Jason Junior, Jason Jr., JJ: prototype of *Jason* robot described above, used from *Alvin* to explore the *Titanic*.

keel: a steel line of plates running lengthwise along the center of the bottom of a ship; "the spine" on which framework of ship is built up.

LIBEC imaging system: sophisticated black-and-white underwater still-camera system developed by U.S. Navy.

lithium hydroxide: compound used inside pressure sphere to cleanse air of carbon dioxide.

low-pressure cyclinders: in reciprocating engines (q.v.) of the type used in the *Titanic,* steam from the boilers was fed first to a high-pressure cylinder, thence to an intermediate-pressure cylinder, and finally to two low-pressure cylinders, in order to produce power. The *Titanic* had two reciprocating engines (port and starboard), thus four low-pressure cylinders.

magnetometer: instrument towed on a long cable near ocean floor that measures disturbances in the earth's magnetic field caused by metal objects.

midship: middle part of ship.

Morse lamp: lamp used to signal in Morse code.

nautical mile: international unit of distance used at sea, equal to about 6080 feet.

plate tectonics: modern theory of continental drift which holds that earth's crust is divided into contiguous, moving plates that carry the embedded continents.

Poop Deck: a raised deck at the very stern of a ship.

port: left-hand side of a ship.

prow: the bow of a ship.

reciprocating engine: in ships, a kind of steam engine in which a steam-driven piston moves up and down in a cylinder, transmitting its motion by a connecting rod and crank to a propeller shaft. A compound engine was a two-cylinder reciprocating engine consisting of a high-pressure and a low-pressure cylinder, getting more drive from the same quantity of steam. The reciprocating engines in the *Titanic* were of the type known as four-cylinder triple-expansion engines; their operation is described under "low-pressure cylinder" above. (See also turbine engine.)

rusticles: very fragile reddish-brown stalactites of rust, hanging down as much as several feet, caused by iron-eating bacteria. These rust features cover much of the wreck of the *Titanic*.

SAR: French acronym for Sonar Acoustique Remorqué, a very accurate deep-towed side-scan sonar (q.v.) developed by the French and able to take the equivalent of visual pictures with sound waves underwater.

Sea MARC I: intermediate-range underwater sonar (q.v.) used for large-area mapping of geological features on ocean floor – developed by Bill Ryan of Lamont-Doherty Geological Observatory.

sea pen: a feather-shaped relation to the jelly fish.

sector-scanning sonar: sonar (q.v.) originally used for detecting mines.

sextant: instrument used in navigation for measuring angular distances of celestial bodies by means of reflection in order to determine latitude and longitude.

ship's chart: map or chart of a portion of sea, showing any coastlines, rocks, shoals, etc., and used to plot and determine ship's course.

side-scan sonar: sonar (q.v.) that can acoustically "see" objects horizontally to each side.

single-ended boiler: boiler with furnaces at one end only, rather than both ends. The *Titanic* had five single-ended boilers, all in boiler room No. 1.

SIT camera: acronym for Silicon Intensified Target, a camera system that magnifies available natural light 10,000 times, making it literally possible to see in the dark with a small amount of light.

sold-state imaging device: camera which uses digital chips for imaging in place of viticon tubes.

sonar: instrument used to detect and locate underwater objects by reflected sound waves (acronym for sound navigation ranging).

sonar interrogation beacon: acoustic device placed on ocean floor which responds to sound signals sent to it from a ship or towed instruments and used to determine location.

SOS: general distress call for use by ship's wireless operators when sending Morse code. It superseded the previous general distress call, CQD, on July 1, 1908. The call consists of the letters S, O, and S sent tight (i.e. without spacing between the letters). This signal was chosen because it could be sent and recognized easily; the letters SOS do not stand for anything except three dots, three dashes and three dots sent tight. (On voice equipment the general distress call is "Mayday.")

speaking tube: tube or length of pipe used on ship for conveying oral commands from bridge to engine room and other parts of ship.

stanchion: upright bar, post, or support.

starboard: right-hand side of ship.

steerage: area of ship allotted to passengers traveling at cheapest rate, usually immigrants.

stern: rear end of ship.

submarine canyon: deep underwater valley.

submersible: submarine vessel which requires a support ship to transport it to and from diving area, and which is recovered each night.

telemetry system: electrical system used for transmitting commands over cable between ship and towed instruments like *Argo* (q.v.).

tow cable: long cable containing copper or fiber optics and used to tow underwater exploration devices.

transducer: device attached to hull of ship or mounted in tow vehicle for transmitting signals underwater.

transponder: underwater acoustic beacon positioned on ocean floor that anchors and tracks navigation of underwater search vehicles, the sonic equivalent of a radio beacon.

tube worms: large worms living in long white tubes around hydrothermal vents (q.v.).

turbine engine: in ships, a kind of steam engine in which steam from the boilers is directed onto blades set at an angle in a rotor connected through gearing to the propeller shaft. The *Titanic* had one turbine engine, mounted amidships and driving the center propeller. Steam exhausted from the low-pressure cylinders of the reciprocating engines was fed into the turbine, to wring the last ounce of drive out of the steam before it went to the condensers.

Well Deck: the lowered deck between the superstructure and the Forecastle or Poop Decks of a ship.

wheelhouse: small covered area on the bridge of a vessel containing the ship's wheel.

windward: area lying in direction from which the wind blows.

worm gear: a long shaft cut with spiral gear teeth along most of its length, used to operate sliding windows and swing out davits.

Index

N.B. numerals in italics refer to captions

DESIGN AND ART DIRECTION: Andrew Smith and Jackie Young/ink
EDITORIAL: Hugh Brewster
EDITORIAL ASSISTANCE: Patrick Crean
                     Catherine Fraccaro
PRODUCTION: Susan Barrable
PRODUCTION ASSISTANCE: Pamela Yong
TYPOGRAPHY: Crocker Bryant Inc.
COLOR SEPARATION,
PRINTING AND BINDING: Arnoldo Mondadori Editore – Verona
MOSAIC ENHANCEMENT: Dodge Color Laboratory

The last photograph ever taken of the Titanic *as she steams off from Queenstown on her fateful maiden voyage.*

THE DISCOVERY OF THE TITANIC was produced simultaneously in ten editions and in eight languages by Madison Press Books under the direction of A.E. Cummings.